Them and Us

*Questions of Citizenship
in a Globalizing World*

ROB KROES

University of Illinois Press

URBANA AND CHICAGO

In memory of Sioe Kie,

the light in my life

Library of Congress Cataloging-in-Publication Data
Kroes, Rob.
Them and us : questions of citizenship in a globalizing world / Rob Kroes.
p.   cm.
Includes bibliographical references and index.
ISBN 0-252-02604-7 (cloth : acid-free paper)
ISBN 0-252-06909-9 (paper : acid-free paper)
1. World citizenship. I. Title.
JZ1320.4.K76   2000
306.2—dc21   00-008322

1 2 3 4 5 C P 5 4 3 2 1

Contents

Acknowledgments

Friends and colleagues—and they are often the same people—contributed much to this book through conversations and comments they made after reading part or all of the manuscript. I thank them all. My greatest debt of gratitude is to the John F. Kennedy Institute for North-American Studies of the Free University in Berlin. A recipient of one of their research grants, I had the use of their marvelous resources. I also found the time and peace of mind in Berlin, in the fall of 1998, to complete the first draft of this book.

Introduction: Cultural Affinities and Political Affiliations

Monsieur Jourdain, he was told, had spoken prose all his life. I am beginning to find out—before anyone tells me—that I have written essays all my life. I am the nonfiction parallel to the short-story writer, not the novelist. More often than not, it is only after I have written several shorter pieces, when I review things I have argued and tried to explain to myself, that I become aware of an underlying thematic coherence. Like a hiker who forgot to bring a map, I stop and look back at places I passed, taking them in from varying angles. Slowly a rather unusual sort of map forms in my mind, as if I were using a kaleidoscope instead of a pair of binoculars. I see shifting configurations of essentially the same colorful fragments rearranging themselves, falling into different patterns as I turn the cylinder. My observations are based on circular movements. I circle around objects that catch my attention, reporting on particular angles, particular points of view. Each report is literally an essay, an attempted approach toward an object of study; the point of each essay, or of a number of them taken together, is also an assay, an attempt to fathom the object in its sense and meaning, at the same time fashioning it to render coherent statements.

The present volume results from the recognition that in much of my recent writing I again had circled around a topic that gradually assumed a face and an identity. It was probably the sociologist in me more than the American studies scholar that had directed my gaze and given coherence to the questions I raised and tried to answer. The thematic thread connecting the writings in this book is one of collective identities, of the ways in which people who caught my interest had grouped themselves together as communities of identity, expressing the interests and affinities that they shared and that set them apart from others. The essays explore feelings of belonging and membership. To the extent that such feelings lead people to organize and act, however, they assume a political dynamic that turns matters of membership into questions of citizenship. The latter word we might take to refer to the area of contestation where groups that define themselves in terms of shared affinities and interests develop a common voice demanding a say as well as a fair hearing within larger social settings that affect their common life. Citizenship, then, is still a matter of membership, but one that transcends the communal bounds and bonds of individual communities. It concerns the larger society of which these communities form a part. It is also a matter of membership in a more political sense of the word. Citizens are those members of a society who are allowed to play a role in matters of state, in those collective agencies and institutions that every society has set up to direct and arrange its collective life, or in words reminiscent of that great state document the American Constitution, "to see to the common defense and well-being of its citizens." Citizenship in that sense has always been the subject of contestation. The state, allegedly the instrument for the expression of the *volonté générale,* the general will of the population, has always been used to set limits to citizenship, to define it as a prerogative for some members of society while excluding others. Such acts are in themselves political decisions and as such reflect balances of power prevailing in society at large. Entire groups have been (and still are) shut out on the basis of criteria such as gender, age, property, class, religion, race, ethnic origin, or years of residence in the country. All such criteria of exclusion have historically formed the basis, in an unavoidable dialectic, for the rise of communal feelings of deprivation and injustice among the excluded and for their organization as groups contesting the reigning views of citizenship. They could seek either inclusion or exit, opting out in the hope of gaining political independence for themselves. The latter option is the more feasible in the case of communities that are grouped regionally and may hope to secede as a region from the larger encompassing state. The former option is the more likely in the case of groups, such as women, that are dispersed within a society.

Citizenship is a topic as old as the history of state formation and political philosophy. As an issue of political contestation, however, it has been articulated much more extensively in the modern era, beginning with the Renaissance, with its radically new views of human agency in history. To the extent that people came to conceive of history as made by men and women rather than given by God, they more readily could conceive of their own destinies as subject to their own individual or collective effort. Still, however time honored citizenship may be as a subject for human reflection, individual authors have always seen their interest spurred by relatively short-term crises and shocks, such as civil wars or revolutions. In the modern era alone, Machiavelli, Hobbes, Locke, the American Founding Fathers, Tocqueville, and

Marx, or more recently Hannah Arendt or Zygmunt Bauman, have all had their writing occasioned by great contemporary cataclysms, most recently the Holocaust or the atrocities of civil war in the Balkans. I do not rank myself among such illustrious names, of course, yet in my case a similar process has been at work at several points in my life.

I remember myself as a sixteen year old, sitting at the radio with my parents and listening in impotent rage to the reports of a Hungarian uprising being stamped down by overwhelming Soviet force. I remember in particular the last Hungarian call for help broadcast to Western audiences, who were unable to engage in anything more than symbolic behavior, such as smashing the windows of Soviet embassies. Yet I remember making a vow to do something more meaningful—and in a way I did. Ten years later, as a political science student, I wrote my master's thesis, in which I used comparative research to argue that the Hungarian uprising must rank as a revolution, albeit an abortive one. My thesis was an attempt to rescue the historical significance of the uprising from official Soviet views that portrayed it as no more than a reactionary revolt inspired by the West. My effort made no historical dent, I am sure, and was slightly derisible as an act of retaliation. Nevertheless, I explored forces that would in fact lead to the demise of the Soviet imperial hold. As a consequence, the effort certainly helped me to make sense of what had taken place by putting it in a larger interpretive frame.

A similar occasion prompted the writings brought together in this book. It was television rather than radio this time, but the feelings of angered impotence at watching the early beginnings of terror and civil war in the former Yugoslavia were equally strong. This time the anger was compounded by my utter incomprehension of the events' sheer atavism. This resurgence of a vicious tribalism in the context of a Europe that might have hoped to have exorcised the demons of its violent history once and for all was something that caught everyone off guard. It not only engendered feelings of individual impotence but also tragically displayed the collective impotence and paralysis of the "New Europe." I decided to use this whole traumatic history as the starting point of my explorations collected here. The analysis of the first chapter takes its cue from these events while at the same time introducing themes that will recur later.

Among these themes two are of central importance when the topic is citizenship: cultural affinities and political affiliations. Seen as two social forces that together make up people's senses of citizenship, they are mutually reinforcing in ideal cases only. Normally they are in tenuous and delicate balance, whereas in worst-case scenarios, like that of Yugoslavia, the central government's squandering of its citizens' political affiliations revived primordial cultural affinities at the regional level. Instead of continuing a Tito-style balancing act, weaving cultural affinities into a workable pattern of political affiliation within the state, which would be seen as transcending the many localisms, President Milosevic responded to the collapse of communism as a legitimating language by appealing to Serbian nationalism in his attempt to cling to power. He thus opened a Pandora's box of rival nationalisms while destroying the political affiliation that had emerged under Tito. Admittedly, Yugoslavia is an extreme case, yet the breakup of the Soviet empire, if not of the rump Russia as we now know it, has caused tragedies of a similar nature.

Nonetheless, neither contemporary Europe organizing itself as the larger European Union, the United States, nor Canada constitutes the other extreme of the full and mutual reinforcement of cultural affinities and political affiliations among a citizenry. They are all examples of the normal midrange of citizenship as a contested concept. In the New Europe the average citizen's political affiliation with the larger transnational structure of governance and administration is clearly the weak spot of the entire project. In reaction, many forms of cultural affinity—some traditional, if not primordial, and others newly invented—offer themselves as rival frameworks for meaningful political affiliation, further threatening the legitimacy of the union's structures. In the United States it is not so much political affiliations as the cultural affinities among the citizenry that are adrift. Within a pattern of relatively stable and entrenched affiliation with the structures and agencies of the republic, groups are vying for control of the meaning of "America" and Americanness, to the point of exploding the concept as a cultural unifier. If pursued to that extreme, it will eventually affect the established pattern of political affiliation, as some critics fear is already happening. I will return to these culture wars at greater length in the following essays, but here it suffices to mention the United States as a case centrally highlighting the force of cultural affinities as a dimension of citizenship. Canada is another enlightening case. It illustrates the continuing weakness of the political affiliation of one part of the population, the Québécois, who see themselves in terms of cultural affinities insufficiently honored and acknowledged by the national government. Ironically, in late-1960s attempts to handle the problem, the Canadian government chose the strategy of a forward flight, proposing to conceive of its French-speaking citizens' cultural peculiarity as only one among a larger pattern of cultural diversity. The word it coined for this view of the cultural makeup of Canadian society was *multiculturalism,* a word that traveled to the United States and now commonly denotes the arena of culture wars that take place there. What in Canada was introduced as a tool of conflict control, containing conflict by pluralizing it in the grand Madisonian manner, is being used in America to describe the many cultural fault lines that cultural contestants are busy opening. It is of further interest here that Canada is almost like an American transplant of the more typically European option of political exit on the basis of a cultural community's regional concentration.

Canada in that sense is a curious historical exception to a pattern of citizenship that one tends more naturally to expect in the Americas. Made up of countries whose populations have all migrated there, the United States being the most complex and varied case in point, the Western Hemisphere seems like the perfect counterpoint to Europe's more stable and certainly less mobile populations when it comes to fathoming the different ways in which people conceive of their citizenship. In this book I have chosen to focus on two rather surprising ways in which this simple dichotomy, America versus Europe, can be problematized. One is to look at the presence of regionalism in the United States, both as a historical experience of its citizens and as a topic of scholarly reflection. It provides us with a perspective on cultural rootedness in a country that facile stereotypes would suggest ought not to have any. From a comparative perspective, however, regionalism in the United States is cast in terms characteristically different from those applicable to Europe. A second way to problematize the dichotomy is to look at immigration in terms of the way people handled the rupture in their lives, breaking away from settings intimately known to them while trying to develop a meaningful sense of citizenship in their country of arrival. Interestingly, as many studies of immigration have shown and as one case study in this book may illustrate, many new immigrants kept up a sense of rootedness and interwovenness with their communities of origin for an amazing length of time. In a sense they lived vicarious lives, propped up through letters, the exchange of gossip, and the use of photographs as visual tools for the intimate stories they had to tell to family members, friends, and neighbors who had stayed behind. The result is a paradox. For many immigrants it proved possible to continue the small-scale lifestyle of the communities they had left simply by extending the communal bonds across the ocean. They transnationalized communities of intimacy in complete naïveté, unaware of the existential feat they were performing. In the end, however, many of them found this approach to be only a psychological tool to ease their transition to a new social setting. It helped them to cope with the pain of rupture while providing time to give sense and meaning to their new social setting and to become functioning citizens in it.

Such a perspective focuses on cultural affinities, but later chapters emphasize the political dimension of citizenship. There I discuss some of the reigning views that have developed in Europe and the United States concerning the political rights of citizenship. To the extent that citizenship is a matter of political affiliation rather than cultural affinity, it has come to rest increasingly on views of the state as a guarantor of freedoms and provider of benefits. A comparative chapter on the human rights tradition in the United States as it differs from European traditions will then take us to slightly more Olympian heights. Clearly, whatever our angle, whether we focus on cultural affinities or political affiliations, we are dealing with the intricate ways in which people structure their worlds, imbuing them with sense and meaning while placing themselves within them. Human cultural creativity is truly central to any consideration of citizenship, yet it is an area that resists intellectual scrutiny and inquiry, a black box that is usually subsumed under the catch-all concept of ideology. If people act on the basis of structured worldviews, well, we have to take their word for it. They are caught up in ideologies, rival and often clashing views that are like so many sociological realities. Yet we cannot leave it at that. I have chosen to look at this black box of ideology in a separate chapter, finding ways to open it and to account for what goes on inside. My starting point is the recent debate in Germany on dual citizenship, a debate forced on the Germans by the presence in their midst of millions of first-, second-, and third-generation immigrants, mostly from Turkey. In a break with its traditional ways of defining citizenship—who is German and who is not—offering the option of dual citizenship to the Turkish minority was the politically agreed-on compromise solution. The debate and furor attending it testified to a rift among the German population between deep-rooted ideological views concerning the nation and Germanness. Interestingly, though, current debates concerning American citizenship reveal parallel patterns of clashing ideological views, as I will argue. Of course, dual citizenship is only the formal, legal expression of a more general, underlying ideology that sees human beings as capable of having multiple identities. I incline toward that view. At some points in my own life I affiliate with the small community in which I live; at other points, particularly when I'm abroad or when the Dutch soccer team confronts the German national team, I feel Dutch. When I temporarily live in the United States, I usually feel European, but sometimes I feel American, for I can share the enthusiasms that move Americans as a nation at high points in their national life. This is not how critics of dual citizenship see it, however. To them, one can be loyally committed to only one body politic and its public interest. Loyalty, for them, is one and indivisible. It is a perfectly legitimate view, held dear by many who conceive of themselves and their fellow citizens in these terms. It cannot be proven wrong in the same way that empirical views of reality can be refuted. Given my personal enthusiasm for a life of multiple identity, I devote this book's last chapters to the transnational dimensions of citizenship.

One of the crucial dilemmas I explore in the chapter on ideology arises because human beings simultaneously thirst for *knowledge* about their stations in life and crave intelligent cues for *action*. Chapter 7, on neopopulism and neoconservatism in the United States, provides a case study. It focuses on the plight of social scientists trying to come up with insights into some of the burning issues of our time while at the same time finding themselves caught in the cross fire of ideological camps. There both the sociologist and

the American studies scholar in me rise to the occasion. That second awareness of myself takes me into a consideration of the ways in which the study
of America in the United States and its counterpart Europe are truly two
different existential projects. Whereas in the United States American studies—almost an ideological project—may help Americans to fathom their
own collective existence, in Europe the scholarly endeavor may well contribute to a sense of citizenship in Europe's various national settings by exploring
critical cultural and political contrasts with the American case. As a further
illustration of this, chapters 9 and 10 explore the ways in which Europeans
have tried to make sense of the American case as an exercise of self-exploration. The process we may well call one of triangulation: when Europeans
explore American culture and life, they always do so with their own national or larger European canvass in mind. Studying America as a contrast, trying to fathom it in its cultural difference and otherness, helps them bring out
more clearly the options open to their national audiences. As the chapter on
French views of American modernity demonstrates, America's guises of both
the politically and the culturally modern showed paths for French ideas of
citizenship to follow or avoid. America, it appears, has historically provided
the French with a larger frame for the exploration of their cultural affinities
and political affiliations. The following chapter, on the changing European
sense of history in the post–World War II era, tries to show how the frame
of reference that Europeans now use to make sense of their collective situation draws on ingredients provided by the worldwide dissemination of
American mass-cultural markers of time and place. Again, we might call this
a case study of the transnational dimensions of citizenship, a transnationalism created not by extending communal bonds across the globe—as in the
case of the immigrants I studied—but rather by creating a world culture
under American auspices that affects the way people in their local and national settings structure their sense of the past. It may well be a process affecting the way they conceive of their citizenship and of the frameworks
defining it. Parts of these two chapters draw on discussions in my previous
book *If You've Seen One, You've Seen the Mall.* They are like modular elements
assembled to serve in a different argument. A natural last step, then, is an
exploration of the ways in which emerging networks of global communication, such as the Internet, affect people's sense of place and cultural rootedness. As I argue in the final chapter, to the extent that we can speak of an
emerging world citizenship, if not of a Netizenship in cyberspace, it may well
be one in a remarkably American guise.

PART 1

Cultural Affinities

1. Supranationalism and Its Discontents

Establishing Shots

The early 1990s still feel like yesterday. Satellites and cable delivered all the time's events right into my living room, from ministerial meetings on the future shape of an integrated Europe to a mixed Serbo-Croatian couple stunned by the vicious return of militant national chauvinisms that their marital union had for many years happily belied. We saw the Balkans atavistically returning to type, a navy shelling coastal resorts that had long seemed to be the gathering points for a post-Marxist, if not postmodern, International—the Tourist International weaving Europe together rather than the Workers' International, which had cut Europe in two. We saw guns blazing away in the trans-Caucasus, either to support resurgent nationalist claims or to suppress them. There were images of a Soviet hegemony peacefully retrenching from Eastern Europe, restoring a pattern of sovereign nationhood while upsetting an established European, if not global, balance of power. There were images, too, of the Soviet Union, the last of the great multinational empires, as it broke up along lines of centrifugal fission, its imperial reach retrenching. We saw Baltic states as the first bits of empire truly to regain their national freedom, reorienting themselves toward a larger Baltic and Scandinavian region that had long been their natural point of reference. Glued to the tube, sipping coffee, nibbling away at biscuits, in the isolated cocoons of our individual homes, we lived through every moment of Germany's changing shape, from the days when the Berlin Wall came tumbling down to recent images of neo-Nazi gangs setting fire to refugee hostels in a frenzy of virulent nativism. "Wir sind ein Volk" was the rallying cry of the many East Germans festively swarming into West Berlin: "We are one people"—to which some West Germans replied, "Wir auch" ("So are we"). Germany's unification was never a foregone conclusion. Quite a few West Germans would have been happy to see the continued existence, side by side, of two independent German states. Yet this was not to be. In a rush toward consolidating the precarious freedom of the East Germans, political wisdom in West Germany dictated the full incorporation of East Germany into its federal structure. It is the only example so far of a larger integrated structure emerging from the breakdown of cold war Europe. At the time, however, it was hard to see it as the harbinger of things to come. As an integration based on common nationality, it was very much in line with trends and stirrings elsewhere.

Despite a general denial of the recent past, with all its forms of integration imposed by the Soviet "Diktat," we witnessed a return to an older map of Europe, where Leningrad was and once again is St. Petersburg. Few were the signs of a forward-looking project that would bring novel forms of transnational integration to Europe. Even worse, the very concept of Europe that would have to underlie any such project of integration seemed more elusive than it had been even a few years before. The cold war partition of Europe may ironically have provided Western Europe with the solid baseline for its project of regional integration, but in the absence of such a negative yardstick, imposed from outside, where does Europe end? What is the meaningful definition of a common cultural space that people would willingly adopt as their collective frame of reference? For the time being we could bring out our old school atlases. Europe had returned to its interbellum form. I choose my words here carefully, ominous as they may sound. We lived through the demise of one modernist attempt at transcending the spirit of petty nationalism, the Leninist version that sought transcendence in the internationalism of its revolutionary ideology forcibly imposed by one-party communist dictatorship. What alternative projects had there been, tested by history, that could guide us in an exploration of the options open to Europe, if we wished to avoid replaying the continent's history? Rephrasing an old wisdom, we might say, "Si vis pacem, evita interbellum." It is time, therefore, to get off our couches, switch off the TV, and look around for ourselves.

The American Project of Transnationalism

Communism has been one daring modernist project for the transcendence of nationalism, but Americanism has been a second, rival project. Each developed its own universalist rhetoric concerning the type of solidarity that would weave humankind into a meaningful community. Each developed its project in opposition to the reigning particularist discourse in Europe in its era of high romanticism, when definitions of the meaningful community tended to be cast increasingly in terms of nationalism. Seen from the perspective of a history of ideas, the opposition is this clear-cut. Yet there are a number of ironies.

Nationalism was in certain respects as much a voluntarist project at transcending earlier forms of communal solidarity as were communism and Americanism. Despite the underlying assumption of the nation as an organic, historically grown community of shared common experience expressed in a common language, recent scholarship has debunked this notion as a mere romanticist invention.[1] Of course, nationalism had its earlier critics. The Dutch historian Johan Huizinga, for instance, called it a puerile affliction and pointed to the recency of the nation as a historical entity, belying the claims that nationalism used to make.[2] Many of the ingredients of nationhood that were vaunted as the age-old common lore tying the folk together as a nation were merely the historicizing constructs developed by nationalizing elites and critically linked to the consolidation of the European structure of independent states in the nineteenth century. When I say "critically linked," I mean to imply two dialectically opposed trends. Sometimes the invention of the nation and of national tradition was intended to provide the state with a legitimizing discourse, as in the case of Germany. At other times, as in the case of multiethnic empires such as Austria, it served the purpose of local élites in their attempts to organize for a "new deal" in the distribution of power within the empire. Hungarian nationalism, for instance, served such a strategic purpose once a sense of Hungarian nationhood had been sufficiently instilled. To that end the Hungarian language was revived at a time when it was on the verge of extinction, and a whole plethora of national rituals was developed, reaffirming the unity, common identity, and common interest of Hungarians within the Austro-Hungarian Empire. These were all modernizing projects, in the sense that they provided the people with a larger framework for the definition of a common identity than had hitherto been available. There was in fact a transcendence of regionalism and localism, much as local ingredients might have been tapped for the elaboration of a larger, overarching common culture.

Given the multiethnic pattern of Europe, however, nationalism as a modernizing project can go only so far. There are natural limits to its rallying appeal, preventing it from ever transcending its own organizing logic. At the same time, it has its built-in fissionary potential, giving rise to the choir of minority national voices, each clamoring for equal rights. Nationalism therefore could never be more than a stage in the attempt to construct a proper rhetoric for the expression of organic solidarity as modernizing forces such as industrialism, urbanization, and increased social mobility began to push

Europe away from a social world meaningfully organized around the local community. This process called for further projects that would make sense of a world increasingly cut adrift from its safe local mooring places.

When I earlier referred to both communism and Americanism as modernist projects of transnationalism, I deliberately chose the word *modernist* rather than *modern*. In its usual application to developments in the arts during the nineteenth and twentieth centuries, the former term refers to the enduring artistic impulse to create new forms and modes of expression that could better reflect a world that had irrevocably entered the era of modernity. In what was truly a Promethean explosion of all accepted forms of art, a new sensibility and aestheticism appeared in an expression of the quintessentially modern self-awareness of the "homeless mind," as Peter Berger called it.[3] From Karl Marx to Karl Polanyi, from Charles Baudelaire to Walter Benjamin, the critical intellect has exerted itself to explore the dimensions of this revolution in the human condition. Emphasizing the aesthetic pleasures, the exhilaration rather than the tragic sense of loss, Baudelaire described the novel type of the "flaneur," the man of the crowd, "the lover of life who makes the whole world into his family." "Away from home" and yet "at home," "at the very centre of the world" and yet "unseen of the world," the flaneur goes on his way "forever in search," "always roaming the great desert of men," "an ego athirst for the non-ego."[4] Precisely this preoccupation with cultural otherness and the multiplication of cultural perspectives it implied have been at the core of the modernist project in the arts.

If we train our ears a little differently, however, can we not recognize in Baudelaire's words the exhilarated cosmopolitanism of a long line of American thinkers who tried to express their sense of "America" as almost a modernist project? From Crèvecoeur's astute question "What then is the American, this New Man?" through James Fenimore Cooper, Ralph Waldo Emerson, Walt Whitman, Frederick Jackson Turner, Emma Lazarus, Mary Antin, Randolph Bourne, and Horace Kallen all the way to later explorations of the Puritan origins of the American self in the work of Sacvan Bercovitch, we have one continuing exploration of a sense of national self that is not predicated on the European idea of the nation. From the early origins of this sense of self—from its *natio,* in the sense of "birth"—there has been an aversion to the idea of historical rootedness and exclusivism, most characteristically in the Puritan, or more generally Calvinist, sense of being "in the world, but not of it." In its most noble expressions, the exploration of the American self gave rise to a national rhetoric that emphasized openness rather than closure, diversity rather than uniformity, and pluralism (if not multiculturalism), rather than a homogenizing view of the melting pot. I want to stress my use of the phrase "most noble." The cosmopolitan version of "Americanism" has always found itself in a critical dialogue with a restrictive reading of the nation's composition and calling, a version ironically known as nativism. Nativism rests on a different guiding myth, one of birth, which has provoked the recurrent impulse in American history to adopt exclusion acts and close the "Golden Door." Nativism in this respect may well be America's version of European nationalism.

At the time of World War I, an anguished individual from war-torn Europe, Romain Rolland, could pin his last, best hope on an America whose mission it was to make a symphony from all those voices that had come to it from all over the world. Rolland's call was published in November 1916, in the first issue of the short-lived but influential cultural journal *The Seven Arts*. At the same time, Randolph Bourne could see the regenerative force of American culture in the "transnationalism" of its population. The contrast is clear: against a Europe that had unleashed the destructive potential of its many nationalisms, America could stand as the model of a society that had successfully escaped from this vortex. It was seen to have done so in essentially four ways: (1) through the open-endedness of its sense of nationhood, stressing consent rather than descent—that is, consent to a set of national ideas and a national language rather than descent from a common set of forebears; (2) through the open-endedness of its federalist system, which has grown from the original thirteen federal states to the present fifty (and the end may not be in sight) and which for most of its history, until well into the 1930s, coalesced around a notably weak center; (3) through the creation of one large economic space, with one currency and one central agency protecting the freedom of interstate commerce; and (4) through the open-endedness of its political citizenship, bestowing full democratic rights on everyone born on American soil or duly naturalized.

* * *

To what extent could Europeans hope to learn from this American venture in transnationalism? Clearly, Europe could never hope to copy America's history of a nation of immigrants. The immigrant, the stranger, may be a prototype of the modern "homeless mind," of the cosmopolitan at home in various worlds at the same time, but outside the modernist centers in the great cities of Europe, there is a lasting mold of geographically distinct nationalities that to the present day forms a potent reservoir of resistance to any project threatening it. Through the increasing interwovenness of its economic structures, Europe may have seen an attendant increase in transborder labor mobility, yet it is a long way away from any drastic dilution of its entrenched pattern of national identities, which are always ready to reassert themselves as critically linked to any viable project of European integration. Equally clearly, federalism and the one open market can appeal to Europeans as elements of the American transnational venture that Europe might hope to borrow. From the rather dreamy-eyed pan-European federalism of the interwar years, Europe has moved to create quasi-federalist forms of integration, doing so through interstate treaties, formative early decisions of the European Court, and a pragmatic incrementalism building on early postwar integrative structures, such as the European Coal and Steel Community. Compared to U.S. federalism, however, Europe's approach entails a lasting incongruity between two organizing principles that yields a lasting uncertainty as to the centrally legitimating concept of sovereignty.

Sovereignty in its classic definition is seen as one and indivisible. Its source, or rather its central repository, has shifted over time, from the divine right of kings, to Parliament, following Britain's Glorious Revolution, to "We the People," following the American Revolution. Americans gradually came to the idea of popular sovereignty once they began considering the separation of powers as well as the federal distribution of power. Sovereignty, being one and indivisible, cannot be affected by such distributive thought and came therefore to be seen as resting with "the people." The radical shift toward a conception of popular sovereignty is yet another testament to the modernist cast of America's attempt at nation building, yet it sits uneasily with a European cast of mind that still sees—and often hotly defends—sovereignty as resting within the various nation-states. Logically nothing would prevent each of these states from federalizing itself (e.g., through devolution), inspired by considerations of subsidiarity (a buzzword in contemporary Europe as much as in 1930s and 1940s Catholic views of political corporatism). Nevertheless, any "transfer" of decision-making powers to levels transcending the individual nation-states would imply an attendant shift in the view of the sovereign people. So far, there has been no ringing call to "we Europeans" equaling the legitimizing and inspirational force of "We the People." In that respect Europe still finds itself caught between different grounds of legitimizing its venture into supranationalism, which may go a long way to account for that venture's overly technocratic and bureaucratic cast. The pragmatism of interstate treaties, creating interstate collaborative structures, stands at right angles to the principle of a sovereign "European" people. "Brussels" (Europe's executive center) and "Strassbourg" (the seat of the European Parliament) are in that sense expressions of two conflicting organizing principles. In the long run, though, we may well expect this built-in tension between the two organizing principles to work itself out in ways where, for example, Belgium or Spain as national entities dissolve into smaller entities, each a constituent part of a larger federal Europe.

The pragmatic aspects of the contemporary European structure, inspired by the logic of rationality and bureaucracy, may make it easier for Europe to adopt the other alluring feature of the American model: the one open market within the geographical reach of the community. There is less need there for democratic legitimization, although the largest negative impact on national sovereignty may come from just such economic integration.

The American case suggests something more, a perennial element of a built-in dialectic that we may otherwise tend to overlook. I have described the American modernist venture in transnationalism as providing a large democratic home to the homeless mind. In doing so I have stressed the cosmopolitan, modernist side of America. It appears as a large, integrative structure of a "Gesellschaft" type, to use the word of the classic German sociologist Ferdinand Tönnies. It is a society of Baudelairean "men in the crowd." If it were solely a Gesellschaft type, however, it would have been unable to satisfy the lasting desire for the integrative forms of the "Gemeinschaft," the consensual community. In fact, America's long history of voluntary associative forms—noted, as were so many other American features, by that astute observer Alexis de Tocqueville—testifies to the strength of this search for Gemeinschaft. Varieties of utopian communitarianism, American religious life, and the recurrent ethnic revivals viewed as nostalgic attempts at "inventing" homes for the homeless all equally illustrate this countertrend to the modernity of American society. Federalism there has never been used to meet this need for the meaningful expression of the cultural identity of local communities. In Europe, though, it may well be worth considering the option of a highly flexible and changeable concept of federalism, supported by democratic majority votes, while at the same time insisting on the protection of the minority rights of consensual communities. After all, minorities will always remain in the midst of whatever majorities make themselves heard.

In that respect it may be useful, although apparently unusual, to refer to a premodern, highly localist version of successful federalism—namely, the Swiss version. It is a shining example of a multiethnic—I hesitate to say multinational—federal order, highly flexible in its capacity to respond to the democratic expression of a local majority's will to set itself up as a separate canton carved out from preexisting ones and happily joining the wider federal structure. This flexibility in the Swiss case may be predicated on the weakness of the political center—no one in Switzerland really gives a hoot about who the president is—yet for comparative purposes, the really crucial point is that localism, the sense of having meaningful control over matters of local interest, is something that political centers, national or supranational, weak or strong, can ignore only at their own peril.

As to the democratic open-endedness of American society, there is one further element to consider. It may appear as if all constituent members of the European community can hold their own against the American example of democratic citizenship. Once again, however, it seems that America's long history of incorporating the immigrant, the quintessential homeless mind—a history forcefully reaffirmed in the Fourteenth Amendment to the

Constitution—is a long way ahead of Europe's. The United States has opted for consent rather than descent in its view of whom to consider as qualifying for citizenship. Europe, however, appears as a hidebound society, tending to elevate descent over consent and from time to time reopening the debate on this matter, as happened in France in 1991.[5] The debate centered on an essay in *Figaro Magazine* in which the former president Giscard d'Estaing argued in favor of traditional views of the "droit du sang," the "ius sanguinis," and against the "droit du sol," the "ius soli," which grants citizenship to those born on the national soil. The debate continues, and not only in France. Among European nations Germany may be the clearest case of a nation conceiving itself in terms of a "ius sanguinis," of a *Volk* based on the bloodline of common descent rather than consent. The recent debate in Germany concerning the citizenship rights of its sizable Turkish ethnic community clearly brought out the tacit assumptions on who could rank as a German. It would be hard to think of a German equivalent to Crèvecoeur's classic question. Who then is this new man, the German? More generally, whatever the underlying views of the people who constitute the nation, there is widespread anguish in the European Union concerning immigration and the presence of strangers in its midst. It is only one token of a wider inclination to conceive of the European community as a beleaguered fortress.

One can easily understand this. In its daring enterprise aimed at overcoming Europe's dismal historical record of internecine wars, the European Union may need time to rest, reflect, and digest. Given the spasmodic changes in the rest of Europe, Germany's ingurgitation of a bankrupt former East Germany, civil war in the Balkans, famine threatening in the former Soviet Union, and possible mass movements of refugees from the east, it is no wonder that we see protective moves to pacify voices of protest within the union itself. One way in which to cast the possible alternatives for further action is to think in terms of a continued widening versus a further deepening of the union. The union stands on the eve of a radical further supranational integration, reaching across a wide range of areas of policy making. At the same time, however, new applicants for membership are knocking on the door—as diverse as the newly independent countries in Eastern Europe, not to mention Turkey.

The new applicants pose many different problems. Most are fledgling democracies with backward economies. Nonetheless, with proper transitional periods of affiliated membership, probably all of them could eventually be fully incorporated without upsetting the union's project at deepening its integrative structures. In the "New Europe," however, the logic of widening offers its own dilemmas. Where does Europe end? Where is there a sense of "we Europeans" as a meaningful expression of a larger sovereign people?

Would Russia ever qualify, extending as it does as far as Vladivostok? Does Turkey really qualify, or is it the true test of a submerged sense of Europe as a Christian world, defining itself against the otherness of the world of Islam? What do these further potential applicants really expect to gain from full membership? Is it the participation in a larger, supranational democratic entity? Is it the economic benefits, expected from membership in a larger economic entity?

I am inclined to say the latter, but even if I am wrong, the community would be wise to go slowly regarding new members and, as a first priority, to try to get its economic act together. This would affect not only its position vis-à-vis widening but also its choices in the area of deepening. I suggest that, rather than move full speed ahead across the full range of programs for integration, the community make a concentrated effort to achieve a fully open internal market together with full-fledged monetary union. Not only would the regime and discipline of such a constellation of economic forces work its own logic internally toward eventual integration in other areas, but it would also create an economically vigorous community that would be able to aid and support Europe's economic laggards. As a thriving and stable economic giant, it could help stabilize, through trade and aid, the explosive reservoir left in the wake of communism's demise.

Conclusion: Transnationalism as a European Project

In the foregoing I have set my consideration of the European present in the context of two daring modernist projects aimed at transnationalism, with my emphasis in the case of Europe on its "democratic deficit," on the absence of a vibrant sense of "we Europeans." Yet I cannot simply leave it at that. Even though the European project of community building through supranational coordinating structures has been a top-down project, insufficiently accompanied by integrative developments "at the basis," the project has undeniably had democratic legitimation through the consent of the various national parliaments. Furthermore, as public opinion data have consistently shown, there has been widespread support among the various national populations for the concept, broadly defined, of European integration. Most clearly, the introduction of the direct election of members of the European Parliament testified to the awareness that the European project needed the institutionalized means for the direct expression of such democratic support. Below this superimposed institutional level, however, what projects or autonomous forces might invigorate the sense of a common European identity? Undeniably, one potent force is economic. To the extent that Europe will transform itself into one large economic market, labor mobility is bound to follow the enlargement of the labor market. The massive effort that goes into creating the legislative and regulatory framework for labor mobility on a European scale will at the same time work to erode the relevance of national borders.

Whatever its precise future shape, the European Union will increasingly become the natural area for Europeans to plan their careers and future lives. Of course, labor mobility has already turned many of those countries into multiethnic societies, a process begun following the rapid economic growth of northwestern European countries during the late 1950s. Even though the pattern of migration may have been geographically skewed, with movement generally from the southern European rim to the North, it has already had its democratizing and Europeanizing effect on nations such as Spain and Portugal, both hidebound, autocratic regimes that at the time were still beyond the democratic European pale. Nevertheless, such intra-European labor mobility has never proceeded under the auspices of a declared European project. "Guest workers" tended to be seen as temporary residents at best, as aliens rather than as fellow Europeans. Historically, however, they have been the proto-Europeans, affecting the sense of nationhood both in their countries of origin and in the receiving nations.

In my opening remarks I rather flippantly referred to tourism as a new International, unifying Europe as one large space for holiday makers to fill. Yet there is a more serious point to be made here. Tourism, much like other forms of our culture of consumption, tends to transcend national borders while at the same time eroding them. Admittedly, tourists abroad usually tend to flock together with fellow nationals, re-creating little Hollands, Germanies, and Englands on the Costa Brava, with restaurants catering to their various national tastes, food brought along from home, and their national newspapers available on the local newsstand.

Nonetheless, even this "low" mass-cultural form includes a number of internationalizing elements. First, psychologically, the very scale on which holidays are now planned points to a sense of Europe as the natural area for leisure activities. Foreign European countries are no longer seen as alien or unsafe, where "you can't drink the water, dear." Second, tourism has changed the cultural landscape of Europe. The Costa Brava may regrettably never be the same, yet as an all-European resort, it, like similar places, has been woven into a larger European cultural landscape, as the European answer to Florida or Arizona. My flippancy, though, had more to do with the fact that tourism is in many ways an epiphenomenon, a dependent variable more than a force in its own right, and not truly capable of weaving countries solidly into the larger cultural space of Europe. The sorry sight of bewildered tourists on their way out of a Yugoslavia that was sliding rapidly toward civil war may serve to bring the point home. The Costa Brava may never be the same, but neither will Sarajevo.

Labor mobility and tourism in the recent past have been examples of unplanned Europeanizing forces, so let me conclude by briefly going into one example of a Europeanizing project sponsored by the European Union and felicitously named after Erasmus. As one who has set up one linkage program, bringing together ten universities in seven European countries, and who also has been more widely involved in assessing the success of other, similar programs, I can say that, yes, there is a lot of red tape, there are too many forms to be filled out, and there is too little money available for students and staff involved in these exchanges; beyond all that, however, this Brussels project is a shining example of Europe producing Europeans. The money spent on it is money well spent. If Europe is on the move, it has to move further in this direction. Only then will the European project rank as a daring—and successful—instance of a transnationalism collectively willed and democratically realized.

2. Trespassing in America: American Views of Borders, Boundaries, and Frontiers

The year 1993 marked the centenary of Frederick Jackson Turner's celebrated "frontier thesis." As we can now clearly see, with the wisdom of a full one hundred years' hindsight, Turner's ideas were only one historian's particular approach toward a problem with which American historians in general have grappled: the problem of America's alleged exceptionalism. There is a long history of views of America that see it as an exception to the established lines of development of Western civilization. In that perspective, America has always been conceived as a counterpoint to Europe and European history. For Turner, the concept of the frontier as used in America offered one such dialectical counterpoint to established European views. A description of spatial mobility rather than of geographical closure, it resembled a "front line" in the military sense rather than a frontier, a *frontière*, a *Grenze*, in the European sense. Nor was this the only contrast. The American frontier was not only dynamic rather than static; in addition, as the forward line of settlement moving across the land, it constantly re-created the pristine encounter of civilization and emptiness, vacancy, and open space, necessitating not just the reproduction but also the constant re-creation of civilized society, as if almost from scratch. This element of constant rejuvenation and renewal, this endless series of new beginnings, led Turner to conceive of the frontier as the classic locus of the regenerative power of a metaphorical "America." Earlier phantasms had already pictured America as a fountain of youth, an alchemist's crucible, or a melting pot.[1] A century earlier Crèvecoeur, a French aristocrat posing as "an American Farmer," had already dwelled on this regenerative power when suggesting an answer to his classic question: "What then is the American, this New Man?" As Turner rephrased it, the frontier had served as the regenerative fount, molding the national character of Americans into its quintessential individualism and democratic egalitarianism. Whereas frontiers in Europe were characteristically cast in the mold of national particularisms, delineating the distinctness of national cultures, the frontier in America stood for the impetuous forward march of universalism, the universalism of human equality and human rights, symbolizing America as the usher of a new world order.

Americans were not alone in this global reading of their national destiny. Throughout the nineteenth and well into the twentieth century, many Europeans optimistically viewed America as holding the promise of a future world based on the values of republicanism and democracy. The Statue of Liberty, a French gift to the United States, was meant to express such underlying affinities. The statue represented the American goddess Columbia, facing Europe and holding up her torch in a symbolic gesture of "liberté éclairant le monde" (freedom illuminating the world). It was only later, in a characteristic act of recontextualization, that Americans came to conceive of the statue as the "Mother of Exiles." It changed the reading of the message that Columbia carried. No longer did her forward stride express the rolling frontier of freedom washing across the globe; she was now seen as standing beside the "Golden Door," a keeper of the gate to freedoms found only inside it. She is reminiscent of a sentry at a border hedging off America as a refuge from a world beyond redemption.

Whether we see America, as Turner did, in terms of a rolling frontier, or rather, in the "Mother of Exiles" reading, as a refuge with a clear outside border, either view can admit an alleged American exceptionalism. On the one hand, as an asylum to those who, in Emma Lazarus's words, are "yearning to be free," it would stand as the shining exception to an unfree and downtrodden world. On the other hand, it would be equally exceptional as a country knowing no bounds, as a kernel around which new patterns of a free world order might crystallize, forcibly challenging Europe's hidebound order of nation-states. Nonetheless, its first guise of a country within its own border, exceptional but self-contained, is nothing that Europeans could not handle or translate back into their Continental customs. It would go through "customs" at no charge. There is a far more rigorous break with entrenched European modes of thought in America's second appearance, as the open-ended country of the Turnerian frontier. Therefore, to compare this notion with the European sense of borders, we would be well advised to focus on America as a clear-cut counterpoint and to take its views of the frontier rather than its border as our central concern.

America's self-conception as an essentially boundless entity of course antedates Turner's ideas of the frontier by several centuries. The Puritans' project of founding "the New Jerusalem," the "city upon a hill" for all the world to see, already implied the characteristic cosmopolitanism of their venture. A further element that stood in the way of any narrow circumscription of their endeavor in geographic terms was their Calvinist sense of "being in the world, but not of it." Their main concern was truly "outer-worldly," even though it may have translated over the years into a Yankee variety of Weber's "inner-wordly ascesis." Ideas going back to that early period, ideas of America as a "redeemer nation" or of its "Manifest Destiny," were all of global reach and relevance. There was an open-endedness to the Puritan project that would characterize later American ventures in state and nation building, even though these were of a strictly secular nature. The very conceptions of state and nation were open-ended. As regards the state, from its founding days American federalism was seen as a tool of political syncretism; its open structure of confederated states has seen the federation's constituent members multiply from the original thirteen to fifty, and they may well increase further. As for the nation, it too was conceived as an associative membership group, open to outside applicants. The precise terms of admission may have been subject to debate, yet they have widened over the years because of the universalism inherent in many of the founding ideas, most potently in the idea of "all men" being "created equal." Groups initially excluded, based on race (e.g., Negroes or Chinese), gender, or age (e.g., those between eighteen and twenty-one years old), now fully partake of the status of citizens of the republic. When a xenophobic nativism was afoot in the mid-nineteenth century, Olympian guardians of the national course such as Walt Whitman and Ralph Waldo Emerson stood up against narrow attempts at closing the border. Theirs was the cosmopolitan view of the American nation, which, as a nation of nations, had the makings of a true world nation.

From the early days of independent statehood, the body of citizens has always been seen as a community based on consent rather than descent, subscribing to a set of principles that defined the United States as a political commonwealth. Rights, freedoms, and interests have always been seen as residing in individuals, providing further open-endedness to the political system. The American democracy was the first to adopt the radically individual one person, one vote principle as the basis for political representation. Admittedly, America's mixed political regime has included other, cross-cutting representational principles, such as the equality of all constituent federal states (where each state is represented by two senators in Congress). Still, in combination with America's breakthrough toward the idea of popular sovereignty, of "We the People" as the collective authorial voice of its central state document, the catalytic logic of individual citizenship was equally at work to erode the traditional views of "virtual representation" that were still the wisdom of the day in Europe. Societal interests seen as emanating from society's estates, hierarchically ordered and patriarchally represented, were exploded to make way for the radically atomistic view of political majorities and the general will as a matter of the simple majority of votes cast in elections.

In this, as in the other instances mentioned previously, we can see a radical modular logic working almost as an analytic solvent eating away the traditional boundaries delineating concepts borrowed from Europe. The universalist "frontier" replacing the particularist, historically grown "border" is only one, critically telling case in point. It illustrates a more general bent of American culture. Europeans, time and again, have been struck by the inherent and irreverent antihistoricism in the American cast of mind. They noticed a tendency in the way Americans approached cultural artifacts, be they material or mental constructs, an inclination to take them in total disregard of context and internal cohesion, literally to take them apart, to look at them afresh, to disassemble them and put them together again at will, as if they were mere construction kits. The Dutch historian Johan Huizinga referred to it as an antimetaphysical attitude. Among the many illustrations he provided in his book of travel impressions, a telling and humorous one refers to the Dewey Decimal System, which had then been adopted for the subject catalogs in many of the larger American libraries. "Time and time again living interconnections [in a body of knowledge] have to be severed for the sake of classification—the human mind made subservient to the decimal order."[2] The point keeps recurring in the work of European critics of American culture. The irreverent attitude toward organic cohesion and historic context, toward the European sense of established hierarchies in social and cultural matters—toward the European sense of borders and boundaries, for that matter—was noticed by French, English, German, Italian, Dutch, and other European observers. Not always was it valued negatively. German socialists in the 1920s, as well as Antonio Gramsci in his *Prison Notebooks,* marveled at the breakthroughs of the American modular approach to industrial production. *Taylorism* and *Fordism* were not necessarily words of opprobrium for them. Moreover, a recent French traveler, Jean Baudrillard, performed a true feat of inversion of cultural standards when, in his book *Amérique,* he celebrated the exhilarating and liberating potential of an American culture that had cast off the oppressive straitjacket of European modes of thought. He went so far (although possibly with his tongue in cheek) as to welcome America's exploding such time-honored binaries as quality versus quantity, real versus fake, and high versus low. He welcomed America as the one true modern nation, endlessly spawning its own simulacra. Similarly, Umberto Eco pointed out that the European landscape may have been flattened, but the European heritage has been replicated a hundred times over on American shores as European culture's last beachhead.[3] Finally, another recent vogue may be equally telling. Nowhere else in the world have French poststructuralist ideas, especially Jacques Derrida's *deconstructionism,* been more accepted than in American academia. Asked how he could account for this success, Derrida exclaimed: "L'Amérique, mais c'est la déconstruction!"[4]

He probably has a point. Recent research in a number of areas, from economic investigations covering American techniques of production, distribution, and marketing to studies of American mass media, architecture, music, and literature, shows the same modular mind at work.[5] It is a matter of an underlying rule of transformation guiding processes wherein America borrows cultural material from Europe. There is a refractive lens interposed somewhere along the path of cultural derivation, breaking up rays of light from Europe into their component colors. As if engaged in a giant recombinant DNA project, America is tinkering with its European heritage in a spirit of Yankee ingenuity, itemizing European culture, regardless of time and place, as consisting of just so many replaceable parts that can be recombined at will. The eclecticism of some of America's classic skyscrapers beautifully illustrates this. There is no compelling inherent logic to the skyscraper's number of floors, no *sectio divina,* or Golden Rule, to define its proportions, no unity of style in its aesthetics. It borrows and quotes freely, ranging across art history from Renaissance to beaux arts, piling mock baroque on top of Palladian pastiche. The skyscraper was already postmodern before it was modern.

In this spirit of blithe *bricolage,* in its antihistoricist and antimetaphysical voluntarism, America has had no truck with the European view of borders as something somehow real and worth fighting wars to maintain. More than mere lines on a map, to Europeans borders define the mythical body of the nation. Never mind, as Hobsbawm and, before him, Huizinga have pointed out, the large dose of voluntarism and invention in the European idea of the nation.[6] A construct it may be, yet as a mobilizing myth, arousing and channeling collective energies—much in the way that Georges Sorel understands the concept of myth[7]—it has proved to be a vital ideological force in the nineteenth and twentieth centuries. The sense of nationhood, the sense of common descent, always translates into the sense of a territory as "home," the homeland, *la Patrie, die Heimat.*[8]

This fusion of descent and territory has never sat well in America. Who but Americans could project feelings of nostalgia onto something as open as the frontier, as when they sing of "home, home on the range"? The places they call home are typically more a matter of consent, like voluntary associations almost freely entered for more or less fleeting moments in their highly mobile lives. The consensual community as Americans know it does of course involve its measure of negotiation; it does require a give and take in every individual's adoption of the established conformist mold. But there is always the option of exit. Americans can always go out in search of more kindred communities. There is less *ascription* and more individual *achievement* in the American sense of home.

There is also an essential vicariousness to it. For their sense of home, Americans can draw on a repertoire of nostalgias, of odes to "home" sung at campfires or behind the steering wheel, like so many replicas of the real thing, true "homesickness." For most Americans, their national narrative is an adopted one; many families did not set foot in America until well after the fabled feats of the national heroes gathered in a pantheon that they now acknowledge as their own. The repeated act of appropriating a national lore and its many regional varieties left behind by those who got there first goes a long way toward accounting for the vicariousness of the American sense of home. Again, the same rule of transformation appears to have been at work: something that to Europeans is quintessentially unique and irreplaceable has been ruthlessly modularized by Americans as just so many replaceable parts. Home comes in umpteen flavors and in as many different wrappings.

The same type of voluntarism that allows Americans to speak of nation building informs their language concerning home. They are always willing to look at a new place as "a home away from home." Woman's role is often described as that of the "homemaker." And what other nation could have conceived the mobile home? Home appears here in its ultimate modular form, never sedentary, never properly rooted, never tied to a territory. It represents the ultimate decoupling of home and land, which for Europeans naturally go together as homeland.

Never in its history has the American republic been willing to condone the reproduction on its soil of quasi-European "homelands" (with the possible exception of the parody of a homeland, the Indian reservations). However much it needed immigrants for the population of its western frontier, welcoming them irrespective of national background, it never allowed colonization and land-development schemes to produce self-governing foreign enclaves. Conceivably these might have joined the union as just so many federal "modules," which some German settlement schemes in the 1820s aimed to do. Such an approach, however, would have threatened America's federalist venture with balkanization, reinvesting it with the territorial rigidity of borders and locking it in a grid of national particularisms while preventing it from developing the universalism of its frontier potential. It would have been perennially beset by the sort of problem that now threatens to break up the Canadian federal structure along its one quasi-European border, that between Québec and the other provinces.

* * *

These, then, are ways in which we can express the different senses of borders in America and Europe. There is an underlying difference in mental mold, a rule of transformation that tends to explode the conceptual boundaries of ideas once they travel from Europe to the United States, fragmenting and modularizing them. Nonetheless, the way I have outlined the contrast no doubt contains an element of ideal-typical construction, which, as Max Weber will always remind us, implies exaggeration. For the sake of balance, then, it may be helpful at this point to mention a number of recent trends in the United States that do assert particular cultural identities while challenging the larger unifying discourse concerning the American identity. The key word in these assertions is *multiculturalism*. What is truly at stake is the established canon of American culture. The challenge is being mounted from many different sides. Historically they can all be traced back to the emancipist stirrings of the 1960s. That decade's heady brew of civil rights and countercultural inspirations has worked its dialectical logic, spawning an ever-increasing number of groups in society clamoring for "equal time," carving out their own cultural space, and erecting their own cultural borders. This is perhaps most noticeable in American academic life. There, in a deconstructionist vein, the established reading of American culture and its historical lines of development tends increasingly to be seen as a patriarchal, hegemonic discourse infused by a perspective that is now recognized and rejected as "white," "male," and "Eurocentric." Historically all attempts at constructing an American canon may have aimed at finding a "usable past" to help Americans get a sense of their collective identity, if not destiny, yet these attempts are now seen as unduly "singularizing." Rather than try to establish *the* canon of American literature, the battle is now waged on behalf of American "literatures." The call is no longer for *one* history of *the* American people but for *histories* of all those *Others* that the one, singular reading tended to ignore.

There is an ironic paradox in this pluralizing drift. The overarching metaphor of the moving frontier may have always been cast in universalist terms, conceiving of the American nation as an open-ended yet consensual community organized around a few central universalist tenets, but its inherent modularizing logic is now striking back with a particularist vengeance. Among the voices clamoring for their own particular niche in American society are those of the Native American, voices from the other side of the frontier, so to speak. The frontier was never the pristine encounter between civilization and vacant space that the traditional narrative portrayed. There are particular stories to be told from "the other side of the fence" that until recently had never found a hearing. In addition, other voices from within American society, minority voices, women's voices, may be going against the one universalist reading of what America is all about, yet in their continuing "deconstruction" of the national myth, they appear to be following a modularizing logic that is as quintessentially "the American way" as is the myth of universalism. How these two conflicting logics will work out historically is as yet unclear.

There is a further paradox. Although the defining lines setting off groups of forgotten Others seem to be straightforward—in other words, drawing those lines may seem to be a matter of recovering the lost histories of women, blacks, Native Americans, and so on—what we see happening is an ever further reduction of group histories in the direction of solipsism. Once the defining boundaries start cutting across one another, how do we meaningfully define the forgotten Others? For example, should we speak simply of women, or do we need histories of black women and white women? Do we need to go further and break up histories of white and black women according to class, ethnic groups, age, marital status, historical period, and regional setting? Where do we end in this particularizing quest? If we follow the implied logic, does it not ultimately take us to the level of every individual's unique life experience? Ironically, the quest for pluralizing will then have ended in so many stories that are quintessentially in the singular mode. Meaningful group boundaries will have shrunk to small solipsistic circles.

Of course, solipsism is nothing new in the history of the American sense of self. Emerson and Whitman carried the "song of themselves" to great solipsistic lengths. In their cases, however, the exploration of their innermost feelings was always in the service of ultimate transcendence, always aimed at reaching out toward mythical union with a larger America. That element of transcendence, of meaningfully relating individual experience to a larger collective existence, appears absent in much contemporary work on life in America. Much as the focus is on Others—which seems to imply a dialectical moment of transcendence—what we see is mostly the presentation of "we the forgotten Others" rather than "we among many Others." In merging the two, one loses the dialectic.

American studies is one area of intellectual endeavor where these trends manifest themselves. American studies has become a "many-splintered thing." But there are signs of a countertrend. Founding fathers of the American studies movement (e.g., Leo Marx) and representatives of later generations (e.g., Sacvan Bercovitch and Werner Sollors), as well as Europeans working in the field (e.g., Günter Lenz), are all in their own ways trying to restore a sense of the larger story, transcending the many particularist ones that are now being spawned. In their hands the study of multiculturalism and ethnicity does go back to the old sense of a dialectical transcendence, of an American culture seen as precisely the outcome of the many transactions and negotiations among the endless variety of Others whose life together has been the quintessence of American society.

Nonetheless, the challenge is not only a matter of academic infighting, of clashing intellectual paradigms. When the battle so centrally concerns the reigning definitions of "America," it is no wonder that the battlelines become political as well. For one thing, the emancipist fervor underlying the attack

on the canon of American culture tends to translate into new social sensi-
tivities and even to harden into prescriptive norms of political correctness
in speech, public behavior, and ways of thinking about "minorities" in America. Nor is it surprising to find reactions to this in terms of "thought polic-
ing" and "new orthodoxies" and to see such trends decried as a threat to the
"freedom of speech" and the tolerance that should go with a liberal society.
Most of these countercharges tend to come from the conservative or neoconservative side of the political spectrum. Nevertheless, as we could learn from
an issue of the *New Republic* devoted to this debate about the American canon, it is not simply a matter of the political left versus the political right. There
is an underlying dimension of humanism that can inspire parties on either
side of the battle. As I already pointed out, the very agenda of multiculturalism goes back to the humanist enthusiasms of the 1960s. On behalf of a widening array of groups, its central inspiration is still to give voice to those who
have lived in silence. There is an equal-rights ethic behind this that is itself
part of a larger American tradition. As its critics keep pointing out, however, there is a danger of doctrinaire overstatement in the multiculturalists' case.
As Irving Howe and Arthur Schlesinger Jr. have argued, no attempt to reori-
ent the American canon for whatever humanist cause should ever ignore the
fact that the humanism of civil liberties and equal rights central to America's political history places America squarely in the history of Western civilization.[9] Advocates of minority rights and multicultural relativism should
never lose sight of a history of ideas that has given them their own voice in
the first place. Rather than draw borders on a cultural map, marking off cultural minorities from one another, they might consider a return to the old
frontier idea, for in fact they are carrying forward a wavelike impulse of ongoing emancipation that is potentially an inspiration to the world. Its origins may lie in Europe, much like the origins of liberty; yet again, like liberty, its inspiration may now radiate from America, "éclairant le monde."

3. Between Globalism and Regionalism: A Comparison of Trends in North America and Europe

To the extent that citizenship implies the drawing of borderlines, their point is always to outline areas that help people to locate their cultural affinities. The word *area* suggests geographical specificity, a place one can point out on a map. The map may well be a mental one, however, and its geography may well be one of the imagination. People are always their own cartographers, moving about in a world arranged according to their needs for affiliation and their senses of affinity. There is no necessary correspondence to the world as atlases show it. In an increasingly interdependent world, the meaningful locale in which people lead their lives may no longer be local. As *globalization* comes to be the word commonly used to refer to the expansion of the scale of human interaction, people are ever more cut adrift from their local moorings. Like Hydra's heads, however, regions keep springing up, reasserting themselves as havens in a heartless world. They may arise under commercial auspices and be known as Marlboro Country, turning into cartographic illusions, yet they will always be there as a necessary accompaniment to the flux and motion of an increasingly interwoven world. In this and the following chapter I will adopt two different perspectives to look at possible ways in which regionalism and globalization connect. In both chapters I view globalization as typically leading to human mobility, to moving beyond the small scale of local communities. People may move psychologically, extending their mental map of the world in which they meaningfully participate as a form of inner migration; they may also move physically, changing place within this larger world as they have come to conceive it. Migration, then, has become the typical behavior attending the process of globalization.

Studying human mobility and migration movements from the perspective of regions and regionalism may appear to be a self-defeating exercise. It may seem like trying to use a still camera to capture motion. After all, regions are commonly seen as the stable mooring points for communal life, giving rise to regionalism as a locally rooted sense of place. Migration appears to be the logical opposite, a force of disintegration upsetting local communities. Nonetheless, one can argue that in two different ways regions can be seen as critically linked to the larger picture of migration history. Ever since the rise of capitalism, from its early mercantile stages to its later industrial and postindustrial manifestations, regionally cohesive forms of social life have felt the impact of these larger forces of social transformation. To the extent that migration was one indication of populations responding to these larger forces, expanding their psychological horizons in the planning of their individual and collective lives and then starting to move within these larger frames of reference, it was always a matter of reorientation within established regional settings. There, within family, friendship, and neighborhood networks, the critical weighing of life chances went on. There decisions were taken on who would move where and for how long. As a result populations were mobilized, moving within a number of concentric circles to nearby or more distant labor markets, within or across national borders. Sometimes these movements were in tune with the seasonal changes in the agricultural demand for labor, producing movements back and forth from their rural points of origin; sometimes they constituted a more radical departure from the home setting. Seen from European settings, America occurred as only one point of orientation, drawing some people from a particular region, whereas others chose different and less distant options. As immigration historians have made abundantly clear, however, whatever the destination of migration flows, the itineraries that immigrants took always turned into information channels along which reports flowed back to the home front, keeping it posted on the opportunities and hardships met at the point of arrival. Thus, depending on such flows of information, chains of migration could build up momentum. Early arrivals in such cases were followed by relatives and friends from their region of origin, joining them in the formation of what immigration historians have felicitously called "transplanted communities." Thus, throughout immigration history, regionally cohesive communities have always played an important role in the precise shape that immigration flows assumed.

There is a second, slightly more paradoxical reason to look at the region and regionalism in connection with processes of migration. The present postindustrial, if not postmodern, setting for migration flows, seen against a backdrop of processes of increasing globalization, has ushered in a strangely abstract world. Geography no longer meaningfully defines someone's place of work; the virtual reality of cyberspace has replaced geography as we knew it. Even a concept such as New York, seen as a nodal point in global networks of information flows, has become in a sense "deterritorialized." It has lost its geographical specificity; people anywhere could see themselves as meaningful players in economic transactions centering on "New York." If this is a correct phenomenology of life in our contemporary world, the current reassertion of regionalism may be seen as a reaction to it, the return of "imagined communities" in the face of worldwide processes eroding the regional specificity of communal life. People have increasingly been cut adrift from a sense of mooring and rootedness; today's regionalism is one attempt among others to reinvent cultural frameworks with which people can meaningfully identify. The logic of the attempt is at right angles to the logic of a world increasingly adrift. In other words, its logic goes against the cosmopolitan rationale for migration as a process necessarily attending our joint itinerary toward the one global village.

This chapter looks specifically at regionalism's return to the European scene. It argues that because nation-states remain the prevalent framework for Europeans' identifications with larger collectivities, Europe may face specific problems coping with the return of regionalism. America provides an interesting counterpoint, one that Europeans may do well to study more closely. In what is essentially a long digression, I explore the ways in which regionalism in the United States has played a continuing role in reflections concerning the nation and the republic. It provides the history of an idea that, for all the possible American exceptionalism, may well have relevance for contemporary Europeans.

The Resurgence of Regionalism in Europe

On both sides of the Atlantic Ocean the geography of nation-states is subject to two pressures working in opposite directions and yet—as I will argue—dialectically joined together. One pressure is transnational, transcending the sphere of sovereignty as claimed by individual nation-states. This pressure pushes nation-states to transfer their national powers to supranational bodies. The other pressure, working in the opposite direction, may then be called infranational, centering on a transfer of national powers downward to local or regional bodies. If the two are dialectically related, then one pressure calls forth the other. They are like complementary pressures keeping each other in check and balance.

The case of postwar Europe offers telling examples. Against the backdrop of two world wars—essentially the most recent cases of the longer European history of individual states trying to establish a hegemony over less powerful neighbors—a group of initially six European states engaged in a concerted effort to break this dismal cycle of history. With a keen sense of the interrelation between economics and power politics, and with critical guidance provided by the Americans through the machinery of the Marshall Plan, these

European states moved toward the joint coordination of their economic policies, a process that in 1957 resulted in the European Economic Community. Better known as the Common Market, its aim was the eventual economic union of its member nations, ultimately leading to political union. The membership was widened in several consecutive steps, and the organization now consists of fifteen member states. Further enlargement is imminent. Moreover, steps have been taken, most recently in the Treaty of Maastricht, to work toward ever greater political union. In the process the participating states have weaned themselves from their age-old habits of economic protectionism and ill-conceived attempts at self-sufficiency; they also have traded in large doses of national sovereignty for a share in collective decision making. In addition, and this time even more strongly under American auspices, consecutive steps have been taken toward liberalizing world trade within the institutional framework of the General Agreement on Tariffs and Trade (GATT). In consequence, with national markets increasingly open to outside competition both inside and outside Europe, the debate concerning the loss of national sovereignty tends to be cast increasingly in terms of globalization rather than Europeanization. In the debate the terms of reference tend to widen from the strictly economic impact of globalization—on employment and wages, the competitive edge of national economies, and growth— toward larger topics such as the globalization of culture and its implied threat to national and local cultural identities. As do all large-scale economic transformations, the current one affects people, individually and collectively, through diminishing their senses of security and control, of mastery over their own lives.

In the midst of this, contemporary democratic states find themselves in a paradoxical quandary. They have given up instruments of independent action to supranational bodies or have simply lost them to the anonymous market forces of the world economy. For all practical purposes, however, they are still the central address for the democratic expression of anguish and concern among their national electorates. Voters see their relative impotence to provide satisfactory answers as a lack of responsiveness, a perception resulting in widespread political alienation and voter realignments. In the case of the European Union, the actual decision-making levels are beyond democratic control, reinforcing the sense of a democratic deficit in the newly emerging Europe. Not surprisingly, then, since neither the national governments nor the new European centers of governance are seen as the meaningful addresses for concerted democratic action, citizens tend to turn inward in their quest for a more meaningful stage for purposeful action. A local sense of shared interest and collective identity is being developed, feeding on such disparate elements as a shared distrust of a remote, unresponsive central government, shared economic grievances, or a more ethnic sense of a local or regional identity that is seen as threatened by homogenizing national or transnational policies or forces. Specifying the causes and effects in this potent brew is a matter of detailed study. In some cases it is clearly the sense of embattled local culture that triggers a wider repertoire of economic and political grievances; in other cases it may well be the other way around. For example, in the case of Québec, Canada, the secessionist program centers on the cultural agenda of the French-speaking community, triggering a wider agenda of economic interests of the province. In the case of the Italian Northern League, the distrust of faraway Rome and the fears of paying more than a fair share toward improving the plight of poorer regions, or of receiving a continuing stream of migrants from the South, have triggered the highly contrived construction of a national entity that goes by the name of Padania, the drainage area of the river Po.

Whatever the precise sequence in the rise of regional emancipation movements, regionalism has come back to haunt democratic politics in its traditional national settings. Ranging from Scotland to Ulster, from Brittany to Catalonia, from Slovakia to the successor states of the former Yugoslavia, in varying degrees of viciousness and in varying local constellations of forces, the region has returned as the geographic referent for meaningful cultural and political affiliation. The word *geographic* is the crucial term in this context. The geographic dimension is the one common element in regionalisms that otherwise show a bewildering range of programs and forms of action. In a sense the return of the region is a throwback to an earlier stage of history when the nation-state was still in the making. Then, in what is commonly conceived as a process of modernization, when—to paraphrase a well-known book title—peasants were turned into Frenchmen,[1] the forces of localism gave way to the larger national framework for politics, centering on national parties or movements that spoke and acted on behalf of large, cross-cutting segments of the national population, such as religious groups, socioeconomic classes, racial groups, and more recently, women. Class, race, gender, religion—such were the unifying criteria for concerted political action on the national level.

But geography has now reasserted itself with a vengeance, like the return of the repressed, as Freud would have it. This latter, Freudian connotation may alert us to the often virulent and irrational nature of regionalist movements, as if it were a matter of pent-up feelings, resentments, and memories long suppressed but never vanished, let alone vanquished. In Europe's age of modernity, elites who were in hegemonic control of the national discourse may have deluded themselves into thinking that regionalism was a thing of the past, that it was premodern. As such it may have been worthy of academic study by social geographers busy mapping local cultures and customs before it was too late. Many European nations have a venerable tradition of folk geography, as we might call it, but it was always conceived in the light of a vanishing stage of history, much as Native Americans were nostalgically seen as the "vanishing race" during the late nineteenth century. Of course, Europe has also spawned scholarly geographical traditions that focused on contemporary trends, where geographers looked at the way that the modernizing process, under the aegis of the nation-state, affected how the population regrouped into new regional patterns. Their interest focused on migration flows, settlement patterns, and regional economic concentrations. Nonetheless, their work rarely, if ever, aimed at a political geography in the sense of producing a map of regions as a matrix of political interests pitted against one another within the nation-state. To the extent that work by European, particularly German, geographers was informed by the study of political interests seen in terms of spatial configurations, their analysis was always at the level of the individual nation-state. More appropriately perhaps, their work was in the service of the nation-state, exploring its *Lebensraum* in the Darwinian terms of a struggle for survival. *Geopolitics* may be the proper word to characterize this focus on the geographical dimension of the *raison d'état*. It was not political geography in the sense of an exploration of political fissures within the body politic of the nation-state. Had there been such a tradition, surely Europeans would have been better prepared for the current reassertion of regional interests in contemporary politics.

Regionalism and Pluralism: Two Lines of American Self-Definition

In what may serve as an excursus, I propose to look at America as a counterpoint to the situation I have argued exists in Europe. For Europe, it may have been natural for historians of the modern era to focus on the daring project of forming its many nation-states and to conceive of it as a stage of history that took Europe beyond regional and local action. The United States has been different from its inception. Almost by default, it was a nation-state at birth, gradually filling a continent the size of Europe. Naturally, given this scale of comparison, the United States knew as much spatially ordered divergence as did Europe, in terms of resources, economic interests, cultural diversity, and rival views of *Lebensraum*. With the sole exception of the secession of the southern states in the early 1860s, however, this divergence never appeared in the language of contrasting national interests.

From the early years of their republic, Americans developed a political discourse centering on the regional configuration of divergent political interests. The perspective of what I previously called a political geography came naturally to American political thought. Yet never was this the sole component. The sense of a spatial ordering of political interests always went hand in hand with an astute perception of social diversity, cutting across the regional lines of fissure. If we think of this combined perspective as a two-vector system, the regional vector might be seen as exerting a horizontal pull, creating a potential for regional alignments and conflicts, whereas the social vector then might be seen as vertical, making for patterns of alliance and conflict irrespective of regional setting. The one tradition in American political thought we may call regionalism; the other, pluralism. In their happy conjunction they have made for an American tradition of political thought that has always had a keen eye for the countervailing potential of accommodation in any matrix of conflict. The American constitutional order and its language of checks and balances expresses the early, pragmatic intimation that, when brought together in one system of governance, pluralism and regionalism can work jointly toward stability rather than division. Regionalism found early expression in America's federal structure of coequal states, represented at the central level in the Senate as a federal chamber, whereas the pluralism of America's social divergence would be reflected in the House of Representatives. In yet other ways, as we all know, America's constitutional machinery is an attempt at balancing and checking the dangers of division lurking in any pure type of political rule, be it a monarchy, an aristocracy, or a democracy. The American Constitution has elements of all three, the monarchical in its presidency, the aristocratic in its Supreme Court, and the democratic in its Congress. The American Founding Fathers were heeding time-honored insights that go back all the way to the wisdom of Plato and Aristotle. Yet they went further in adopting ideas of a separation of powers and in diversifying democratic mandates given by the electorate. Elected independently, the president, the Senate, and the House of Representatives each represent divergent configurations of the American democratic public. Through the logic of the varying electoral systems, the Senate tends to overrepresent the less populous states in the union, whereas the majority that votes a president into office is more reflective of the large population concentrations and therefore tends to be more urban than rural. This whole intricate machinery is meant to serve the one central purpose of forestalling, if not altogether avoiding, the eventual decline of republican order.

Ironically, it was an outsider, the French visitor Alexis de Tocqueville, who in his analysis of the viability of American democracy saw the source of political stability less in the intricate machinery of republican institutions than in the pluralism of American society itself. There, in the forms of American social life, the associative habits of the American citizens, Tocqueville saw the stabilizing potential of America's social pluralism. Free to associate with others in the pursuit of their manifold interests, Americans would never feel forced to align themselves along one overriding line of conflict, dividing society "against itself," as Lincoln would have said. Nevertheless, Tocqueville was neither the only nor even the first person to acknowledge sources of political stability outside the strictly political sphere. An American Founding Father, James Madison, had expressed similar insights before him, but with a characteristic difference: in addition to extolling the stabilizing qualities of social pluralism, Madison also strongly emphasized regional pluralism. Thus, in *Federalist Paper 10*, Madison pointed out: "Extend the sphere and you take in a greater variety of parties and interests; you make it less probable that a majority of the whole will have a common motive to invade the rights of other citizens." We might call this not political theory but sociological pragmatism. The emphasis rests less on central principles and values, such as republican virtue or Lockean liberalism, than on the structural conditions for their survival. As Daniel Boorstin put it some forty years ago, the genius of American political reflection lies in making "sociology do for political theory," merging "the descriptive and the normative,"[2] while taking political principles as a matter of consensus, as "given."

This pragmatic assessment of diversity, in both its social and regional forms, has often been linked to America's exceptional geographic location, particularly by outside observers. Thus British author Dennis W. Brogan attributed America's appreciation and acceptance of sectionalism to its "comparative absence of outside pressure; it is a luxury that an isolated people can permit itself."[3] Yet another British author, M. J. C. Vile, put it thus: "Americans have been able to afford the luxury of localism and never having been subject to the same pressures as European countries, at any rate until the present century, they have rejected the idea of an undivided all-powerful national sovereign, they have insisted that on some matters the final power of decision lies in the *local* community."[4]

Against this background it is not surprising that Americans have produced an intellectual tradition in the study of regionalism that differs in characteristic ways from European traditions. This is not to say that there are no parallels. Whatever its specific national setting, regionalism as an intellectual endeavor is always by its nature descriptive. Its quest is always for the delineation of entities that are both spatially distinct and internally homogeneous. As with any such project, the object of research may occasionally lead the researcher astray. There is always the danger that the everyday, naïve experience of regional difference may lead us beyond the careful documentation of such difference into the preconceived idea that the region is something "out there," waiting to be discovered. It is the classic pitfall of conceptual realism, *Begriffsrealismus,* where the very fact that we have a notion of the region means that it must exist in reality. The history of regional geography in both Europe and America offers clear illustrations of this mistaken quest.

As I argued before, however, there are characteristic differences as well. The most telling clue in this respect may be the use of the word *sectionalism,* which perhaps indicates Americans' intuitive sense that regional variety should always be conceived dialectically. Moving beyond regionalism as the attempt to grasp the full extent of regionally enclosed homogeneity, sectionalism looks at regional diversity in terms of its problematic relation to national unity. As Max Lerner once put it: "The section may be the region in its political aspect, but it has divisive overtones, while the region has cohesive ones."[5] The implied dialectics comes out even more clearly in his observation that "this pluralism [of regions] is one of the facts that gives Americans their impulse to cohesion."[6] The concept of section in this sense goes back to the work of Frederick Jackson Turner, who introduced and elaborated the concept in his later publications.[7] I will return to sectionalism in a moment, but first I turn to American regionalism as a purely descriptive tradition.

Characterizing a large territory in terms of its regional features is of course a well-established tool of description. Recall Julius Caesar's famous opening line, "Gallia omnis divisa est in partes tres" (All Gaul is divided in three parts). Regionalization for the sake of orderly presentation is a recurring feature in the description of America as well, appearing in popular genres such as journalism, travelogues, and tourist guides. Ever since the early years of the American republic, however, regionalism has also been used in a more disciplined way, guided by concerns such as what criteria to use or how to establish the validity of research findings. The oldest tradition is that of geographers who set out to group data concerning climate, soil, and social structure in regional patterns. Jedidiah Morse, the father of American geography, was among the first who tried to produce a satisfactory regional map of the United States. On the basis of the existing political structure of individual federal states, he tried to group these in terms of geographical characteristics. His approach was still rather intuitive and impressionistic. As the number of states grew, he came to often ingenious revisions of his scheme. Many geographers after him continued to work in this vein. Thus in 1870 Steinwehr and Brinton devised a scheme of sections on the basis of "natural divisions," using criteria of physical geography. Their approach was new in that they no longer took the existing map of states and territories as their starting point.[8] In 1898 Redway and Hinman, in their *Natural Advanced Geography*, introduced the concept of "industrial sections"; they combined differences in surface structure, climate, and soil with five main products of human toil, which together resulted in their scheme of regions.[9] At about the same time—1895—John Wesley Powell, the director of the U.S. Geographical Survey, published his *Physiographic Regions of the U.S.* It presents an ordering of strictly physiographic material, irrespective of differences in social structure or state borders. The book's central feature was the frequent use of cartographic techniques.[10] Later years produced a great many works, both physiographic and more generally geographic, that illustrate the enduring vogue of this kind of regionalism.

This tradition accompanied a second development. Its early rise is linked to George Tucker, a professor at the University of Virginia. In 1843 he published a survey of census material from the preceding fifty years. On the one hand, he used a fivefold division based on climate, product, and the dominant "habits and pursuits" of the population to present his material. On the other, he came up with a fourfold scheme based on geographical location and the presence or absence of slavery to present data concerning population size, density, and increase. His approach clearly shows an attempt to systematically analyze correlations among the disparate data.[11] Later on, in the twentieth century, this would lead to the use of more sophisticated statistical techniques of data reduction, such as factor analysis and principal components analysis. A leap forward in this tradition came in the 1870s with the use of statistical cartography. Ever since then this has remained a standard tool for the presentation of census material. It allows the visual representation of disparate data on a single map, showing their spatial coincidence. In particular, this technique has become an important instrument for devising new regional schemes as well as for discarding old ones. Its adoption meant a definite farewell to older, qualitative-impressionist approaches.

An important figure in this development is Henri Garnett of the U.S. Census Bureau. His publication *Natural Groupings of the U.S.* was seminal. His ideas have gained currency through their adoption by *Scribner's Statistical Atlas* (1883) and *Scribner's Historical Atlas* (1890).[12] Drawing on the rich store of data contained in the census bureau's reports, this representational technique made it possible to visualize selected aspects of American society, such as patterns of consumption and production or economic relations in agriculture as they appeared from the relative numbers of tenants, share-croppers, and landowners. The variety of agricultural products could be shown in the same way, using the dot-map technique. Classic examples are the publications of the U.S. Bureau of Agricultural Economics, directed by O. B. Baker; particularly noteworthy are his *Atlas of American Agriculture*,[13] and his compendium *A Graphic Summary of American Agriculture Based Largely on the Census*.[14] Baker's work is one of the most meticulous attempts at producing regional schemes that were neither too comprehensive nor too ambitious. The results of his efforts are precise, valid, and broadly useful. In addition, economists and demographers, also drawing on census material, have used similar techniques of representation, resulting in yet other regional schemes.[15]

* * *

There is yet a third main tradition in American regionalism, which we can trace back to a group of historians at the University of Wisconsin. Undoubtedly the most famous among them is Frederick Jackson Turner. They added election data and voting patterns in Congress to the kind of material used by geographers or collected for the U.S. Census in their search for regions as meaningful entities of social and political life. An early publication in this vein is Humphrey J. Desmond's article "The Sectional Feature in American Politics." Desmond based his analysis on election data from 1796–1884. One quotation may serve to give the reader a sense of his argument: "A federal government attempting to do a great many things in a great many directions is sure to arouse warring interests and clashing influences. And in a country which reaches from the Atlantic to the Pacific and touches the Tropics, and stretches out to the land of the midnight sun, all such interests are more or less geographical and sectional."[16] This strong emphasis on geographical elements characterized the Wisconsin school more generally in its approach to American history. Here perhaps most clearly we can see the lurking danger of a *Begriffsrealistische* exaggeration of the regionalist approach. As the Desmond quotation illustrates, he deductively concludes that the very expanse of the United States necessarily implies the role of regionally based interest groups. He thus logically infers the importance of the region. The task for historians is therefore to conduct research that shows these regions as they "really" exist. It comes as no surprise, then, to see historians of the Wisconsin school refer to "*underlying* sectional areas" that, for instance, Libby, a student of Turner, proposes "to bring to light."[17]

Looking at these historians, we can see the various lines of regionalist thought coming together. Thus Turner argued for combining analytic techniques as developed so far with a view to delineate the "natural," nonstate areas. I will return later to the precise interpretative thrust that Turner gave to his views of section and sectionalism. On occasion he linked them to his concept of the frontier, but especially in his later work, he used them in a more general sense. In Turner's approach in particular, the concept of section develops its full claims as regards the implied realism of the concept and its centrality in the gravitational field of political vectors. At one point Turner argues: "Our sections are becoming more and more the American version of European nations. . . . we have become a nation comparable to all Europe in area, with separate geographic provinces which equal great European nations. We are in this sense an empire, a federation of sections, a union of potential nations."[18] Elsewhere Turner compares Congress to the League of Nations.[19]

In this context I should also mention the regionalist tradition that flourished at the University of North Carolina during the 1930s. It was inspired mainly by H. W. Odum, who undertook what was perhaps the most ambitious attempt to delineate the socioeconomic regions of the United States. One assumption guiding the endeavor was that such regions are characterized by, among other things, their own "way of life." Therefore the research aimed at establishing a regional consciousness centering on a specific pattern of values. The American South had a long tradition in such cultural self-definition, although other regions show similar impulses. Particularly

Odum's *American Regionalism,* coauthored with H. W. Moore, aims to delineate the "major social regions" of the United States: "Such a region to be
definitive, must approximate the largest degree of homogeneity for the largest
number of purposes."[20] This approach was less influential within American
social sciences than one might have expected. Nonetheless, at the University
of North Carolina—before World War II perhaps the most enlightened and
progressive southern university—Odum's work stimulated the further elaboration of the theme of a distinct cultural identity of the South, a region
unlike any other. The North Carolina approach inspired such excellent studies
as R. B. Vance's *Human Factors in Cotton Culture* (Chapel Hill, 1929) and his
Human Geography of the South (Chapel Hill, 1933).

Nevertheless, protest had already been stirring against the increasing arrogation of analytic powers claimed by regionalism. Thus in 1914, N. M. Fenneman had argued that "no one set of sub-divisions of a continent can be
made to serve in all discussions. The scheme of sub-divisions must vary according to the things discussed."[21] He thus stimulated a discussion about the
sense and uses of regionalism that would culminate at the 1933 and 1934 an-
nual conventions of the Association of American Geographers. In 1937 John
Leighly called regional geography "unscientific"; he deemed it impossible "to
synthesize arbitrarily selected heterogeneous facts."[22] This, according to him,
was the work of the artist, not the scientist.

Undoubtedly regionalism as a scholarly exercise had made itself vulnera-
ble to such attacks, as the following quotations from a much-used textbook
of the period indicate: "Dividing a continent into regions is a matter of 'scientific generalizing' and is not, as someone once remarked, 'merely a peda-
gogical device to facilitate the presentation of geographical material to classes of students'"—a statement that, a little further on, the textbook itself
undermined by saying: "The authors of this book have consulted maps made
by all these methods [for delineating manufacturing districts] but the most
important criterion utilized has been the regionalist's 'feel' of the area."[23] Thus,
the ambitious claims for regionalism were maintained while at the same time
regionalism was made the esoteric domain of initiated insiders. Such exag-
gerated claims, ironically, appear to have been canonized in the unsatisfacto-
ry definition of *regionalism* by *Webster's Third Unabridged Dictionary.* Regionalism, according to *Webster's,* is "the study of regional societies as distinct
geographical and socio-cultural complexes esp. in their relationship to other
regions and to composite national societies of which they form a part."

It is beyond dispute, however, that in its more modest ambition as a descriptive method, regionalism remains a useful tool for analyzing geographical diversity within American society. This approach has produced several
good histories of special regions of the United States, such as the South or
the West.[24] A classic example is Walter Prescott Webb's work *The Great Plains,*

in which the author chose to focus his historical analysis on a region defined by its physiographic characteristics.[25] One rather exceptional case among American historians with a geographical perspective was Ellen Churchill Semple. Semple was a student of Friedrich Ratzel in Germany and the author of *American History and Its Geographic Condition* (New York, 1933), a work in which she merged the perspectives of German *Anthropogeographie* and American regionalism.

In this survey of regionalism as a descriptive tradition, I should also mention the study of linguistic regions, a field commonly known as linguistic regionalism. Hans Kurath, one of the leading early lights in the field, defined the program for linguistic regionalism as "the construction of a refined scheme of dialect areas based upon lexical, phonetic, and morphological isoglosses."[26] Objecting to the approach thus defined, critics have argued that it neglects the social dimension of linguistic diversity. As Glenda Pickford put it in 1956: "Geography is only one factor reflected in linguistic diversity . . . ; in America, it is *not* the most important." She argued on behalf of a "modernized, sociologically-minded American dialectology," an approach that came to fruition later and is now known as sociolinguistics.[27] Nonetheless, as Hans Galinsky, a German scholar in the field, argued in 1972, the distinction between the social and the geographical is not as unambiguous as it may seem. As he put it: "Ein Problem stellt sich sofort: Sind die sozialdialektischen Erscheinungen nationweit verbreitet, d.h. sind sie soziale Differenzierungen einer Gemeinsprache, oder sind auch sie, wenn nicht der absoluten, so doch der relativen Verbreitung nach, z.B. in Form besonderer Konzentration, und der Entstehung nach regional bzw. sub-regional gebunden? Sind also Sozialdialekte im Grunde soziale Differenzierungen von Regional-dialekten?"[28]

* * *

Since the debates in the 1930s regionalism has shed its delusions of conceptual realism. It is now predominantly a descriptive tool put to pragmatic uses. The increasing demand for regionalist knowledge as a tool for administrative purposes, particularly since the Roosevelt era, has played an important role in this shift. Turner may have toyed with the idea that regionalist insights into the interplay between social life and its geographical and geophysical conditions should constitute the basis for a new delineation of the states as federal entities, yet regionalism failed to turn this into a practical guideline until 1940. As one publication argued: "These sub-divisions of the U.S. should be of value to administrations concerned with planning programs to fit specific areas and situations and with laying out the territory for decentralizing administrative functions."[29]

In the same spirit J. W. Fesler wrote a working paper for the Committee on Administrative Management, set up by President Roosevelt. In this paper, entitled "Executive Management and the Federal Field Service," he warned against the undue standardization of federal regions in view of the great diversity of federal functions and regional problems.[30] Fesler's recommendations influenced the later decentralization of federal policy as well as the creation of regional development committees and interstate compacts for regional development. The most spectacular example of this trend is the Tennessee Valley project. With a view to the large-scale economic and social rehabilitation of the southern Appalachian region, clearly only federal government planning could transcend established state borders to embrace the entire Tennessee River region, including tributaries. The Tennessee Valley Authority, set up to implement this project, was a political innovation. As the discussions preceding its enactment show, the agency was seen as infringing on established state powers and therefore hotly contested as a constitutional anomaly.[31]

When, following Louis Wirth, we conceive of "planning regions" as attempts "to shape the most appropriate units of organization for collective needs,"[32] it is clear that this form of regional approach is inherently politically innovative, trying to adapt the framework for policy implementation to specific policy objectives. To the extent that the approach is suggestive of innovations, these will have to be won against the inertia of entrenched political powers. It is small wonder, then, that the Tennessee Valley Authority is still a rather unique case of such innovation.

The use of the regionalist approach for purposes of political administration clearly illustrates the more pragmatic turn that regionalism has taken. In this approach regions are now being delineated either as the locus of specific problems to be solved by specific policies or as the locus of concentration for activities whose administration could be handled more efficiently by one coordinating body. An illustration of the latter could be the Port of New York Authority, which is a publicly chartered agency with binding authority over transportation, whether by sea, air, or underground rail, centering on New York City but affecting neighboring areas in New Jersey and Connecticut. As early as 1935 some seventy federal government bureaus used one hundred different regional maps designed to fit their specific policy objectives.[33] Following the rapid expansion of urban areas after World War II, the problem of delineating regional entities for policy purposes has increasingly become one of drawing metropolitan regions to be used for metropolitan regional plans.[34]

Regionalism, Sectionalism, and Pluralism

I now turn to regionalism, sectionalism, and pluralism. "Sectionalism in American politics has always been to some degree a cartographic illusion. . . .

[It] conceals the fact that within each region a minority exists which remains unmoved by appeals to the predominant sectional interest." These words were written in 1942 by V. O. Key.[35] They express a sense that has always been present in American political thought. Madison's words from *Federalist Paper 10* that I quoted earlier already reflect this basic insight of pluralism: the more diverse the interests among the population are, the more limited the disruptive potential of each single clash of interests will be. Tellingly, however, the regional matrix for the pluralism of interests repeatedly forces itself on observers as being the most salient. Thus it was also Madison who said: "The great danger to our general government is the great southern and northern interests of the continent, being opposed to each other. Look to the votes in Congress, and most of them stand divided by the geography, not according to the size of the state."[36] Washington as well, in his farewell address, pointed to the possibility of parties forming on geographic grounds: North against South and the Atlantic border against the West. Such awareness had, in the days of the Confederation, inspired the Northwest Ordinance of 1787: newly acquired territories in the West would not be added to any of the existing states, an act designed to prevent states from acquiring hegemony over others.

Despite the emphasis on the geographic appearance of the harmony or conflict of interests, however, the core intimation of pluralism is always there: the greater the variety of interests, the smaller the likelihood of division. Half a century after the generation of the Founding Fathers, when the opposition of North against South grew ever more acute and a regional sense of identity—particularly in the South—began to resemble ever more closely a sense of nationhood, pluralism continued to inform southern thinking. The clearest illustration is John Calhoun's theory of "concurrent majorities." As A. O. Spain, Calhoun's intellectual biographer, argued in 1952:

> Calhoun developed the idea of a concurrent majority in opposition to the simple numerical majority of normal democratic theory. Society is composed of different and conflicting interests, and a "constitutional" system of government is one in which the majority view *within each interest* was taken into account, not merely the numerical majority of the country taken as a simple unit. For Calhoun the important interests in the U.S were almost exclusively geographical, resulting mainly from differences in climate, soil, situation, industry and production. . . . Each interest must be able to exercise a "veto" over decisions vitally affecting that interest.[37]

Apart from the regional emphasis, and disregarding Calhoun's highly partisan polemical purpose (he wrote in defense of the South's "peculiar institution"), the argument appears as if inspired by America's political pluralists of a full century later. The logic of Calhoun's argument should have taken him toward a consideration of the social pluralism within the South. It should

have led him to ask whether majorities among the various segments of southern society concurred in the course the South was taking. Calhoun of course
was not sufficiently disinterested to pursue his argument along those lines.
He wrote on behalf of a South whose voting white citizenry was, to him, the
one relevant entity; if it did not concur—on a state-by-state basis—with federal policies, it should be seen as having vetoed them. In Calhoun's partisan
view, the Constitution as a compact between the states led to his assertion
of the right of secession. Now clearly, secession is a feasible political option
only when the sole basis for the distribution of interests and interest groups
is geographic. Equally clearly, such a case can exist only in the realm of conceptual constructs. In reality interests are never distributed along solely geographic lines. Every local setting houses interests that are ordered vertically,
cutting across regional interests. Twentieth-century pluralists have tended to
focus more on the effects of such cross-cutting, more so, at least, than the
traditional regionalists did.

Similar intuitions have guided the work of the Wisconsin school historians. They characteristically look at sections in terms of both their divisive-
ness and their power to bind, but individual authors exhibit telling differences in the way they made up the balance. Thus on the one hand, Humphrey
J. Desmond[38] argued that "the Constitution, though a compact between the
states, was essentially a treaty of alliance between two great sections having
opposite civilizations and diverse interests"—a view that clearly emphasizes
contrast and conflict within the union; on the other hand, Turner, in his view
of the West as a third distinct region, underlined its potential for mediation
and cooperation. As Turner himself put it: "The frontier stretched along the
Western border like a cord of union . . . [and] in its economic and social
characteristics . . . works against sectionalism and disunion."[39] Almost as a
paradox we can recognize the basic idea of pluralism: the crosscutting of
sections is seen to prevent sectionalism.

This recurring insight is truly a basic component of American political
wisdom. It connects the early federalists, the sectionalists, and the pluralists
of our century. More systematically than before, though, the regional appearance of conflicts of interests may now be seen as one configuration among
others—as only one pattern occasioning the formation of alignments and
oppositions. Among the post–World War II pluralists, attention has shifted
away from the spatial patterns and toward more vertical ones, in a variety of
settings, centering on interests of class, race, gender, ethnicity, religion, lifestyles, and generations. Moreover, more clearly than before, an awareness has
risen that the region as such can be seen to have interests, for instance, in its
relation to a political center or in terms of its place in distributive systems of
political power and resources. In that sense the region appears as more than

the mere spatial configuration of truly nongeographic interests. Seminal work exploring these geographic dimensions of political conflict was done by Edward Shils and Alvin Gouldner.[40] Particularly Shils's analytic concept of center versus periphery and Gouldner's analysis of aspects of reciprocity and autonomy in the way systems relate to subsystems have stimulated research into the spatial aspects of political arrangements. Some authors have gone as far as to project center-periphery ideas onto the larger canvass of the Western Hemisphere in their studies of exploitation and underdevelopment, an approach popular in the heyday of Marxist studies of American imperialism. Whether the language was one of center versus periphery or of metropole versus satellite, it may have seemed as if the Western Hemisphere had become the arena for a new American sectionalism. More recently, with the anguished debate about a globalization of world culture, if not its Americanization, the arena may well have become the whole globe. Consequently, I return to Europe and explore some of the ways in which processes of globalization have affected Europeans.

L'Europe des Régions?

John Stuart Mill despised small-nation nationalism. "Nobody can suppose that it is not more beneficial for a Breton or a Basque of French Navarre to be . . . a member of the French nationality, admitted on equal terms to all the privileges of French citizenship . . . , than to sulk on his own rocks, the half-savage relic of past times, revolving in his own little mental orbit, without participation or interest in the general movement of the world."[41] Mill expresses the enlightenment enthusiasm for a cosmopolitan citizenship, connecting individuals to "the general movement of the world." The logic of this view seems to lead to a transcendence of even the large-nation nationalism toward a universal world citizenship, and indeed such was the thrust of American and European Enlightenment views of the "rights of man" as world citizen. In the following century, however, Europe would never get beyond the nation as the largest viable setting for this modernizing project. It did succeed in breaking down the small horizons of localism and regionalism that had defined the sphere of communal life for the average human being until then. European nineteenth-century nationalism was in that sense a halfway station, leading people away from local affiliation and toward the larger entity of the nation. As I have argued before, only two modernizing projects—Americanism and socialism—then aimed at taking the process further, toward a truly transnational stage. As the recent collapse of the Soviet empire shows, however, at least the socialist (or more precisely, the communist) attempt at establishing a transnational empire has broken down along the many lines of fissure of local identities. The one common language of the larger empire, Russian, is giving way to the variety of local languages and to a reassertion of local cultural identities.

In contrast to America, where, as I have already argued, regions threaten to become nations, Europe may now be a space where nations may threaten to break down into regions. This applies not only to those parts of Europe where the collapse of a political regime ushers in an era of fragmentation, as in the former Soviet Union or the former Yugoslavia, but also to those parts of Europe that since World War II have been engaged in the daring leap toward transnationalism that the construction of the European Union constitutes. For reasons that I outlined in the first part of my argument, regional identities below the level of established nation-state structures are resurfacing. The interesting feature in this latter case is that the principal factor behind the reassertion of regional identities has not been the collapse of political structures that were felt to be oppressive. Rather, it seems that many of the demands for devolution, if not for actual regional autonomy, have been facilitated by the evolving larger structures of European authority, such as the European Court, the European Commission, and the European Parliament. Many claims for the acknowledgment of regional identities are set within the larger context of the European Community. The question therefore may well be whether the future Europe is not more likely to be one of an "Europe des régions" than an "Europe des nations," to paraphrase Gaullist language. In fact, in a development parallel to those I have traced for America, regions within Europe may well come to be seen as more natural entities for policy formation and implementation than are the established nation-state structures. Such a revision would entail a drastic revamping of the map of Europe not only in terms of economic activities, markets, and interdependencies but also in terms of entities that local populations see as providing solidarity and cultural identity. The Dutch entrepreneur Alfred Heineken instigated a project aimed at devising precisely such a map of a Europe of regions, regrouping population segments according to such criteria.[42] Subsidiarity has become one of the buzzwords in an emerging European Union trying to find the regional scheme for the devolution of governmental tasks from the central European level downward, but it may well be that the established nation-state structures are too much a relic of the past, sitting awkwardly in the way of meaningful devolution of government functions.

Surely this quest for a new map of Europe may seem to make sense when it comes to the more efficient administration of government tasks. Criteria of administrative efficiency could be impartially weighed against the claims of existing national government structures. In that sense there is a clear case for a federalization of British government along the lines of the federal German structure. It may go a long way to accommodate claims for greater administrative autonomy on the part of, for instance, Scotland. Nevertheless, the case is not as clear-cut when it comes to the cultural dimension of the regional resurgence, with its claims for the reinstatement of local languages on a par with established national languages. That takes us back to the qualms expressed in John Stuart Mill's curt dismissal of small nationalisms. In particular, the claims for a revival of local cultures, centered on claims made on behalf of regional languages, seem to involve an antimodernist reaction directed against the globalizing tendencies, particularly in the cultural realm, that engulf all contemporary societies.

Migration and Regionalism

If one valid reading of the resurgence of regionalism is to see it as a cultural retrenchment in the face of globalizing tendencies, migration as one manifestation of these larger trends may have particular force in giving these trends their concrete bite at the local level. The grounds for anti-immigration activism may be many, casting immigrants as a threat to employment opportunities and wage levels in the economic sphere or to the continued functioning of entitlement programs in the political sphere, yet a sense of cultural threat always adds something to such discourse. Immigrants are the strangers endangering the cultural integrity of a people's native territory. Nativism therefore is a felicitous word for anti-immigration sentiments. It helps to bring out the aspects of established cultural communities developing strategies of excluding outsiders while narrowing down the definitions of who ranks as an insider. On occasion it may work to reinforce views of the nation, narrowly conceived, as in the case of the "One Hundred Percent Americanism" crusade earlier in this century or in the slogan of "Germany for the Germans" bellowed by young anti-immigration protesters more recently. More generally, however, when it comes to drawing cultural lines, producing binary schemes that oppose "them" and "us," the cultural entity that is presented as pure and homogeneous and in need of defense is most commonly the native ground of regions. Regions in that sense may be the strongest bulwarks against the threat of cultural miscegenation. The nation, although etymologically akin to the word *nativism*, is too much a product of the age of modernity, too much imbued with ideals of cosmopolitanism, to provide the natural language and frame of reference for a defense of cultural localism. In the present context of anti-immigration movements, therefore, the region stands as the natural bastion against cultural invasion. The logic of the regionalist discourse, defending and defining the regional identity in exclusionist terms, stands at right angles to the logic of migration movements and the discourse of multiculturalism. Thus, immigration and the concept of multiculturalism challenge Québécois separatism more than they do Canadian nationhood. Similarly, European claims of cultural specificity, even claims as contrived and artificial as those in the case of northern Italian separatism, always involve immigration. The rift between central government policies and regionalist movements occurs most patently where central governments, implementing policies designed to integrate refugees and asylum seekers, disperse them across the national territory, thus confronting local communities with the advent of strangers in their midst. More often than not, the reaction is one of alienation from central government policies, reinforcing demands of local autonomy.

How does America fit into this pattern? Clearly, as this excursion into the American awareness of regions as meaningful configurations of political, economic, and cultural interests has shown, there is an American tradition of pluralism that recognizes the geographic component of interest politics in a sophisticated way. The excursion explored a peculiarly American history of ideas concerning the region and regionalism. Rather than constitute a threat to the continued cohesion of the nation-state, regionalism was seen as a stabilizing factor according to the central Madisonian maxim of pluralism, which holds that the greater the diversity, the less the likelihood of fissure along one main dividing line. Regionalism therefore never was the dormant repertoire that it became in Europe, where until recently it was seen as a relic of the past, set on a course of eventual extinction. In the United States regionalism has always provided one way among many others in which Americans could express their sense of identity, constituting one point along a continuum rather than a polar opposite to identification with the nation. Not surprisingly, then, regionalism in the United States has not become a rallying point for anti-immigration forces or more generally for movements resisting the encroachments of globalization. If there is a parallel to Europe's resurgence of regionalism, it is the rise of ethnic awareness. The claims made on behalf of a multivocal America may well be considered the current parallel to the quest for authentic voices that, in Europe, are rooted in the region. There is an irony here, in the sense that in Europe the voice of regionalism may be understood as speaking on behalf of ethnic identities seen as geographically located. In that sense Europe's many ethnicities reflect an older Europe, predating the impact of forces of modernization, industrialization, urbanization, and large-scale migration movements. In the United States, however, the many ethnic voices reflect precisely those transformations. They would never have been heard had the United States not been the nation of immigrants that it is.

4. Immigrants and Transnational Localism: A Focus on Photography

At the end of the last chapter, I left the immigrant as a stranger in the midst of societies of arrival. My focus there was on the response of the host society retrenching behind exclusionary lines of a revived regionalism. In this chapter I change perspective and look at the ways in which regional affiliations may have sustained immigrants in their new settings, connecting them to relatives, friends, and neighbors in their areas of origin. They expressed these continuing bonds through letters sent home, trying to preserve a sense of intimacy with those who had stayed behind. They also added a touch of closeness by using photography as a visual aid to provide vicarious eye contact. There is an enticing directness to these photographs; they suggest a density of information, even though the rich and manifold meanings they held for their recipients may have faded a century or more down the road. Later observers can only try to re-create the role photographs played in preserving virtual communities of intimacy spanning half the globe.

* * *

We all know the great photographic icons of American immigration. We can, at the flick of a mental switch, call forth the images of immigrants setting foot on Ellis Island, carrying their meager belongings in a bundle. In a strange intimacy, we see the faces of immigrants in repose yet anticipating the imminent encounter with their new country. We remember Lewis Hine's *Madonna of Ellis Island* or Alfred Stieglitz's *Steerage*.[1] There have been millions of immigrants like them, yet we have a sense of knowing them all and having shared their experiences. Photography has the strange power to catch the fleeting moment while at the same time condensing into one representation the great anonymous processes of history, with their casts of thousands or even millions caught up in war, migration, industrialization, and urbanization. We look at these pictures and have a feeling of a "democratic vista" restored, of a meaningful communion with unknown and untold others. They and their stories are untold no longer. In its iconic powers, photography has the Whitmanesque force of a democratic art.

Even though photographic icons belong to the public domain, even though they have become public representations that powerfully control our collective imagination of vast and impersonal events, they are not unlike the individual human beings frozen in their frames. Just as millions of unseen others hide behind the faces of those whom we will never forget, so do millions of photographs lurk behind the glossy radiance of the pictures that have reached iconic status. They have not penetrated into the public domain, nor were many of them ever intended to do so. They functioned always on a level of communication much more private than that of the pictures of Hine or Stieglitz, whose impulse was documentary, the making of a public statement. When Stieglitz reflected in an almost transcendentalist vein on what had moved him when he took the picture that would become known as *The Steerage,* he said: "I saw shapes relating to one another—a picture of shapes, and underlying it, a new vision that held me: simple people, the feeling of ship, ocean, sky: a sense of release that I was away from the mob called rich." Private his emotion may have been, yet it was one of public communion, one moreover that he meant to turn into public communication. "Some months later, after *The Steerage* was printed, I felt satisfied, something I have not been very often. When it was published, I felt that if all my photographs were lost and I were represented only by *The Steerage,* that would be quite all right."[2] This single photograph would then have sufficed as Stieglitz's public statement, affirming his calling as an artist. It would forever "represent" him through its representation of an act of democratic communion.

As I already said, however, most photographic representations of the immigrants functioned on a different level of communication. They were part of highly private exchanges meant to convey their messages within private networks of relatives and friends. They added a visual element to ongoing written exchanges and could derive their precise reading only from that context. The icons that we all know how to read are like the photographs in the window display of an archive storing millions of pictures whose reading has become uncertain. It is an archive of almost Borges-like dimensions, a maze of many nooks and niches, stacked with uncataloged boxes of words and images, fragments of stories, that we may no longer be able to piece together. Occasionally there are guides, ghostlike figures who have only their memories to live by and who can bring words and pictures together again. One such guide emerges from the pages of Louis Adamic's *Laughing in the Jun-*

gle, an old and frail migrant who returned from the United States to the old country in what, until recently, we knew as Yugoslavia. At one point Adamic remembers the day from his youth when he sat beside this old man, listening to his stories about work in the mines and the steel industry and looking at photographs that the old man had brought home with him, including shots of New York: "'The day before I sailed home I walked in the streets'—he pointed at the picture—'where the buildings are tallest—and I looked up, and I can hardly describe my feelings. I realized that there was much of our work and strength, frozen in the greatness of America. I felt that, although I was going home . . . , I was actually leaving myself in America.'"[3] More often than not, however, such explanatory voices have gone silent. We are left facing photographs that no longer tell their own story. We are no longer able to re-create the recognition they evoked at both ends of lines of communication maintained between immigrants and those who had stayed behind. Such photographs have become the silent documents of an anonymous past.

Thus at Calvin College (Grand Rapids, Mich.), the center of learning for the Christian-Reformed Dutch American community, visitors to the archives of the Historical Collection at Heritage Hall come on many photographs whose sitters are referred to as "unidentified persons." Many of the older pictures are studio photographs, giving us the name of the studio in ornate lettering. The sitters have dressed for the occasion and are set against backdrops redolent of luxurious mansions. They were Stieglitz's "simple people" who briefly identified with "the mob called rich." Who did these early immigrants want to impress? Were these photographs ever sent to relatives in the home country? Did they simply serve to provide embellished family memoirs in their vicarious display of a life of ease and luxury?

We will never know. What we do know is that these photographs belong to an era and a genre of studio portraiture where photography was made subservient to the creation of an illusion. The new medium of mechanical reproduction reproduced for the many the pictorial aura of ease, refinement, and culture that only the wealthy could afford in the heyday of painting. If this was democracy, it was the democracy of illusion. Costumes, stage props, and backdrops were all provided by the studio. The sitters willingly subjected themselves to the choreographic rules and stage direction that had governed family paintings ever since the seventeenth century. The mold of self-presentation was definitely patriarchal, although it came in two varieties. In the cases where husband and wife had their photograph taken, the husband is usually seated with his wife standing beside him. An extreme version of this choreography is a photograph of an old woman standing beside an empty chair: she was a widow. In a sense, however, the dead husband was still there, defining her role and position. Occasionally the woman is seated with the husband standing by her side, the good provider and protector in one. In studio portraits of parents and their children, the parents are usually seated, with the children standing.

These photographs may show us reality as a fiction, but it was not necessarily one consciously fabricated to mislead the home front in the old country. The representational code underlying this particular genre of studio photography was widely known: this was what people, in both Europe and America, expected portraits to look like. Nonetheless, the mere fact that people could have their pictures taken proved not only that they could afford this relative luxury but also that even in their pioneer existence in America they could enjoy the amenities of a modern technical civilization. Studio photography was never far behind the frontier of settlement. Studio photographs were not solely a big-city phenomenon; many are the photographs taken in small towns all across the United States. The sittings may have required the immigrants to make a day trip to the nearest small town and back, yet the message was clear: civilization was never far. Theirs was not a life in the wilderness.

Of course, there were cases where the use of studio props did serve the purpose of willful fabulation, where the fictitious overstatement did go beyond the representational conventions that sitters and beholders shared in common. In his study of immigrants from southern Italy, *Il pane dalle sette croste,* P. Cresci mentions a genre of studio photographs that show the immigrants holding a bicycle or casually leaning on a motorcar.[4] More often than not these were the studio's property, used to convey an image of material well-being that may have been a dream as distant to the immigrants as to their Italian relatives. Such photographs are a clear case of theatrical impression management. They were the visual accompaniment to the glowing overstatement in many of the immigrants' letters.

In general all these photographs, not just those intended to overstate circumstances, were accompanied by words, either scribbled on their back or sent along in letters. Language added to the photographic information, contextualizing it by giving names, ages, and color of eyes or hair or by referring to the occasion, such as a baptism or a wedding anniversary. They were all matters of private relevance, providing the recipients with literally a closer look at their distant relatives and friends. Words were meant to add focus and detail to the photographic image, yet they could function only within the wider unspoken context of established relations of kinship or friendship. Outsiders, strangers to such intimate relationships, could never hope to get the full message. The situation is far worse for later observers, such as students of immigration history: the passing of time and generations has filtered if not erased family recollections, it has caused the loss of letters and photographs, and it has severed the links that meaningfully connected each to the other. Vital context has eroded massively. We are left with the mere fragments of what was once a meaningful and ongoing communication across the Atlantic.

Yet the fragments remain all around. The "archive" of immigration history is tentacular, reaching as far as the catchment area of American immigration. Letters and photographs, half-forgotten, half-remembered, are still kept by individual families all across that area. Occasional conversations as much as concentrated research efforts can result in lucky strikes. Thus one day a Polish colleague, Jerzy Topolski, who spent a year with me at the Netherlands Institute for Advanced Research and who knew of my research interest, told me that he knew of photographs of distant relatives in late nineteenth-century America that family members in Poland still kept. A little later that year he brought them from Poland. They were studio photographs, from Chicago and New York, all with the amber hue that tied them to the "Brown Decade" era. There were more markers of time, place, and country of origin. For example, in addition to the name and address of the studio, which were prominently featured below the image, handwritten notes on the back added information of a more private nature. The notes were in Polish, but as Professor Topolski pointed out to me, it was a variety of Polish as spoken in Silesia, with a clear admixture of Germanisms, such as literal translations of German words or German idioms. Thus a simple message such as "Son Joseph, 22 years old, 24th July 1896," gave away the region of origin: the phrase "22 years old" (the Polish message used that word order) parallels the German "22 Jahre alt," an order not found in standard Polish. Similarly the Polish word used for *picture* is a literal translation of the German word *Aufnahme* (which means "a recording"). Once again, the word strikes a contemporary Polish reader as a marker of Silesian Polish.

At the time the brief notes must have sufficed to put the various persons shown in the photographs within a network of relatives living on both sides of the Atlantic. Such immediate genealogical mapping no longer occurs among their present-day offspring. The photographs are the faded effigies of relatives who have themselves faded from memory. No longer able to call forth a repertoire of anecdotes and stories, set in a context of silence, these photographs are not unlike weathered tombstones, the mute markers of family history. This comes out most tellingly in one of the Polish photographs. It is the portrait of a young woman showing just her head and shoulders, in the style of a sculptor's bust, the image reduced to an oval and the rest retouched to nothingness. The impression is one of an image emerging in clear focus from an enveloping mist. The little photograph was taken by Hartley's Studio in Chicago. The name is partly hidden by the flowers and leaves of an ornate wreath that encircles the picture, for this is in fact a photograph of a photograph, once again taken by Hartley's. Below the wreath there is a rectangular shape suggesting the heavy stone lid of a grave. The whole is definitely a studio arrangement. More than any other photograph it conveys the sense of the past as lying irretrievably across the River Styx, in the domain of the dead. The handwriting on the back dryly informs us that the woman was named Elisabeth. "When died she was 24 years, 3 months, and thirteen days old."

In a sense the other photographs are not that much different. They are all images of people who have long since died, regardless of what the handwriting tells us. "Son Joseph, 22 years old, 24th July 1896": a proud, princely Pole stares us in the face, a self-assured young man, dressed—or so it seems—for a night at the opera. "First communion," it says on the back of a photograph of a young girl. She wears an elaborate white dress; there is a flow of fine white tulle covering her hair. Her left hand rests on a light, rattan stand; her right hand holds the Bible. She looks us straight in the face, her life ahead of her. "Granddaughter Gertruda Pallow, daughter of Franzisek. She was 4 years old in January 1896"—a photograph of a darling young girl, dressed like a little princess, that was sent to her grandmother in Poland. The picture is all that the grandmother may have ever seen of the girl, frozen for all time at age four. None of these photographs has been wreathed and rephotographed as the picture of Elisabeth was. They were never intended to carry a message of death, yet to us they have the same quality of a memento mori. The passing of time has placed them irrevocably in that genre.

Only the living memory of those beholding a photograph can bring the sitters back to life. I was reminded of this when reading a story by James Schaap, a Dutch American author. The story tells us of a young man who has come to see his grandmother on her deathbed. He enters the bedroom. "Nameless faces lined the walls, and an old Dutch couple peered at me from an ornate oval frame hung above the headboard. I always loved that room, for there was excitement here, the fascination of experiences long past. I loved to sneak in as a boy, to sit alone on the bed and look around." Now, for the first time, he is not alone. In her final days his grandmother tells him about the past before it is too late, about "the nameless faces" on the wall, her father and mother. "What was your mother like, Grandma? Like you?" Slowly, in answer to his queries, she brings the past back to life, telling a story that she had kept to herself all along, about a disastrous fire on board an immigrant ship crossing Lake Michigan en route to Sheboygan. The father died fighting the fire; the mother died looking for one of her daughters. The portrait of his grandmother's parents comes to life: "I glanced at the portrait. I had seen it often before. It had come from Grandma's uncle in Holland. He was seated on a chair as big as a throne, his wife's hand rested on his shoulder as she stood soberly at his side." As the drama unfolds, the tale of his grandmother's parents' deaths but also of his grandmother's journey back in time, reviving the story, the grandson keeps looking up at the picture. "I tried to imagine [them] as Grandma spoke."[5] They are no longer nameless faces.

When I was reading the story, there was a strange sense of déjà vu, of something half-forgotten pushing to resurface. Suddenly there it was. A book in which a Dutch amateur historian pieces together his forebears' emigration histories refers to the same tragic event on Lake Michigan.[6] I had heard the story before and had gone through the same emotions as had the young man in Schaap's story listening to his grandmother. I had also been looking at photographs of people who had been in the fire. They were reproduced in the book, relatives and friends of relatives of the author. In his act of filiopietism, he manages to draw outsiders like me into a quasi-familial circle, where "nameless faces" are being restored to their place in history through stories told by their distant offspring.

* * *

Since the photographs in these transatlantic exchanges acquired their full meaning and sense only in a context of written words, one of two things usually happened with the passing of time. Either we find photographs that time has cut loose from their accompanying annotation, or we are left only with the annotations, cryptic references to pictures that originally must have been enclosed with the letter. Many are the people who in acts of filiopietism have sat down to collect and order what is left of the communications their relatives sent across the Atlantic. They have sorted out such letters as have remained and provided copies to official immigration archives in their home countries or the United States. More often than not, however, these are mere fragments of exchanges that went on for years, if not decades.

One task that immigration research has set itself is archival: to bring together as many of these fragments as can be found. The results have been impressive. Massive amounts of immigrant letters have been collected, ordered, and made available for research. Large selections have been published, both in the United States and in the main countries of emigration in Europe.[7] Larger collections are available in immigration archives in all those countries. Nonetheless, much of this material is still as labyrinthine as before. Serendipity still reigns supreme; researchers in the field keep stumbling on unmined treasures. No single researcher can claim to have seen it all or even to have gone over a representative sample. Yet there is always the temptation to come up with some tentative general statements. Consequently, with all due provisos, let me give some general impressions before I go into greater detail.

My own work in immigration history has been mostly concerned with Dutch immigrants in the United States and Canada.[8] In the course of my research I have come upon hundreds of letters, if not thousands, and there are new finds all the time. On that basis, and also on the basis of such collections of letters as have been published in other countries, it seems safe to say that photographic information played only a marginal role. Entire exchanges between family members, even those that went on for decades, have no reference at all to photographs. A collection of Dutch immigrant letters published by Herbert J. Brinks never once mentions photographs in its selected fragments. Moreover, only a few of the book's many photographic illustrations are clear cases of pictures sent to the home country. Thus there is one example of those stilted studio photographs that I already described as forming a genre. We see husband and wife, the man sitting, the woman standing by his side, both looking as if they have just swallowed a broomstick. The caption, in quotation marks, reads: "In this letter I send you my portrait and that of my husband. I can also send you the children, but then it may be a little too heavy."[9] Another picture, from about 1906, is taken outdoors, on an unpaved street, with a group of people posing alongside a hearse. According to the legend, the photograph was taken on the occasion of the burial of a young immigrant in Grand Rapids and was intended for his mother in the Netherlands. The photograph is more in the vein of documentary reportage than the highly stylized studio picture of the deceased Polish woman, yet again the photographic image served to document one of life's irreversible moments, such as birth, baptism, and death.

One explanation for the relative scarcity of visual images in the letters that Herbert Brinks used or those with which I myself have mostly worked may have to do with religion. After all, these are letters from a staunchly Calvinist immigrant population, that is, a group that tends to conceive of itself as the people of the Word, averse to any form of visual representation. As descendants of iconoclasts, as worshipers in white-washed churches devoid of imagery, the mechanical muse of photography may have been just another idol to them. Nevertheless, the relative scarcity of written references to enclosed pictures, irrespective of the sender's religion, is too widespread for this explanation to hold.

To the extent that we find photographs mentioned in immigrant letters, what does this tell us about their communicative value and function? Consider a few examples. I have one set of letters exchanged between members of the Te Selle family from 1865 to 1911—that is, from photography's early period. The earliest mention of a photograph is in a letter from 1869, scribbled in the margin and added as almost an afterthought: "Here is a protrait [misspellings in original] of our little Dela. She is now eleven months old. She sits on a chair but it was difficult to keep her still for so long." Another note in the margin adds: "I took the letter to the post office but then it was too heavy. I will send the protrait with G. Lammers." In an 1873 letter sent from Winterswijk, in the Netherlands, to relatives who also lived in the Netherlands, there were originally two enclosures, a letter from an elderly uncle in America and his photograph. In the little accompanying note we read: "So I send you this letter, and also the portrait, so you can see him on it, and also read in this letter how he is doing. Also you can perhaps send it to your other sister who would also like to have it and see it." In June 1873 the same old uncle writes a long letter, again from Holland, Sheboygan County, Wisconsin. Following a pious dissertation ("And Blessed are we if we hear, do and maintain what God says in his word. But also we know that there is an other, who is called Devil, Satan, Old Snake, the Seducer, Lord of Darkness, God of this, our century."), there are a few bits of news about a granddaughter's marriage and the weather. Then, despite the orthodox old-Calvinist introduction, there is this line: "Also I feel the urge to send you the portrait of my Deceased Wife; we had only one portrait of my wife, and this very same one we had duplicated which we now send you." Again his nephew in the Netherlands passes on the letter and the portrait to his uncle's sister and brother-in-law. "The portrait is yours to keep," he adds.

In 1883 there is a reference to a different kind of visual information, not a portrait of a family member, but a picture of a wind-driven water pump. "This autumn we had a water wind pump put on our well. Now we don't have to draw the water for the cattle ourselves any more. It cost a hundred dollars. Here on this little print you see its picture." Then, in a letter of October 1892, there is the anxious query for an acknowledgment of receipt: "On February 2 this year I have sent all the potrets [*sic*] of my children and of my son-in-law with the request to write back soon, but then later on we got a letter from you which made me conclude that you hadn't received it. Then I have done it again once more but if they have gone lost again at sea I don't know." Apparently the enclosure of photographs must have been an act of great significance, worthy of repetition and the cause of worried inquiry.

This one collection of thirty-five letters, spanning a total of forty-seven years, is fairly representative of other such correspondences. The references to photographs are few, and most of them related to portraits. Apparently the main informative function of photographic enclosures was to maintain a sense of visual proximity among family members in spite of geographic distance. This sense is vividly evoked in a letter sent from Santa Monica to Leeuwarden in the Dutch province of Friesland:

> Dear nephew, I have received "in good order" the photographs that were passed on to me from Yakima. After I had received your letter I looked forward eagerly to seeing them and so, as you can understand, it made an unusual impression on me "to see" a likeness[10] of my next of kin. After such a long absence. Your mother I could not recognize as the sister which I had pictured in my "memory." Her appearance, it seemed to me, had changed. Your father seemed to me more or less the same as I remembered him. A little older but the same

"jovial" person. I value the possession of the photographs and thank you for the interest and "attention to send them" to me.[11]

Pictures of inanimate matter, be it natural scenery, machinery (such as the windmill mentioned previously), or the built environment, hardly figure at all in immigrant letters. They are more likely to show up in business-related correspondence or publications. Thus the *Noord-Amerikaansche Hypotheekbank* (the North American Mortgage Bank), which operated from Leeuwarden, the capital of the province of Friesland, and had representatives in two Dutch immigration centers, North Yakima, Washington, and Bozeman, Montana, produced an advertisement folder with two photographs and the following two legends: "Picking apples in one of the valleys in Washington" and "Harvest and threshing combine at work in Eastern Washington." It also gave the names of its two representatives in the United States. Clearly people looked at such visual information with different eyes, with a view to business opportunity and migration possibilities. Of course, there were many channels conveying precisely such information: shipping lines, land development corporations, and migration societies. Such information, however, was not what people expected to be carried by the much more private lines of communication that connected friends and family members across the Atlantic.

Context was not the only consideration governing content, however. During the early years of both photography and large-scale Dutch migration, economic considerations affected the selective nature of photographic information as well. Having portraits made and sending them across the ocean was relatively costly. A letter from Michigan City, Indiana, dated June 5, 1894, is quite explicit on this point: "Had we not had such a bad time, we would have had our pictures taken this summer: but now this will have to wait a while." Economic means permitting, however, family portraits were the first priority in the exchange of pictures. The same correspondent, in a later letter sent from Holland, Michigan, in 1900, is exultant: "Dear Brother and Sister, With joy and gratitude we received your letter with portrait. We were overjoyed for now we could behold your family from afar: of Freerk we could not very well see that it werst thou. It is eight years hence since we saw each other."

Further evidence that family members were the favorite subject of photographic information comes from the later period, when price was no longer a limiting factor. When immigrants became better off following their years of hardship, and when photography itself had come within reach of the general public, family pictures were still by far the leading genre. The constraints were now set not by economics but by the technology of the early amateur cameras. Exposure time practically prevented indoor photography, but even outdoors the light was not always sufficient. "Last Sunday we have taken pictures of the children. We would take a few more the next Sunday but it was a dark day so we have to wait until the following Sunday. As soon as they are ready, we will send them to you. Monica is quite a girl already and Anna comes along nicely."

Photography had moved outside the confines of the studio and into the private realm of the family garden. The focus was still on family members, but explanatory notes now increasingly referred to details of the setting as well, such as "our house," "our front porch," or "our garden patch." One legend reads: "This is our house, we built it." Nevertheless, the recipients of such pictures still set their eyes most eagerly on the human presence. Writers on both sides of the ocean commented on tiny details of physical appearance. Color of hair and eyes, signs of aging, and family resemblances were standard topics in the exchanges accompanying this photographic communication. Photographs went from hand to hand among family members at the receiving end. "Dear cousin, . . . have you received the portrait already of the little sisters? We sent six to aunt Klaasje; if you don't have them yet you can expect them every day now. Can you tell who they resemble? Not me, that much I can see myself." A letter from Chicago written in the late 1920s by an American daughter-in-law married to a Dutch immigrant comments: "You all look so good on the picture, older of course but aren't we all getting older every day. Mother is much thinner but Dad he almost looks the same except for the gray hair."

In this later age of the amateur snapshot, there is a greater informality in the way people had themselves represented. People in their everyday clothes doing little chores around the house form a common theme: "Father feeding the chickens." Nonetheless, there are clear echoes of earlier strategies of self-representation. People often still dressed up for the occasion and stiffly posed for the photograph. The choreographies may be vaguely remembered and awkwardly executed, yet in the family groupings on the front porch we can recognize the prescriptions and styles of self-representation that reigned supreme in the era of the studio photograph.

Yet another, highly practical function of photographic information is apparent in much post–World War II correspondence. Following the news of the wartime ordeal and of postwar scarcity in the Netherlands, immigrant relatives in the United States assumed the role of good providers. Postwar correspondences frequently refer to packages sent to the Netherlands, carrying clothes, bicycle tires, and other goods that were in short supply. Long discussions of what kind of clothes would fit whom were a recurrent feature. Photography played its part in these discussions, informing people about such mundane matters as size and physical build: "Just imagine that I had thought Wiebe's size to be halfway between Pieter and Ulbe. That is why there was never anything his size in what I sent you"; "Your mother is much more heavy-set than I am. Otherwise she is my size."

* * *

The photographs that I have considered were always of a highly private nature. They added to the exchange of intimate news between family members and close friends. They gave those at the receiving end a closer look at their correspondents and their immediate settings, their homes, their gardens, and the streets on which they lived. It was the closest technical approximation to actual family reunions. In fact, family reunions at the immigrants' end, after families had become dispersed across the United States over two or three generations, were a favorite item of photographic reportage to the old country.

Playing their role within highly private networks, however, all such photographs were only one highly specialized element in the transmission of visual images of the new country to those who had stayed behind. They represented only a slice of life, albeit one that no other genre of photography could convey. In addition, the varieties of public photography, published in weekly magazines and similar sources, carried information about the United States. Yet another category of "official" photographic information was that put out by the Dutch government in the postwar period, when for the first time in the history of Dutch emigration, the government adopted an official emigration policy in conjunction with the period's two main countries of destination, Canada and Australia. The Dutch government now acted as the main sponsor and coordinator of what had hitherto been an unplanned, voluntarist process. A woman married to a Dutch immigrant and living in Canada remembered that her husband came up with the idea to immigrate to Canada after seeing a large billboard, a piece of the Canadian government's recruitment propaganda. She described it as "a beautiful poster . . . a golden grainfield, waving in the breeze," with the obligatory happy and prosperous young emigrant family standing in the middle of it.[12]

Generation after generation of immigrants has been drawn toward America under the impact of such public images, advertising the lures and attractions of the new country and casting America in the light of a land of promise and bounty. When confronted with the realities of American life, many must have felt a sharp disillusionment. As James Schaap tells us in another of his tales of Dutch American immigrant life: "De Kruyf had read about the scandals. He had seen the giant paintings of America when they had all lived in the old country. People from all over Europe had been cheated. He knew many who had come to this country with nothing but a picture from a lantern slide in their minds, thinking themselves somehow heirs to the riches of the new paradise." Collective experiences like these may have made the immigrants more distrustful of pictorial representations, more keenly aware of the confidence games behind much of the public imagery about Ameri-

ca, yet the immigrants did not turn away from photography and its recording potential as such. If anything, they relied more on photographic records
that they themselves produced and choreographed for their own private use
and that of their distant relatives in the old country. When we try to fathom
the role these family photographs played, we should never lose this sense of
context. The stories told by these highly private photographs, stored by immigrant families and circulated along with their letters among friends and
relatives in their home countries, were always private answers to the sobering reality of immigrant life. They offered as much a constructed, retouched,
manipulated view of life in America as did the pictures that circulated in the
public realm. Yet they served a totally different psychological purpose. They
could shore up the hopes and spirits of immigrants at times when their great
expectations, fostered by one form or another of land development interests,
threatened to collapse.

"Sign of a Promise," the title story of the James Schaap collection,[13] includes a moving vignette that beautifully illustrates this role and place of
private photographs in the life of immigrants. The author takes us to the
pioneer house of a Dutch American family struggling to survive on the prairie
frontier in northwestern Iowa. They have recently moved there in the restless search for success that had earlier taken them to Wisconsin and Minne-
sota. They are alone, the first in their part of the world to break the prairie
soil. It has been raining for days, washing away the result of days of backbreak-
ing work. The woman stands behind the window, looking out: "And the sky,
spewing incessant rain, seemed to combine with the desert of grass to destroy whoever, whatever tried to exist there. The endless miles of prairie
seemed to her a Godless expanse, and all the prayers she had learned as a child,
no matter how loudly she could cry them to the heavens, could not bring her
any closer to the God she had known in the old country. This land was so
wide, so vast, so everlasting, that she felt her best prayers rise in futility . . .
to a God who had never minded this region of creation." Forlorn and for-
saken, forgotten by a God who is normally the last hope and refuge for people of her religious background, the woman is in utter despair.

> She turned from the window and looked back to the family portrait that hung
> on the mud wall. It had been taken in Wisconsin. She had wanted it immedi-
> ately after their arrival in America to send to her parents in Holland, for she
> knew their concern and felt that they would be reassured by the clean faces and
> the Sunday clothes of the children. They knew very little of America. Some of
> the stories they had heard were like those of the land of Canaan—a land most
> bountiful, full of opportunity. But others were fearful, accounts of drought,
> storms, savages, violence, strange and horrid stories of people who didn't know
> the Lord. The family picture had helped, she knew, for it showed them tidy and

happy, wearing the smiles that reflected the hopes and jubilation of a life filled with new opportunities. She knew they would like it, for she liked it. This was the way she imagined things.[14]

The last line is amazingly perceptive. It catches the meaning of photographs that immigrants had taken of themselves, presenting an ideal view of themselves to family members in the old country, but more important, to themselves as well. Family photographs in that sense are not pictures of the present or records of the past; they are visions of the future. They document the hopes and anticipations of immigrants they themselves harbored, not those conjured up by outside interests. If the latter are a reservoir of disappointment and despair, the former are the repertoire of hope.

* * *

For a wide variety of reasons, then, photographs have continued to play their role as a source of private information, for the earlier immigrant families as much as for the tens of thousands who left the Netherlands in the postwar period. Immigration itself began to taper off in the late 1950s, precisely when the Dutch national economy began to gather steam. Then, with prosperity coming to the home country, along with the technological revolution in international travel facilities, a final ironic twist occurred in photography's role as a means of private communication. All those amateur historians of family migration who in filiopietistic enthusiasm have husbanded the store of information, who have typed out the letters and arranged the photographs neatly in albums, have one final surprise for the researcher who has come to see them. The photo album's final few pages are likely to include an image of the host amid his distant American relatives. The visitor looks at the host and points at the picture: "That's you there!" The host nods in agreement. Yes, he has gone across the ocean, not as an immigrant, but as a tourist. He has decided to close the circle and go see for himself. Yet the reunion with family members, whose memories have been kept alive over the years through his loving, archival work, is a memorable event in its own right. It is worthy of the same medium of photography that had kept earlier generations posted in an age when emigration appeared to be a definite farewell.

PART 2

Political Affiliations

5. The Human Rights Tradition in the United States

Individualism and Civil Rights

Certain trends in the historiography of the early American republic suggest that intellectual traditions other than Lockean thought and Puritanism influenced the Founding Fathers' generation. The English Whig tradition, the Scottish Enlightenment, and the Machiavellian view as transmitted through Montesquieu have all been suggested as providing an intellectual context to the extreme individualism of the Lockean and Puritan worldviews. The latter views indeed stressed man as a self-contained entity, fully cognizant of his individual interests and centrally motivated by them in his social actions. Locke saw him as conceptually separate from society, if not actually predating it. The Puritans, too, saw him in isolation, directly confronting divine scrutiny. Despite these recent attempts to redraw the intellectual world of the Founding Fathers, the accepted view still portrays their political thinking, as well as the classic texts to which it gave rise—the Declaration of Independence and the Constitution, including the Bill of Rights—as imbued with the spirit of individualism.[1] It was the spirit of the time.

Or was it? Strictly speaking, to use the word *individualism* is to project a view not current until later. Individualism is essentially a romantic concept, in either the heroic version that Burckhardt gave it or its more pessimistic Tocquevillean version. Much as the intellectuals of the Founding Fathers' generation centered their attention on individuals and their pursuit of rational interests, they always saw such individuals as acting in a social context. The thought of men such as James Madison, Alexander Hamilton, John Adams, and Thomas Jefferson always critically hinged on the relation between individual liberty and the preservation of the republic. If we look at it this way, we can see more clearly the role played by classical political philosophy and its emphasis on collective political life in a republic. Thus, if we look beyond the Lockean opening statement of inalienable rights in the Declaration of Independence and go over its list of specific grievances, we enter an intellectual world that is reminiscent of late medieval and early modern political thought on the right to resist tyrants. Much like that other remarkable declaration of independence, the Dutch Act of Abjuration two centuries earlier, the American document appeals to local freedoms that were corporate in character rather than individual. Indeed, some of the vaunted rights guaranteed in the first ten amendments to the Constitution are not individual in any Lockean sense. They are more exactly social freedoms, such as the freedom of religion or the freedom of assembly. They are organizational guarantees, more on the level of ordered public life than on any individual level conceived as outside politics or society. Moreover, whatever their specific thrust, the first ten amendments are as relational as later ones in the area of civil rights. They all define rights and freedoms within an institutional context. They do not so much define the rights and freedoms in any abstract sense as worthy causes put to paper; rather, they define them within a republican context providing the instruments for their protection. They cannot be fully understood unless we bring to bear the weight of political reflection on issues such as the separation of powers or the institution of the Supreme Court as the pinnacle of an independent judiciary. Such concerns for the pluralization of political power—or, as in Madison's case, for the pluralization of organized interests in society—all expressed one more central concern: how to prevent the newly established republican order from sliding back into despotism. If there is a continued focus on individuals, it is in their role as citizens within the institutional context of a republic.

Nevertheless, what makes the United States a separate case in the history and development of human rights, on the levels of both thought and implementation, is the longevity of the individualist frame of mind in American society. Until the present day the U.S. Supreme Court, as the supreme guardian of the citizens' civil rights, testifies to this individualist outlook in its decisions. In fact, it may have become more radically individualist over the years. Whereas individuals, in the parlance of the Founding Fathers, were conceived in their role as citizens, participating in the body politic on an equal footing, they were at the same time seen in their corporate nature as heads of households, representing the corporate bodies of their families, and as owners of property, representing, as Marcus Cunliffe has put it, a propertarian view of sociopolitical stability.[2] With the reapportionment cases of the 1960s, affirming the radical egalitarianism of the "one man, one vote" principle, the Court moved toward a more drastically atomistic view of individualism.

Individualism, then, provides one line of legal and political thought in the

United States, but there are others that have tended to move human rights conceptions away from their initial individualist, civil rights cast. In his universalist ideas of the right of national self-determination, Woodrow Wilson transposed traditional individualist ideas of civil equality onto the world stage of individual nations, thus providing nationalist and anticolonialist stirrings around the world with a powerful vocabulary. Franklin Roosevelt, with his proposed Bill of Social and Economic Rights, subsequently outlined ideas that were later integrated into such internationally approved texts as the Universal Declaration of Human Rights.

Domestically, however, the legal status of such ideas never equaled that of the entrenched civil rights texts. Still, despite their inherent individualism, these texts have proved remarkably flexible, capable of development not only toward more radically individualist extremes. They have also been made to apply to the radically transformed matrix of social inequality of modern industrial society, sustaining legal opinion as it pertains to the rights of collectivities. As I will argue at length later, the area of race relations and discrimination has offered strategic ground for the development of civil rights thought in more collectivist directions, applying it to group relations rather than relations among separate individuals.

Civil Rights: The American Way

The American Declaration of Independence of 1776 invoked a number of truths held to be self-evident: "That all Men are created equal, that they are endowed by their Creator with certain unalienable rights, that among these are Life, Liberty, and the Pursuit of Happiness—That to secure these Rights, Governments are instituted among Men, deriving their just Powers from the Consent of the Governed." Moving beyond earlier appeals to the British homeland, which had all been cast in terms of the rights of Englishmen, it chose to conceive of the American separation from England in the light of universal rights. Some fifteen years later, when Americans had reached agreement on the constitutional arrangements for their republic, they decided to add to their new constitution of 1787 several amendments commonly known as the Bill of Rights. Although in one sense this was the latest outcome of a line of development dating back to the Magna Carta, it was at the same time a highly contemporary document, equal to the French revolutionary Declaration of the Rights of Man in expressing the spirit of the time. As such, it is one of the classic versions of early views of human rights, centering on the individual in his political role as citizen.

In that sense the rights cited are truly civil rights. On the one hand, they guarantee freedoms: they outline spheres of freedom for the individual citizen outside the reach of the government, but within society, such as the free-

dom of speech and religion. On the other hand, they also set procedural standards for cases where government does affect the life of the individual citizen, thus avoiding arbitrariness in such situations. In this case equality rather
than freedom is the guiding principle. Individual equality before the law, the
equal protection of the law vis-à-vis every individual citizen, serves as the
basic guideline for government action. Both kinds of rights, the classic freedoms as much as the rights safeguarding equality, aim at protecting the citizen from the potential misuse of government power. At the same time, the
protection of equality vests a high purpose in government, assigning to it the
duty to ensure that the protection of the law extends equally to all individual citizens.

For about two centuries now these classic civil rights have guided political
life in the United States. Their precise sense and meaning have changed through
the years, and later texts have been added, but all in all there has been a remarkable continuity, an unbroken line of growth and development. Paradoxically,
however, this growth has proceeded in two rather contradictory directions, one
increasingly individualist and the other ever-more collectivist.

When asked what the Constitution means in any given case, we can offer
only opinions. In the United States the operative opinion is that of the Supreme Court, or a majority of it. The opinions are given at such remote dis-
tances of time and circumstance from the original text that they depend on
inference, generally colored by the reigning worldviews of a later age. On
occasion, however, the Court feels bound to expound on first principles, as
happened when the problem of legislative apportionment arose with *Baker
v. Carr* in 1962. Two years later, in *Reynolds v. Sims,* Chief Justice Earl Warren
found occasion for a definitive pronouncement of constitutional principle:
"Legislators represent people, not trees or acres. Legislators are elected by
voters, not farms or cities or economic interests." It had been argued that
certain interests deserve to be given special consideration in the electoral
system; to this the chief justice replied that it is "inconceivable that a State
law to the effect that, in counting votes for legislators, the votes for citizens
in one part of the State would be multiplied by two, or five, or ten, while votes
for other persons in another area would be counted only at face value, could
be constitutionally sustainable."[3]

These decisions were fundamental in the literal sense. They aimed at restoring the American system of government to its foundations. They put into
effect a doctrine well understood by the generation of the founders, that to
survive, a republic must return periodically to its founding principles—a
wisdom as old as Aristotelian thought and transmitted through Machiavelli's well-known injunction to the Italian republics to "redurre ai principii"
(to take back to principles). Ironically, in going back to first principles, Chief
Justice Warren put his own construction on them, casting their implied in-

dividualism in a far more radically atomizing light. Whereas political thought in the early years of the republic had conceived of individual voters as representatives of larger corporate entities (e.g., families or landed estates comprising those living on them) that together constituted the body politic, the Supreme Court in the 1960s chose to see individual voters as representing their own individual interests. Individual voters therefore should be seen as politically equivalent, entitled to the Court's protection of their equal right to the vote, that is, of their right to an equal representation of their individual interests.

This recent interpretation is only one outcome of a line of development that tended to take an increasingly individualist legal view of social relations, shedding what corporatist notions may have been implied in earlier views. Thus, an earlier stage of individualist reconstruction, in the latter part of the nineteenth century, saw the novel phenomenon of the industrial corporation conceived not along more traditional lines as an organization entrusted "by the Public" with productive functions on behalf of the commonweal but rather purely as private property—or more radically still, as a private actor, entitled to the full protection of its rights as an individual entity. Of course, the ideological implications here differ widely from those inspiring Earl Warren's view of the individual voter, yet both are equally illustrative of the atomizing logic that remained submerged in the Founding Fathers' earlier views of civil liberties and equality.

As I said, however, an opposed line of development is discernible, one that leads toward a greater awareness of corporate bodies, or at least aggregate categories, as relevant to legal thought and political reflection. Here again it can be said that later developments have a conceptual link to earlier political thought. I have already pointed to the implied corporate view of the individual voter. A telling case in point is the original version of article 1, section 2, of the Constitution, apportioning representatives among the various states according to their respective numbers of inhabitants, "which shall be determined by adding to the whole number of free persons . . . three fifths of all other persons." This is the famous compromise formula, aimed at giving the slaveholding states added political weight at the federal level by granting their free "electors" a weighted vote. From its inception the "Republic of the Free and the Equal" has been aware of inequality in its midst, its legal language allowing for the existence of different categories among its inhabitants. It has always been a source of creative tension, giving rise to a line of legal and political thought quite separate from the heritage of individualism.

Perhaps it is putting it a little too strongly to use the metaphor of a line of thought, which suggests unbroken continuity. After all, America had to undergo the cataclysm of the Civil War before its public came to see the existence of distinct and unequal categories of inhabitants on American soil in the light of the inspiring creed of liberties and equality. To be precise, through the adoption of the famous Civil War amendments to the Constitution, the protection of the initial civil rights amendments, as a high federal calling, was extended to the entire category of newly freed American blacks. In addition to extending this protection to a whole category of citizens, moreover, these new amendments widened the federal reach, explicitly denying to the individual states the right to make laws abridging the constitutional rights of citizens of the United States. Thus the onslaught on entrenched social inequality was doubly corporatist: not only did it apply to the entire body of black citizens; it also directly affected the corporate balance of power between the federation and the states. The problem of the equal protection of citizens of all races has ever since remained the responsibility of the federal government. In due course other patterns of group inequalities in society have been deemed equally deserving of government action, including inequalities based on national origin, religion, and sex. Changes in the climate of opinion in society at large have always played their part in this gradual extension of the federal role in the area of group inequalities. Later on I will consider some of the more recent developments in this area, but first I propose to look more closely at these American trends in the application of civil rights from a comparative perspective.

Civil Rights and the International Human Rights Debate

In our era, with its clashing ideological systems, somewhat disparaging views of human rights in their classic version of civil rights have not been uncommon. People have tended to slight them as merely old hat, representative of an age of individualism that can no longer speak to the modern world, with its complex patterns of social differentiation. Others have tended to see them as merely formal rights, unable ever to affect the substance of social inequality. In the eyes of radical antiliberals they were the mere class privileges of an entrenched bourgeoisie. Both reproaches—of the individualism and the formalism of classic civil rights—deliberately ignore or at best simply fail to consider American civil rights history. Given the context of strife for ideological primacy in the days of the cold war, it is small wonder that many of these slights tended to come from the communist world or its sympathizers. Against the classic civil rights, boasted by the so-called Free World, the Soviet Union tended to field its brand of social and economic rights, which it alleged to have secured for its citizens.

Such arrogation of guardianship in the area of what became known as second-generation human rights is not quite sustained by historical fact. As it is, the United States has been among the leading contributors to the evolution of international thought on human rights. Not only did President

Woodrow Wilson intend his concepts of a universal world order to incorporate the classic civil rights into a body of international law, but in his ideas concerning nations' rights to self-determination, he also expanded the sphere of individual rights to apply to separate national actors on the international stage. Later, in 1941, President Franklin D. Roosevelt proclaimed his "Four Freedoms" and thus linked such classic liberties as freedom of speech and freedom of worship with more recent conceptions of social rights, such as freedom from want. What he had in mind were "economic understandings which will secure to every nation a healthy peacetime life for its inhabitants." Ideas such as these, later supplemented by Roosevelt's "Economic Bill of Rights" of 1944, soon developed into a more coherent view of social and economic rights that as a second generation of human rights would add to the classic first generation not as replacements but in a happy symbiosis.

When the General Assembly of the United Nations voted to adopt the Universal Declaration of the Rights of Man in 1948, both generations were incorporated in the text. This amalgam was partly a political compromise, the outcome of pressure from member nations that tended to withhold the protection of classic civil rights from their citizenry, but other forces affected it as well. The Universal Declaration was fully as expressive of changing views in the United States as well.

More recently a new rights debate has gathered momentum in United Nations circles. This debate, inspired by a number of Third World countries, centers on the need for yet a third generation of human rights, one concerning the rights of nations. The consequent discussions have included proposals concerning nations' rights to economic development, to peace, to a healthy natural environment, to the sole authority over their natural resources, and finally to the common cultural heritage of humankind.

These are all worthy causes and concerns, but it is difficult not to see this as a forward flight when so much remains to be done in the area of first-generation human rights in so many regions and countries of the world. There are those who reproachfully remind people in the West that emphasizing those classic rights is in fact a case of cultural imperialism, of imposing Western values on countries whose national ways and traditions are not receptive to them. Rather surprisingly, out of a misguided sense of cultural relativism, leading thinkers in the West sometimes make this point their own.[4] In fact, however, such a humble renunciation of Western arrogance is merely Western arrogance in a different guise, resting on the tacit assumption that the protection of individual human rights is something solely for the West to conceive and enjoy.

The current discussion concerning second and third generations of human rights, interesting as it is, requires a thorough understanding of the way the classic first generation has developed, of the high and demanding mission it assigns both to contemporary national governments and to the international community, an understanding that proceeds from a universalist viewpoint rather than the disparaging one of a tepid cultural relativism.

Taking the United States as a case that might help us to explore these more general issues, at least two points deserve further discussion. Both involve seeing how and why the classic civil rights have retained their monopoly hold on the American human rights scene, despite that country's important contribution to international human rights ideas. We will have to ask ourselves why the United States, a cosignatory to many international human rights treaties, has been slow to ratify them and make them into national law. We will also have to see what equivalent law, if any, has developed in the United States in the absence of texts reflecting present-day international human rights views.

International Human Rights Treaties and American Law

At best the United States has been tardy in ratifying international human rights treaties. The Senate did not consent to ratify the treaty concerning the prevention and punishment of genocide until 1986, a full thirty-five years after it became international law. Obvious political motives, such as the fear of finding itself in the dock on account of racial segregation in the South or, later, the Vietnam War, had prevented ratification at an earlier date, but there seems to be a further, more general reason for America's tardiness. In its actions on the Genocide Treaty and similar recent issues, the Senate has exhibited a recurrent pattern of adding "reservations, declarations, [and] understandings" to the treaty texts. Thus one of the main reservations added to the Genocide Treaty stipulates that the American Constitution as interpreted by the Supreme Court will be superordinate to the treaty. A reservation of similar portent, regarding treaty articles that individual citizens could use as legal grounds in litigation, requires prior national legislation that would turn treaty provisions into national law. The clear aim is to prevent international treaties, once ratified, from becoming "self-executing," superseding the national lawmaking powers. Finally, a general reservation added to all treaty texts stipulates that all obligations incurred under the treaty will be binding on the federal government only. Here's the rub, it seems. Irrespective of whether an international treaty explicitly extends its reach to the component parts of a federal state—and some do—the prevailing fear among the many political and legal opponents to the ratification of international human rights treaties seems to lie in the treaties' alleged breach of federal arrangements as codified in the Constitution.

What legal grounds do these people have for their opposition? The Constitution itself clearly vests the treaty-making powers in what has sometimes been called the fourth branch of government, the president plus two-thirds of the Senate. Combining as it does the chief executive with the federal chamber, representing the separate states, this would logically seem to imply the assent of the individual states to international treaty obligations. For a while, however, it appeared as if the Tenth Amendment, reserving to the states those powers not granted to the federal government, could offer a way out. Some argued that the federal government could not use its ratification of treaties to gain powers over the states without their consent. As early as 1920, however, in *Missouri v. Holland,* the Supreme Court decided that "valid treaties of course are as binding within the territorial limits of the states as they are elsewhere throughout the dominion of the United States." The treaty in this case concerned the protection of migratory birds trekking across the international border with Canada and threatened with extinction. If their protection was considered a matter of national interest, transcending the autonomy of the individual states, why then is the protection of human rights through international treaties still an object of so much trepidation?

Within the United States the drift in the protection of rights and liberties has been toward an ever-greater role for the federal government. Ever since the incorporation of the classic guarantees of "due process of law" in the Fourteenth Amendment, the federal government has had a supervisory role, especially in such areas as penal law and criminal procedures, which had previously been left to the sole authority of the individual states. There was nothing automatic about this extension of reach, however. It has taken many Supreme Court decisions, especially during the 1960s and 1970s, for the full implications of the Fourteenth Amendment to take effect.[5]

Arguably the single most important legal ground for the extension of federal sway over the separate states, in widely varied areas including human rights, has been the Constitution's Interstate Commerce Clause: "The Congress shall have power . . . to regulate commerce among the several states." Thus the antidiscrimination sections of the Civil Rights Act of 1964 were upheld by the Supreme Court on the basis of the Commerce Clause. As Justice Clark, writing for the Court, put it,[6] federal law should be deemed duly applicable if the activity it is meant to regulate "affected commerce which concerns more states than one and has a real and substantial relation to the national interest." A criterion as elastic as "affecting commerce" leaves few areas of state authority immune to federal intervention.

Nevertheless, in 1978, when President Carter sought senatorial consent to four international human rights treaties, he made the following reservation in his accompanying letter of transmittal: "The United States shall implement all the provisions of the convention over whose subject matter the Federal government exercises legislative and judicial administration; with respect to the provisions over whose subject matter constituent units exercise jurisdiction, the Federal Government shall take appropriate measures, to the end that the component authorities of the constituent units may take appropriate measures for the fulfillment of the Convenant."[7] Once again a "federal state reservation" was made, despite the drastic changes that the federal-state re- lation had undergone. Such reservations seem to be no longer needed as a strong political argument, meant to accommodate oppositional sentiment in the Senate and in the country at large.

Second-Generation Rights: The American Equivalent

Among the international human rights treaties still pending in the Senate is one concerning "economic, cultural, and social rights." Neither it nor any equivalent text has yet been incorporated into the body of U.S. law. Unlike the Dutch Constitution, for example, which in its latest version enumerates social rights alongside the classic civil rights, the American Constitution is still squarely within the classic civil rights tradition. As I have shown, how- ever, from the beginning this tradition has been informed by both individu- alist views of society and corporatist conceptions. A body of law and juris- prudence that in a sense merges the two has developed since the Civil War. It has gradually extended civil rights views and ideas concerning equal pro- tection as a government responsibility, making them apply to entrenched patterns of inequality in society. This trend has taken a quantum leap since the 1950s, when, following the Supreme Court's watershed decision in *Brown v. Board of Education,* sustained judicial, legislative, and executive activism began a massive onslaught on patterns of social discrimination. Racial dis- crimination was the initial focus of attention. Later on discrimination in general, in ethnic relations and in relations between the sexes, became the overriding interest. Social inequality, seen as the outcome of a history of patterned discrimination, became the central yardstick for a government policy, sustained by the judicial branch, of so-called affirmative action. Across a wide range of social areas such as housing, education, employment, and career patterns, government provided guidelines aimed at restoring a prop- er balance, or mix, of races, ethnicities, and sexes. Government intervened in its own sphere as much as beyond, touching a great many areas of social activity. It did all this in its role as final guarantor of the "equal protection of the law."

This history of remedial governmental intervention in group inequalities makes it clear that human rights policies in the United States have under- gone a dramatic change on the basis of time-hallowed ideas concerning lib- erties and inequality. From their initial individualist mold they have evolved to apply to complex processes of group interaction and social inequality. The intricate balance of liberties and equality (or perhaps liberties versus equality) has shifted toward equality at the price of restricting liberties. Through affirmative action government imposes courses of action that people might not have chosen to take.

This dramatic and drastic change, roughly coinciding with America's somewhat belated introduction of large-scale welfare-state programs, has not gone unnoticed. In fact, a highly vocal opposition has emerged, rejecting the affirmative-action approach precisely on account of its alleged infringement on the time-hallowed individualist cast of egalitarian thought in the United States.[8] Many of those who challenge affirmative-action decisions in court base their case on the very same equal protection clauses that have undergirded the affirmative-action approach itself. It makes for an intriguing creative tension within a shared universe of legal discourse that continually affects the precise balance between liberty and equality.

Does all this mean that in America the classic civil rights have evolved to function as what in other parts of the world goes by the name of social rights? Some people would say no on purely formal grounds. According to them, classic civil rights are negative; they proscribe actions, especially on the part of the government, rather than prescribe them. Social rights are positive in the sense that government should act toward certain social and economic goals. There is some truth in this rejoinder. If discrimination is taken to be the key operative term in the American case of affirmative action, government in the final analysis is still acting to protect individual human rights, ordering people to desist and refrain from discriminating against individuals.

But the American government does more. As I have said before, its responsibility for the equal protection of the law has always assigned it a positive duty, but it can take this duty in several ways. Over the last thirty years the government has actively sought to eradicate the outcomes of a long history of discrimination in a number of different areas of social life. It is acting as any government should once it has the positive goals of social rights assigned to it. The irony is that more often than not, a "Bill of Social Rights" remains a dead letter, whereas in the absence of such a bill, the American government has actively pursued the high goal of social equality.

America and the Welfare State

The foregoing analysis, looking at the way in which legal thought in the United States developed in response to contemporary views of social problems and social policy, has in a sense been taking an inside view. It has borrowed the language and perspective of a society that, more so than any European country, approaches problems of social policy legalistically. In that sense the analysis may have been overly formal and insufficiently sociological. To this criticism I reply that one cannot begin to grasp the historical experience of a country such as the United States without playing the role of a vicarious insider.

Nonetheless, there are those who, on the basis of comparative views of contemporary welfare states, are inclined to disparage trends in civil rights thinking such as those I have been exploring. To them, what is striking about America's record in the area of social policies is its underdevelopment as a welfare state. There are many glaring cases of poverty and injustice outside the protective reach of welfare-state programs. On a number of indicators of social health and welfare, the United States lags behind countries in Europe. Yet one should try to see this in perspective.

One way to conceive of the welfare state is by referring to government practices of allocating a certain percentage of the gross national product to welfare. The definition of welfare includes all public expenditures for health, education, income maintenance, deferred income, and funds for community development, including housing allocations. In one area—education—the United States has long been leading Europe in the expansion and democratization of its public education system. In other areas, however, the United States has expanded its welfare expenditures more slowly than have major Western European nations. But the gap has been closing. By 1970 welfare expenditures in the Federal Republic of Germany (then West Germany) had reached 19.5 percent of the gross national product, and in France it was 20.9 percent, while the comparable figure for the United States was 15.3 percent, reaching 18.5 percent by 1979. By the latter year, social welfare costs consumed 55.0 percent of the federal government's budget and 56.8 percent of outlays at all government levels.[9] At this time in the United States as well as in European countries, both the political right and left began to voice a critique of the welfare state, a critique occasioned by a great number of various welfare-state systems' unforeseen and unintended consequences. Henceforth public debate and policy-making circles would focus not on ways to expand the system but on ways to contain it, if not reduce it. The latter part of the following chapter discusses this period, from the late 1970s on. Ironically, as I will argue there, the United States may have changed from the relative laggard that it was in introducing welfare-state programs to a model for other countries to follow. Whatever the precise relation between them, however, both the United States and European countries have come to view controlling the costs of the welfare state as a central concern. The expenses are not limited to the programs' direct costs but include the costs of the huge government bureaucracies that have arisen to administer the programs. Their costs are technically an overhead of the welfare system and should be taken into account if we want to assess the overall share of the gross national product taken up by the system. Much of this growth is fairly recent; for the United States, it can be dated to the Kennedy-Johnson years, where it coincided with the emergence of affirmative-action programs. Indeed, these programs can be seen as a nonpecuniary variant of essentially the same interventionist conception of the contemporary state. The state, in this view, is the natural vehicle for collective action, expressing society's sense of solidarity in programs meant to assist individuals in realizing their personal goals, their dignity, and their self-esteem.

It is quite remarkable that such a view of the state's role has sunk any roots in the United States. Ever since the advent of the nation-state in Europe, the state has always been seen there as the natural instrument for realizing collective aspirations, whatever their object, be it national aggrandizement through war or the establishment of justice through social welfare. In the United States, however, the natural avenue for collective action has long been the voluntary association rather than the state, a matter of civil rather than political initiative. Not until the Progressive Era, and more particularly the state's mobilization of collective energy during World War I, did activists, reformers, and intellectuals begin to consider the state as an instrument for positive collective action. It took another fifteen years, under the impact of the Great Depression and Roosevelt's New Deal, for the modern state to develop on American soil. In a place where, according to European standards, the state had been virtually nonexistent as late as the 1920s, a total transformation of the political stage had taken place by the end of the 1930s. The New Deal was in fact the first sustained manifestation of state activism in response to pressing social problems. Yet the change of mind implied here did not come overnight. In the enactment of the Social Security Act of 1935, the first law of its kind in the United States, organized labor played only a minor role, mainly because of labor's ambivalence about the benefits of a national welfare system.[10] Thus an organized interest that one would have expected to be among the main proponents and supporters of the idea of social security stood aloof because of its entrenched aversion toward government interference.

The New Deal, followed by World War II, made America safe for the welfare-state idea. Both crises formed threshold periods critical for the idea's adoption. Trends in intellectual life concerning the essential manipulability of the social system (e.g., the idea of social engineering among social scientists or Keynesianism in economics) further tended to confirm the newfound role of the modern state.

As I pointed out before, however, during the 1970s, at the time of its fastest expansion, the welfare state came under attack both in Europe and the United States. Attempts at checking its growth, or even at curtailing its reach, have been relatively unsuccessful. Many of its entitlement programs have proved politically sacrosanct. Much of the growth in expenditure is automatic, due to the indexing of benefits and to increases in the number of entitled recipients. The only retrenchment in the United States during the Reagan administration was in the means-tested programs for the most needy. The share of such program went down from 22 percent to 17 percent of all federal welfare expenditures.[11]

The Right to a Cultural Identity: Cultural Affinities Revisited

So far I have been exploring human rights traditions in the United States, which offers a contrast to Europe in the way in which human rights conceptions have operated. I now propose to explore one more area where there are telling differences between Europe and the United States: the rights of minorities to their own cultural identities. In a fairly recent development in the West and elsewhere, regional and other cultural minorities have been trying to promote their case for cultural autonomy by presenting it as a human rights issue. In their view, it is clearly a case of a collective right, adhering to groups rather than individuals, not unlike the right to national self-determination. Generally speaking, theirs is only one specific instance of the wider problem of the tyranny of a majority, a topic equally urgent to Madison and Tocqueville. Nevertheless, the country of Madison has handled problems of cultural diversity differently than has the European world that Tocqueville addressed.

Whereas Europe went the way of the independent nation-state, each harboring one or more quasi-national minorities, the United States, quintessentially an immigrant nation, can be seen as a multination state. Its national minorities are the defining characteristic of its national identity. Seeking unity in diversity, it has always had to walk the tightrope between a narrow and oppressive Americanism and a more cosmopolitan and diverse sense of itself. Vigilant nativism has always served to keep a centrifugal cultural pluralism in check. Ironically, wave after wave of immigrants have willingly undergone this pressure toward their Americanization. More often than not, they experienced it as a rite of passage, an emancipation if not a regeneration, in which they willingly traded in the ascribed cultural identity of their countries of origin for the newly achieved status of Americans. Despite the outside pressures exerted on them, their Americanization was characteristically an act of individual voluntarism. The pressures that existed were hardly ever of a totalitarian kind, working toward total assimilation in every sphere of life. On the whole, the same spirit that had informed the constitutional view of spheres of life beyond the reach of politics and public life was evident here. If Americans should be free in their religious lives or their choices of voluntary associations to arrange their social lives, they should be equally free to use any language or to keep any national or ethnic tradition alive in their homes, neighborhoods, presses, and social organizations. National standards were uncompromisingly enforced only in those spheres commonly deemed to constitute the public life of the republic. In education and politics the language should be English; in politics the guiding ideas should be American, not "un-American." Over time the combined impact of these freedoms and pressures produced a remarkable amalgam, a vigorous sense of nationhood and ethnicity.

Recent developments have been particularly relevant to the alleged collective rights to a cultural identity acknowledged by others. In many quarters we have been witnessing a militant reassertion of ethnic identity accompanied by attempts to re-create separate cultural histories from the "master narrative" of "the American people." Various factors have been at work. For one thing, the cultural revolution of the 1960s, stressing the quest for cultural identity and self-fulfillment, has made for greater cultural relativism. It may have been a case of third-generation immigrant children reclaiming an ethnic heritage that their parents and grandparents had neglected. In addition, the policy of affirmative action, designed to bring the victims of discrimination within the mainstream of American life, has caused other groups in society to rally defensively around themes of ethnicity. There is a paradox here. Although privileged ethnic groups may have seen their entrenched collective positions in society threatened by the onslaught of positive discrimination, their defense was often cast in the language of individual rights. They protested against the alleged "un-Americanism" of a government policy that seeks to establish equality among groups rather than among individuals. As one of the leading early polemicists, Nathan Glazer, put it: "Those who in the 1960s thought equality demanded that no person be required to give his race or ethnic group in applications for admission to schools and employment now think that it is essential, in order to achieve equality, that every person be required to do so. Troubling and difficult questions have been raised as government, to achieve a greater equality, begins itself to impose limits on the dreams and aspirations of individuals on the basis of their race or ethnic group."[12]

Clearly, the assertion of group cultural identities has posed quintessentially American dilemmas. Old debates about the defining characteristics of a common American nationhood have resurfaced, doing so most patently in the case of an ethnic group that may have proved most resistant to forces of Americanization: Hispanic Americans. Given the shift toward greater cultural relativism and the official affirmative-action support to the reassertion of group cultural identities, bilingualism has been on the march in public education as well as more generally in the area of public communication. But the trend has not remained unopposed. In 1984 California voted in favor of a proposition establishing English as the sole official language. Never before had the affirmation of the common core of a national political culture been sought through legal codification.[13]

Similar trends toward cultural relativism in intellectual life have occurred in academic curricula. If America is truly a nation of nations, some are of the opinion that there is little point in neglecting their varied contributions to world culture, universally conceived. Thus, at universities across the country, the "Great Classics" are now selected not according to their contribution to Western culture, seen as a line of gestation culminating in America, but rather on the basis of a global catholicism. The dilemma this poses to a national culture like America's is evident. Cosmopolitanism as a value sees itself—as it has throughout American intellectual history—opposed once more to the value attached to a vibrant, vital core of a common national culture. The outcome is as yet uncertain, and essentially for Americans to work out. To outside observers such as myself, however, the debate is of crucial relevance. If the United States, among contemporary nation-states, is the one most truly representing a global melting pot, it is only the harbinger of trends in store for all of us in our global village.

6. Ideology: Black Box or the Logic of Our Ideas?

Dual Citizenship and Ideology

The world may be turning into a global village, but this does not mean that its inhabitants are becoming world citizens. If anything, the trend is in the opposite direction. The number of independent states organizing the world's inhabitants in terms of citizenship and nationality has increased relentlessly, particularly in the twentieth century. Indeed, it grows yearly with every empire that falls apart and every ethnic group that secedes and sets up its own state. World citizenship may be a dream inspired by the universalism of human rights and human equality, but the particularism of group identities struggling for independent nationhood is an everyday reality of undeniably greater strength. The one clear exception to this trend is the daring transnational venture of the European Union, which is attempting to transcend the halfway covenant tying citizenship to nationhood. Ironically, even though it is an exception, many view it as the true expression of modern views of citizenship. By that yardstick, the tragedy unfolding in the former Yugoslavia and other parts of the world appears to be an atavism, a relapse into a bygone stage of world history. Precisely such modern views inspired the Western world's military intervention in the Balkan conflicts, an intervention followed by attempts at establishing, if not restoring, a sense of multiethnic citizenship among people who had been at each others' throats for the previous decade. The Western project may be a tragic misreading of the particularist drift of history and may well come to naught.

Interestingly, the tension between ingrained readings of nationality and citizenship in a particularist vein and a universalist, transnational view is constantly at play even within the European Union, despite its transnational

ideals. A telling recent case is Germany's 1998 debate concerning the citizenship rights of its immigrant population, mostly hailing from Turkey. The
immigrants number in the millions, some of them third-generation inhabitants of Germany. Technically they are all still citizens of Turkey and have
Turkish passports. They are not citizens of Germany. What does this mean?
The problem is not that, as a group of resident aliens living and working in
Germany, they are excluded from the government services and entitlement
programs that many see as the benefits of citizenship. They are not. Like the
Germans, they enjoy these rights and pay for them. The problem boils down
to two basic ingredients of citizenship that resident aliens lack. One is the
right to a place in the world that one calls home, a state that one can enter
and leave at will. For the Turkish minority in Germany, this is not the core
problem. As Turkish nationals, Turkey is their home. Until recently they had
no choice, even if they or their German-born children and grandchildren
thought of Germany as their home. The other, more crucial, ingredient of
citizenship is the right to political participation, such as voting or serving in
public office—the right, in other words, to play a role in the collective deter-
mination of public life and the public weal. The very logic of the evolving
European Union, with its distant goal of a larger European citizenship, stands
at right angles to the exclusion of millions on the basis of the highly particularist definition of citizenship long prevailing in Germany.

The German view of citizenship operative until recently is not unlike that
in many parts of the world and may well be in line with the particularist drift
of current world history. It is based on an ethnic, if not tribal, sense of the
nation. One inherits citizenship through descent, not through an act of voluntary affiliation. Anyone who can trace his or her lineage back to German
forebears can claim German citizenship, even if the family has lived elsewhere
for generations. The underlying logic is commonly known as the *ius sanguinis*, a bloodline connecting one to the mythic body of the German nation.
The rival view is that of the *ius soli*, the right to citizenship on the basis of
one's place of birth. It implies a more open view of who helps to constitute
the body of citizens making up a nation. Countries such as France and the
United States have given powerful expression to this sense of citizenship ever
since the Enlightenment. They both cast themselves as the true bearers of
Enlightenment enthusiasms concerning the "Rights of Man," as the language
of the time expressed it. Ironically, both nations now derive their senses of
national identity from those lofty ideals, particularizing what is in essence
universalist, turning universal ideals into the defining mark of Frenchness
and Americanness. Things are different in the case of Germany. Recently,
however, the new governing Green-Socialist coalition, with the support of
the small Liberal Party, has broken up the established mold of the German
nationality.

The solution they introduced was dual citizenship, allowing Turks born in Germany to hold citizenship in both Turkey and Germany. Opposition forces came out in strength, in street protests and in the media, to counter this development. The more intelligent voices on their side deplored the absence of a true public debate, reminding their opponents of democracy as "government by discussion."[1] One such individual, Peter Graf Kielmansegg, argues that views of democracy and citizenship stand in two philosophical traditions that are tenuously related.[2] One is the liberal tradition, going back to John Locke, which conceives of political participation as inspired by the pursuit of individual interests. The other he traces back to Jean-Jacques Rousseau; it stands in the tradition of republicanism, which sees political participation as geared centrally toward the common interest—literally, the res publica. The latter tradition sees the citizen as disinterested, imbued with a civic sense of duty toward the common weal. Kielmansegg acknowledges the first, Lockean tradition, especially in its Anglo-Saxon guise, as having carried everything before it, dominating the modern discourse on what democracy is all about. It tends to make people forget about the other side of the coin, the citizens' commitment to the public interest.

Kielmansegg then moves on to a discussion of the ways dual citizenship can be seen to work. As Rousseau might say, how can one serve two masters at the same time? How can one truly be committed to two states at the same time? Commitment implies involvement, deep emotional affiliation with the collective history and fate of a political community with which one identifies. As Kielmansegg sees it, people can meaningfully identify in this way with only one such community. He refers to the peculiar plight of the Germans, who are aware of international pressure pushing them to work the collective memory of their national past, both its horrors and its greatness, into their sense of nationhood. How can others, immigrants and cultural minorities, share in this momentous task? How can they, in that demanding sense, fully become citizens of Germany?

At that point a truly conservative reading of national identity comes to the fore, truly conservative in the sense that the father of conservatism, Edmund Burke, was a conservative. Against the daring modernists of his age, the Enlightenment heroes who saw history as makable and who conceived of individual human beings as the true agents of history, free to mold it at will, Burke pointed to patterns of organic growth and cohesion, the manifold bonds that history had woven to envelop human social life. If history thus understood is the main determinant of communal bonds, no outsiders can ever join the circle. They do not share the stock of collective memories that make for a sense of community. Of course, one may disagree, arguing that the human mind is gifted with the creative ability to enter the store of memories shared by others. After all, this is what the history of America's immigrants is all about. They have all adopted America's Founding Fathers as a meaningful part of their life histories, and they have done so in individual acts of voluntary affiliation, testifying to the power of consent over the force of descent. Therefore, one would not expect to find a parallel to Kielmansegg's narrow reading of nationhood in American discussions concerning citizenship. Nevertheless, America's history of nativism, its rejection of "strangers in the land," to quote the title of John Higham's classic study of the subject, points up many such parallels.[3] Nor is nativism only a thing of the past in America. Conservative readings of the American nation as a community of shared memories that no outsider can truly enter do occur in recent debates about the citizenship rights of immigrants.[4] Burke is alive and well in the United States and appears in many guises, ranging from the intellectually honest to the vulgar and self-serving.

Whether the debates I have briefly explored here refer to Locke, Burke, or Rousseau, they all point to the fact that people's views of citizenship are never a clear-cut matter of science, to be decided by irrefutable proof. They are always a matter of underlying worldviews, of the ways in which people structure their perceptions and evaluations. The test is always whether something makes sense and can meaningfully fit in their views of the world. No scientific proof or evidence can refute this. To the extent that *ideology* is a word denoting the ordered worldviews of human beings, it refers to a mental realm that is remarkably immune to the findings of science. Yet people can live with ideology *and* the scientific worldview at the same time. They neatly set apart the logics of science and ideology as separate compartments that give direction to their lives. They will not step out a thirteenth-floor window unless they are pushed or committing suicide, for they remember Newton and the apple. At other moments, however, they will cut a neighbor's throat because he is different from them: they remember Cain and Abel, too. Given that ideology is a strong force and crucially related to the topic of citizenship, I propose in the following to gauge its inner logic.

Ideology and Truth

We all know and use the word *ideology*. It pops up in many different settings, in barrooms and on barricades. It has scholarly and vernacular uses, like many other words that students of society share with a larger lay public. This sharing of a language, however, does not always make for easier understanding across the dividing line. The situation is like that of the United States and Britain, two nations—as a common witticism has it—separated by a common language. In much the same way that the English language has developed differently in different historical and social settings, the concept of ideology has had different careers depending on who used it and in what context.

Whatever form it has taken, however, the concept of ideology itself has always been contested. It is never used or defined in quite the same way by all the parties in conflict. There is a polemical side to the word *ideology* used as a rhetorical tool. Those who use it this way always mean to unmask the other party's worldview as mere ideology, something that merely serves self-interest, while claiming pure disinterestedness for their own party. Thus, *we* have a worldview, but *they* have an ideology. The very logic of this situation makes it unstable. It is never long before the opposing party strikes back by simply reversing the polemical thrust. It is *they,* not *we,* who stand on the side of disinterestedness and objectivity. The inherent dialectics of these battle-lines may be seen as opposing ideology and truth, as philosophers would have it, or ideology and science, as social scientists would argue. In such polemical uses, ideology is always something that typifies the opponent. Nevertheless, there are also those in the intellectual history of the West who, as self-styled ideologues, have opted for a life in the labyrinth of ideology. They lead lives centered on the critical review of ideas and values as these structure and guide human societies. As critics of ideas, however, they are equally exposed to contradictions, for they pretend to see through other people's ideologies as cases of "false consciousness," as no more than the outward reflection or justification of their social position, while at the same time maintaining that they themselves are beyond such historical conditioning. The dialectics can therefore also be seen as occurring between ideology and what we might call historicism. The latter position is a romantic-era reaction to the rationalism of the Enlightenment and its claims for the universalism of human values. Historicism highlights the transient, time-related nature of all human knowledge. Ideologues in that sense are children of the Enlightenment, trying to save some of the universalist enthusiasms of that age from the utter relativism of the historicists.

In all the preceding, the crucial point is the status of human knowledge as it relates to the powers of human observation and thought. The emergence of the concept of ideology and its later career find their place along a line of development beginning in the Renaissance with the gradual liberation of human thought from tradition and the teachings of the Church—the liberation, in short, of the human individual as a knowing subject. The breakthrough occurred along a wide front. With the Reformation, individual believers participating in organized church life began to resist the dogmatic hegemony of the Church as well as the separation between a trained clergy and an uninitiate lay body of believers. They found justification for doing so in their individual senses of direct communion with God. It was a case of religious individuation that found its institutional reflection in the mushrooming of a great many sectarian churches. Similarly, outside the sphere of religion, the rise of the natural sciences as we know them was won against the opposition of religious authorities who claimed to know God's plan with the world from divine revelation.

Casting off this imposed religious authority was a long process. It had to be challenged on two fronts. The first challenge was to the nature of knowledge as flowing from divine revelation. Henceforth the accumulation of knowledge would be secularized, humanized, and based on the powers of observation. Human reason geared toward the acquisition and interpretation of knowledge based on experience, if not experiment, had put itself in the place of divine revelation. That in itself was a momentous change, affecting many of the established balances of society. If the traditional unified worldview portrayed not only knowledge of the world and its origins but also the authority of secular rulers as given from God, then rebellion against the divine origin of religious teachings could not help but spill over into the area of established state authority. Sir Francis Bacon and like-minded individuals were well aware, and wary, of these implications. In his analysis of the deleterious effects of established prejudices—"idols," he called them—on human knowledge, Bacon therefore hastened to point out that his analysis applied *only* to the sphere of science.[5]

The second challenge was not to divine revelation as the source of all knowledge. Instead, it focused on the contents of what was allegedly revealed: the divine plan structuring the world. This view—or rather, belief—that the world exhibits a God-given order was harder to eradicate and still survives. Its persistence may well be due to a basic quandary confronting the scientific quest for knowledge: how to account for the patterns of order and logic, if not the signs of a master intelligence, that science continues to discover in the universe? Early German historicism found one way to cope with this quandary. For all the revolutionary potential of its daring insight into history as a force shaping human knowledge, it chose to ignore this insight's radical implications. When confronted with the various forms that religion and philosophy have taken throughout history, German historicism refused to surrender to a tragic view of human knowledge as utterly relativist, choosing instead to see the transcending unity of a divine plan in this variety, a plan unfolding itself step by step. Only later, when historians could no longer see any line or plan at all, could the German historian Wilhelm Dilthey speak of an *"Anarchie der Überzeugungen"* (an anarchy of points of view) without any shared meaning or coherence.

A similar trajectory can be discerned in the ways in which the concept of ideology has been used and understood. What started out as an innocent reflection on the impediments to pure knowledge gradually assumed the tragic allure of a fall from grace. I am using a biblical metaphor here, but one that seems highly appropriate. In Genesis the tree of *knowledge* symbolizes the expulsion from a paradisiacal order, condemning human beings to fend for themselves. Old as this premonition may have been, it once again came true. Francis Bacon's early reflections on human prejudice would prove to be only one early stage in the modern history of thinking about thinking. That history would inexorably move from a liberation of thought, and from the exhilaration attending that stage, to the ultimate demolition of the last fundaments of knowledge.

The innocence and optimism of the early stage lasted well into the Enlightenment, particularly in France, where the philosophes won a remarkable measure of intellectual freedom in the face of the censoring traditions of church and state. They achieved this in a historical alliance with an emerging bourgeois class trying to extend its social sphere of action. The philosophes gave this movement intellectual ammunition and in that sense were the first on the stage of history to represent the quintessentially modern character of the *intellectual,* the man or woman of words rather than of action, able to keep a critical distance from current social developments yet also to perceive their sense, direction, and coherence and to turn them into programs for action.

In their intellectual engagements, scientific and critical pursuits were like birds of a feather. We can see this illustrated particularly well in the case of Condorcet and Destutt de Tracy. Resisting established authorities, which they dismissed as merely transmitting the self-confirming prejudices of entrenched elites (as their contemporary Helvétius put it, "The prejudices of the great are the laws of the small"),[6] they set out to develop a scientific epistemology free from prejudice and based on sensory observations for the formation of its ideas.

According to this program, it should be possible to discover the foundations of proper ideas in human beings and, consequently, the proper ordering of such human beings within a larger political order. Destutt de Tracy conceived of this scientific endeavor as the basis for all other thought concerning state and society; he chose to call it *idéologie,* the science of ideas. We can still clearly see the extent to which the scientific program fed into a plan for social action in Destutt's view. The two programs could still blithely live together; no tension had yet shown up between them. That would not last much longer.

Marx, Paradoxes, and Dilemmas

With Karl Marx the concept of ideology would enter the next stage of its career. Marx borrowed the word from Destutt but gave it a drastic new twist. From a remedy, as it had been in Destutt's hands, it now turned into an instrument of diagnosis. As a concept it came to stand for knowledge systematically distorted, for the twisted representation of reality that Destutt had meant to remedy with his "science des idées." Nevertheless, Marx's analytic aims were of the same order as Condorcet's and Destutt's, of great moralists such as Holbach and Helvétius, or of Marx's contemporary Schopenhauer. With great linguistic virtuosity and polemical acuity, Marx, too, set out to denounce current social ideas for what they were: mere strategies to legitimate narrow group or individual interests. In his ruthless unmasking of all such unabashed apologetics, Marx did not shrink from taking aim at famous British thinkers of his time, such as Edmund Burke or Thomas R. Malthus.

Nonetheless, Marx saw ideology as more than a veiled apologetics to be exposed by individuals who, like Marx himself, were able to see through them. As Marx conceived of it, ideology assumed a different meaning and a different analytic thrust of great epistemological consequence. The implications may have been unforeseen and would open up a tragic rift in Marx's thinking. A first step had been taken down a road at whose end knowledge would turn against itself, one where knowing subjects would lose their last foothold. This second, more ominous meaning appears in Marx's treatises on scientific economics, a field developed by predecessors and contemporaries such as Adam Smith and David Ricardo, authors whose work Marx esteemed highly. By putting their work in historical context, however, he demolished its pretense of general and universal validity. Here Marx is the historicist: he acknowledges that the classical economists gave the perfect theoretical analysis of novel social trends and forces. He construed their work as the scientific reflection of the emerging market economy of early capitalism. As such, however, it was tied to that stage of history, despite its claims to formulate the general laws that guide economic life. This tension between the arrogation of general validity and the actual conditions that history set to such validity led Marx to deride the reigning economic wisdom of his day as an instance of "false consciousness," an ideology rather than enduring scientific truth.

* * *

If one cocks one's ears, one can hear a time bomb ticking away, for the unmasking of classical economics' pretense can be based only on a rival pretense: the claim that one has a better insight into the laws of economic life than did the great liberal economists. In that connection, Marx is not only a historicist in the way he takes aim at Smith and Ricardo but also what we might call a finalist, a man who believes he can see farther than any of his predecessors—indeed, so far that he can perceive the final course of history. Clearly there is an anomaly here. The way that Marx merges the role of historicist in his critiques of the liberal economics of his time with that of the finalist pretending to transcend the constraints of time and place is a first illustration of what I called the tragic rift in Marx's oeuvre.

Marx may have been decrying other people's science as mere ideology, but he was able at the same time to preserve his belief in the powers of science.

Marx did believe that it was within the powers of the human mind to fathom the laws of motion not only of the universe but of social life as well. In
that sense Marx is very much a child of the Enlightenment. A classic early
statement of the power of human knowledge, again from Francis Bacon,
holds that "human knowledge and human power meet in one; for where the
cause is not known, the effects cannot be produced. Nature to be commanded
must be obeyed; and that which in contemplation is as the cause is in oper-
ation as the rule."[7] This notion might be taken as informing all of Marx's
scientific work.

Submission and command are each other's preconditions: to exert command over objective processes, one must be capable of replaying those processes before one's inner eye, almost literally reflecting them before reflecting on them. Marx did qualify this exercise of free discretion and command
as based on scientific insight, however. For one thing, in his most radical
moments, Marx conceived of scientific insights, like all other ideas, as never
more than the reflection of objectively given and knowable social relations,
centering on the basic social matrix of economic production, its technological stage of development, and the accompanying patterns of ownership of
the means of production. This view, when applied to itself, can be seen to
harbor a paradox: Epimenides' classical paradox of the Cretan who called all
Cretans liars. Nor is this all. Marx did not shrink from adding a further paradox. If history truly is subject to the unchanging course that Marx thought
he had uncovered, a course that turns every historical actor into its blind
perpetrator irrespective of objective class position or subjective intention, if
indeed Marx's arrogation of scientific authority to support his reading of
history fully applies, then scientific knowledge can no longer make for humans' informed control of their collective destiny. No longer can there be a
point to sustained collective action meant to change the established pattern
of social relations.

Yet the determinist, or finalist, in Marx was only a part of his split person-
ality. There was also the voluntarist in him, the man who believed in the free
exercise of human discretion. Throughout his work as a scholar and a political activist, this latter persona vied with the determinist. As a determinist,
he acknowledged the proletariat as the historical agent for the final *Aufhe-
bung,* the ultimate transcendence of society's class contradictions and all that
they entailed in terms not only of an organized state, production, and market relations but also of people's alienation from their work and from themselves. At the same time, however, he did not quite trust the proletariat to
fulfill its historical role on its own predetermined initiative. The proletariat,
in Marx's analysis, is too much the captive of the pervasive "false consciousness" of capitalist society. An extrahistorical agent must be called forth, like
a deus ex machina, to help the proletariat fulfill its mission.

Time and time again Marx argues that this role of awakening the proletariat to its true class interest falls to what he himself calls "bourgeois ideologues," individuals able to rise above their objective class interests and to
act as the self-conscious vanguard leading the proletariat toward its ultimate
victory, organizing and educating it for the task. Thus, the voluntarist in Marx
keeps taking over precisely at those moments when his scientific insights into
the character of false consciousness under conditions of capitalist class relations seem to turn against his belief in the power of scientific analysis.

Ideology and Truth: Three Forms of the Dilemma

Ever since Marx, no form of reflection on the problems of human societies
could ignore these paradoxes and dilemmas. Henceforth the deconstruction
of the bases for true knowledge that had been wrought by the growing insight into the forces distorting knowledge continued apace. The process led
to a variety of suggestions on the best way to cope with these paradoxes. The
systematic reductionism that kept eroding the claims for truth made on behalf of human knowledge, seeing them as no more than the semblance of
legitimation of narrow interests, continued throughout the nineteenth century. With Friedrich Nietzsche the very concept of truth fell prey to this erosive process. Such a result stood at quite a distance from Hegel's claim that
his philosophy gave shape to the historical self-realization and self-awareness
of the human mind in its timeless and absolute contours.

It was Marx, a student of Hegel's, who had subjected the grand Hegelian
synthesis to his own materialist reductionism. According to Marx, from the
moment when social relations of production involve a separation between
manual and intellectual labor, human consciousness can begin to conceive
of itself as something different from the mere consciousness of the practi-
cality of everyday arrangements (ein Bewußtsein der bestehenden Praxis).
Only then can it pretend "really to represent something, without representing something real" (to state matters in one of those stylistic inversions at
which Marx was a master).[8] Human consciousness is then able to turn away
from the world and to move toward the creation of allegedly "pure" theory,
theology, philosophy, ethics, and so on. Marx brought his dialectical vision
of human social life's historical stages to bear on all such emanations of pure
human thought, with their semblance and pretense of universality and perennial validity, as well as their pretense of representing a natural order. This
vision relentlessly dissolves "things" into "processes" and shows all forms of
social and cultural life, such as the idea of justice or ideas of the true state
and the true religion, in the dual aspect of their historically necessary rise and
equally necessary demise. The tragic rift in Marx's thought, as pointed out
before, consists precisely in the corrosive force of this vision set against Marx's
rationalist belief in science and truth.

Toward the end of the nineteenth century, Nietzsche subjected the concept of truth itself to an ideological and sociological reductionism. He considered truth to be no more than the outcome of human understandings,
inspired by the need, common to all human beings, to construct a shared
worldview that will help them to make sense of their own lives. The "true
world" is no more than an illusion; it suffices that we believe ourselves to
possess the truth. In other words, truths prove themselves to be such through
their effects, not through the logic of evidence. The true and the effective have
become identical.

Nietzsche, like Marx, points to the human need to create the fiction of a
stable, real world, a fiction centering on key concepts such as unity and entity, or continuity and being, but also and most important, meaning and
purpose. Concepts such as these allow human beings to interpret the world
and make sense of it. This human need—or "will," as Nietzsche called it—
to make life bearable by giving sense and meaning to it resulted in the fiction
of a "true world," a world that, ironically, is thought to "make sense" in its
own right. Even when rulers and the ruled are confronting each other in
conflicts centering on ideas and ideals such as justice, freedom, equality, these
ideas are no more than the expression of the "will to power" (der Wille zur
Macht) that is driving both contending parties. They have no intrinsic validity, no inherent truth.

We should bear in mind, however, that for all his relentless drive to dis-
credit and denounce, Nietzsche himself was propelled by a quest for truth.
As he put it himself, his insight into the decadent spirituality of the Western
world was "von Wahrheit und Wissenschaft am strengsten bestätigt und
aufrechterhalten [most rigorously tested and confirmed by truth and sci-
ence]."[9] Nevertheless, the whole gist of Nietzsche's insights seems to gain-
say this assertion; the very logic of his argument cannot fail to bring down
such holy pillars as "Truth" and "Science." One might expect that Nietzsche's
work, having laid to waste the entire intellectual landscape of its day, would
have resulted in utter disillusionment. Yet Nietzsche's ideas have been hailed
by generations of thinkers in Europe precisely for being liberatory. That, too,
one might argue, is a form of truth. If communities of like-minded spirits
chose to read Nietzsche this way, if they saw a liberating thrust in his work,
then their interpretation was their truth, in an appropriately Nietzschean way.

Both Marx and Nietzsche pointed to the way in which what are truly ongoing processes congeal into fixed, institutional forms, a transformation to
be understood in terms of class conflict or the will to power. As both authors
saw it, this tendency produced institutional structures that seemed to lead
their own lives and that, despite their having been made by humans, constituted a realm beyond the reach and control of human beings. Instead of being
subject to the exercise of the human will, they had turned human beings into

objects themselves. In their autonomy and inner logic, in their sets of rules and regulations, these institutional structures formed an unmovable whole to which human beings can only subject themselves. Marx denied this independent existence. He viewed these institutions as no more than the formal reflections of human self-alienation, a dismal doubling of the world into forms that further reinforce human subjection and alienation. Like Nietzsche's deconstruction of *Geistesgebilde* (intellectual structures), Marx's dismissal of all such forms, such as the law, meant first and foremost the invalidation of everything that had seemed fixed, natural, timeless, and universal. Ideology—of a Marxist or Nietzschean inspiration—therefore may give rise to a sense of human freedom. It may inspire a feeling that people can be the masters of their own lives and destinies. Thus the dilemma of ideology and truth as presented here may well translate into the dilemma of ideology and freedom, even in the case where the concept of truth has been broken beyond repair.

The continued onslaught on the concept of truth, in its naively rationalist form as something out there waiting to be recognized, has had a lasting effect on all who have studied human life. The reduction of objective truth to varieties of subjectivity—such as people's place in society, their interests, their will to power—would henceforth doom every acquisition of social knowledge to captivity in the iron cage of subjectivity, felt more or less strongly as a prison, but certainly seen as inescapable.

Classic sociologists such as Émile Durkheim, Max Weber, and Karl Mannheim sought a way out of the predicament of the lone subject; they set the terms for a debate that continues until the present day. Each of these three sociologists tended to emphasize one of the dilemmas introduced by the unsettling idea of ideology. Durkheim focused on the relation between ideology and science; Weber, on the relation between ideology and freedom; and Mannheim, on the relation between ideology and historicism. Let me repeat here that each of these dilemmas in its own way represents the underlying fundamental dilemma of ideology and truth: how can knowing subjects ever reach a stage of insights and views shared with others.

Durkheim's Way Out

Of the three authors mentioned, Durkheim perhaps most clearly represents the staunch and undaunted counterpoint to the undermining of human knowledge brought by ideology. A strong believer in a social science modeled after the natural sciences, he took up a thread that runs all the way back to Enlightenment optimism. In a way Marx did the same when he tried to model socialism in a scientific vein, but unlike Marx, Durkheim never experienced the drama of thought turned against itself. His belief in the scientific method as the proper means for acquiring knowledge never wavered.

He flatly rejected any reductionism that portrays social and cultural phenomena as no more than the false appearance of underlying interests. He argued that social reality is sui generis and can be understood in its continuity, order, and change only through the ordering of *social facts* in terms of causes and effects. In his escape from the cage of subjectivity, he nearly ended up in the cage of objectivity. Thus an inverted reductionism began to loom, the view that the individual is no more than a particular appearance of social facts—such as cultural values and norms or a particular language—that exist independently of the individuals who give expression to them.

Thus to Durkheim, even a quintessentially private act such as suicide can be understood in terms of social facts and the pressure they bring to bear on individual human beings. One such phenomenon, as Durkheim showed, is the erosion of patterns of norms and expectations under the impact of rapid changes in the social division of labor and in social mobility. An awareness of this breakdown of what he called organic solidarity, causing widespread anomie (another of Durkheim's key concepts), led Durkheim to commit himself to the social problems of his age. Older forms expressive of organic solidarity (e.g., religions) had allowed individual members of society to see their positions in society as meaningfully related to the larger social order. Durkheim's sociological insights showed him that these forms no longer functioned properly precisely because of the social fabric's increased complexity and density. Durkheim is an ideologue here to the extent that he harbored the hope that social science as he conceived of it might in the future function to restore a view of coherence and meaning. In other words, like Marx, Durkheim hoped that his ideas would have an impact on society. If there was a rift in Durkheim's case, a tragic sense of dilemma, it was due to the fact that his scientific research provided him with insights that seemed to run counter to his high hopes. The rift, in other words, was between his ideological commitment to the problems of contemporary society and what he saw as society's last, best hope: science.

Weber's Way Out

In his studies of the society of his day, Weber tended to emphasize the tension between ideology and freedom. First of all, Weber did not view the cage of subjectivity as a prison. Weber's views of humanity differed drastically from those of Marx at his most determinist or Durkheim at his most collectivist. Weber defines "man" in his subjectivity as the free creator of values, capable of actively interpreting and influencing life and its meanings. Human beings engaged in this endeavor form social settings imbued with meaning and relevance. This condition of human society grants the student of society a degree of freedom unavailable to the student of nature. Social scientists can use a blend of recognition and interpretation to enter the meaningful world of others; thus, they may hope to reconstruct its typical cultural configuration around a number of central values. Weber therefore rejects reductionism, choosing instead to accept the human mind's multitude of manifestations in their own inner logic and mutual affinities, as illustrated in his famous study of the affinity between two historically specific phenomena: Protestantism and early capitalism.

Weber's view of the constraints of subjectivity differs from Marx's or Durkheim's. Although Weber's view of social science allows and even requires values to be known and understood, their validity or correctness cannot be shown with the tools of science. This is the specific form of relativism that Weber gave to his analysis of the constraints of subjectivity. One can study values in their effects, in the relations of means to goals as people have historically applied these in their various social arrangements. Nevertheless, however much each observer as a moral being tends to bring his or her values and commitments to bear on research questions (an instance of what Weber called *Wertbezogenheit,* or "moral involvement"), as a scientist he or she will have to refrain from letting moral judgment interfere with intellectual understanding. The individual values of the researcher should be kept separate from the research process; in that sense science should be value free.

Thus, this distanced methodology requires the social scientist to step aside from the social life under study. The role of politician or ideologue, both involved in the broader social debates about values and goals, differs from that of the social scientist, even though both roles may coincide in single individuals. The discourse of science appeals differently to the human mind and is subject to rules of argumentation distinct from those of the ideological debate. In the latter case the argument must of course be firmly based in a knowledge of society and its problems, yet its aim is *persuasion,* giving an audience reasons to work toward a common goal. Value judgments are central to the entire intellectual transaction. In scientific discourse, however, the central aim is to *convince* on the basis of agreed rules of evidence and proof. Thus, people can be made to agree to the conclusions of a scientific argument despite the different values they may cherish as individuals. Here, it seems, lies the special contribution that social scientists can make to the value-centered discourse of political debate. To the extent that every attempt at ideological suasion always sketches maps showing how to get from here to there, relating means to ends, the scientist may disagree as to the ends but, as a connoisseur of social interconnections, may well advise as to the means and their efficacy. We can recognize here the social scientist as policy adviser, a role increasingly common in our contemporary world.

Undeniably, however, this combination of roles, the one prescribing intellectual distance and the other assuming a moral commitment to political issues, brings its own dilemmas. It certainly does so in the case of Weber, who tended to emphasize the freedom of human individuals as creators of cultural values. On the basis of his studies of social relations of power, Weber, like Marx, found that human beings not only set up organizational structures of command and control but in most cases surrender their freedom in submission to those structures. Even though these structures may have been aimed at realizing collective values, even though they may have been—in Weber's own words—*wertrational* (value rational), the social apparatus of control and command may have become so complex, opaque, and impenetrable as to seem an alien outside objectivity imposing itself on society. The paradox is unavoidable. Not caught in subjectivity, capable of the free realization of social values, human beings have been caught in an iron cage of objectivity, a structure of their own creation but nevertheless beyond their control. This somber insight in social trends and developments, linked to the methodological commandment to abstain from moral judgment, confronts the social scientist with characteristic moral dilemmas.

Mannheim's Way Out

As the twentieth century moved along, these moral dilemmas only gained in poignancy. Weber's analysis of the structures of social control turning against the citizens foreshadowed later discussions of totalitarianism in the 1930s and 1940s, or for that matter of the welfare state in the 1970s and 1980s. The problems of society in the interwar period, the breakdown of liberal market economics and democratic politics, and the rising totalitarianism of fascist, national-socialist, or communist varieties led German sociologist Karl Mannheim to consider yet another way out of the basic dilemma of ideology and truth, a dilemma that he understood as one of ideology and historicism.

Mannheim shared the mood of cultural pessimism prevalent among many of his contemporaries, such as Oswald Spengler, José Ortega y Gasset, and Johan Huizinga, yet his pessimism had a twist all its own. In the face of a mass society that had lost all its integrating social frameworks and was no longer a functioning civil society, neither science nor critical philosophy could come up with viable remedies. In a radical version of Marx's ideas, Mannheim argued that all thinking is fully determined by the historical and social position of the thinker. Once again human beings are imprisoned, this time caught in what we might call the subjectivity of history. Mannheim's view is a radical version of nineteenth-century historicism, apparently offering no way out.

Nonetheless, Mannheim repeated Marx's escape act and surmounted his determinism by an exercise of free will. Using a phrase coined by his fellow German sociologist Alfred Weber, Mannheim posits the existence of a *"freischwebende Intelligenz"* (a free-floating intelligentsia), a class of intellectuals sufficiently free from the socioeconomic relations in which their contemporaries are caught to allow them to transcend the total *Seinsbedingung* (social determinacy) of their thinking. This methodological trick offered Mannheim a way out of a dilemma of his own making. As a self-appointed member of this free-floating intelligentsia, Mannheim could then move on to render a "diagnosis of his time" (to paraphrase the title of one of his books) and to design a program for social change based on a mixture of political democracy and economic planning.

Thus we can see how, of the thinkers discussed here, Mannhein was alone in opting for the role of ideologue to shake off his subservience to historicism—the role, in other words, of the *intellectual,* who in critically analyzing society's predicaments and designing programs for change is able both to act on a sense of moral commitment and to keep scientific distance. We can recognize here the fundamental freedom of critical reason, which Weber had postulated and which Marx had hesitantly smuggled in despite his historical determinism. In his person and his work, Mannheim combined the roles that Weber had distinguished and only tenuously held together.

The Intellectual as a Historical Type

In his unagonized embrace of the role of intellectual—or of ideologue—Mannheim took a position that had been the object of left-wing political reflection since the days of Marx. The bourgeois ideologue who aligned him- or herself on the side of revolution, and who in Marx's analysis had appeared like a deus ex machina on the historical stage, inspired later socialist thinkers, such as Karl Kautsky, Robert Lafargue, Robert Michels, Henriette Roland Holst, Theodor Geiger, and Hendrik de Man, to consider the outlines of a sociology of the intellectual. That line of reflection parallels the history of the concept of ideology and of the many philosophical dilemmas that it entailed for human knowledge. The reassertion of critical reason's autonomy from the entrenched forces of tradition or imposed modes of thought enforced through censorship was not itself an autonomous movement in intellectual history, following its own predetermined course and logic, despite Hegel's pronouncements on the matter. Quite the contrary: it was a history intimately interwoven with social transformations to which intellectuals of many stripes provided the critical accompaniment.

With the rise of a bourgeois society within the established late-feudal and strongly agrarian setting of a hierarchy of social estates, along with the rise of a market economy and the attendant spread of literacy and a bourgeois press, new social options opened up for the literati, the specialists in matters of the mind. Earlier on they had always been enmeshed in the established structures of authority, in the service of church or state. Now, for the first time, they could lead independent lives wielding their own pens. In gaining these positions in society, they shared interests with the emerging bourgeois class in a joint struggle against entrenched impediments to the free exchange of opinion, the free trade in goods, and the free movement of people. The rise of an independent social status for intellectuals cannot be understood in isolation from this historical alliance with the emerging bourgeoisie.

That alliance would become more strained when, after the bourgeois revolutions in Europe, the bourgeoisie took control of the powers of the state. Henceforth there would be a continuing tension between the newly gained freedom rights—a constituent part of all successful bourgeois revolutions—and the need for a language to obfuscate, or legitimize, the newly entrenched capitalist mode of production. Intellectuals as a group were subject to those capitalist relations in their professional lives, as journalists working for capitalist owner-publishers or as teachers having to confront an official bourgeois ideology in matters of academic freedom. Therefore, it is not so much their objective relationship to the means of production that accounts for their lives in the interstices of society and their abilities to "float freely." They were in fact as much sellers of goods as were others in society. Instead, the intellectuals' demanding and obstinate code of honor set them apart as a social group.

Their cultural commitment to disinterested and unsparing critical reflection on historical and social interrelations and tensions made intellectuals appear to be voluntary members of a new, secular version of the medieval mendicant orders. This metaphor may help us to fathom the intellectuals' special social station better than can words such as *class* or *estate*. Just as medieval monastic orders were an organizational response to the dialectical tension between allowing doctrinal diversity and preserving church unity as one overarching organization, bourgeois societies made room for the various orders of intellectuals as islands of ideological diversity within the larger organizational unity of the capitalist bourgeois state. This arrangement reflected the always ambivalent relation between the economically and politically powerful bourgeoisie and the intellectuals, who were the gadflies of those in power yet also the monopoly purveyors of the specialized knowledge on which the growing organizations in political and economic life had to rely. The class line between bourgeois and non-bourgeois, between ally and opponent, could therefore run right through the intellectuals' ranks.

I should at this point mention that the word *intellectuals* is more recent than their appearance as a historical type. The French philosophes could certainly be counted among their number, yet the term was not used until the late nineteenth century. Even then, it referred broadly to the general category of nonmanual labor, also known then as the "new middle class"; for instance, Karl Kautsky used it this way. To indicate intellectuals as we understand them, a word derived from Russian usage—*intelligentsia*—was more current. Only at the time of the Dreyfuss case in France, when a large number of writers, journalists, and other public figures rallied in protest, did the word *intellectuels* gain currency, denoting a group with a shared sense of social mission and critical responsibility.

The End of Ideologies

Mannheim referred to intellectuals as a "free-floating intelligentsia" in an attempt to capture both the social ambivalence of their position and the clarity of their cultural mission. He himself tried to live up to this vision in the choice he made for democracy and planning. In both respects he may have programmatically opened the way toward the "historic compromise," that great, historic reconciliation between intellectuals and the late capitalist state. The problems of social reform in Western democracies during the Great Depression were conducive to early experiments with welfare-state ideas and forms of economic planning without infringing—as the totalitarian dictatorships of the day then did—on the established rights and freedoms of democracy. This combination of factors offered intellectuals their chance to join in the effort while clinging to the ethos of their secular "order." This trend would not gain momentum across the democratic West until after World War II, however, at which time the voices of an estranged wholesale critique and rejection of the prevailing order, from left and right, began to fall silent, more so as the total failure of the totalitarian alternative became apparent. In their new role as experts and policy advisers, intellectuals had gained access to the corridors of power. The road that Mannheim had indicated for intellectuals to follow, merging the Weberian roles of scientist and ideologue, would lead to a view of science as applied and subordinated, putting itself in the service of the reigning policy consensus supporting the welfare-state project. Thus the late 1950s saw the rise of the view that the times marked "the end of ideology," an era characterized by applied science, depoliticization, and pragmatic policies.

As it turned out, this was no more than an instance of historical myopia, an optical illusion. From a larger perspective, it may be clear that the onslaught on tradition and authority as sources of knowledge led to a road of critical exploration that unmasked everything standing in the way of pure knowledge of objective reality, such as prejudice, false consciousness, and interests. As I have shown, this exploration resulted in the quintessentially modern consciousness of the subjectivity of all knowledge. It was a consciousness that gained common currency and became part of common culture. For the continued human quest for knowledge, it assumed the form of a cultural assignment: as knowing subjects human beings should always be aware of and account for their subjectivity. Their knowledge should always reflect back on itself; it must be reflexive knowledge. The age in which this awareness gathered strength, from the late 1960s onward, we might justly call the age of ideology, almost as a badge of honor. From being a slur or a slight, the reproach of false consciousness, the term has now become an exhortation to think through the premises of one's own thought. As an assignment and a mission it delineates a mental and intellectual habitus that touches on both Weberian spheres of intellectual activity: knowing and understanding. Both would need the continued questioning of implicit, tacit, or half-conscious premises. In the social sciences the reflection on paradigms—on the underlying constructions of humanity and society guiding one's outlook on reality—is one sign that this mission has been taken up. In philosophy and cultural studies similar trends are apparent up to the present day, with writers subjecting the very language we use to rigorous deconstruction and unveiling the quasi-natural and so far unreflected matrix of our thought and perception. From all such reflection on the uses and consequences of our structures of knowledge, from the late 1960s call for relevance and critical science to the present-day debates concerning multiculturalism and cultural otherness, it is apparent that students of culture and society have become aware of their role as intellectuals, involved in crucial social debates concerning the condition of human society, nationally and internationally.

The Contents of Ideology

The ideological view of reality resembles the scientific view, as I argued before. Both rest on ordered knowledge of the world, and both are informed by the problematic nature of knowledge. Like scientific debates, ideological debates start from the premise of human freedom and creativity in the questions asked and answers found. That freedom offers a way out of each thinking individual's subjective enclosure, inviting interaction and exchange. Following the train of other people's thoughts and confronting them with one's own form the area of what is known as intersubjectivity, a mutual intellectual understanding based on a shared skepsis as to final and objective knowledge. In certain respects, however, the ideological project differs from the scientific one. It is meant to serve a purpose for human beings as thinking subjects different from that of science.

Science provides us with working knowledge about the world; it produces an inner mirror image of the world ordered according to criteria of causal coherence and allows each of us to reflect the world and reflect on it mentally. Only through such inner reflection are we able to think ahead, to foresee the consequences of our actions and to interact with nature and our fellow human beings intelligently. Our intelligence is not there, ready to use at birth, but shapes itself in the experience of and interactions with our environment. The order inherent in that environment will gradually be mirrored in the inner world of our intelligence. Jean Piaget, a psychologist who studied this inner development, takes this mirroring hypothesis to great lengths, suggesting a highly original way out of the dilemmas of objectivity and subjectivity. Be that as it may, in general we can say that intelligent knowledge—and scientific knowledge is only a specific and more demanding form of it—constitutes a vital condition for human action.

A related but different human need is to find sense and meaning in the world, the need to create a meaningful cosmology. That need was long served by traditional symbolic systems such as mythology and religion, but with human thought's gradual emancipation from tradition and doctrinal authority as sources of knowledge, they too lost their place as providers of meaning. It was especially this trend, the human mind's pretension to know better than history, against which Edmund Burke, that great early ideologue of conservatism, raised his voice.

But he could no longer stem the tide: the self-awareness of human reason—to put it in Hegelian terms—as the prime instrument for the acquisition of knowledge also meant that henceforth human reason alone must answer questions as to the sense and meaning of life. That implication truly made the era of ideologies come into its own as the era of worldly religions. Only then could people begin to conceive of their societies as called to such higher tasks as the fulfillment of central human values, such as liberty, equality, and fraternity—the secular creed of the French Revolution. The utterly novel, historically unheard-of nature of this led Hegel to make this statement: "Es war [noch] nicht gesehen worden, daß der Mensch sich auf dem Kopf, das ist auf den Gedanken stellt, und die Wirklichkeit nach diesem erbaut [It had not been seen yet that man stands on his head, i.e., bases himself on his thought, and builds up reality accordingly]."[10]

The Great Ideologies

Ideologies, centered on human values, show tenuous relationships among themselves in more than one way. One reason for this tension is the underlying mutual antagonism of the social classes, each of which carries one of these ideologies. Another reason is the tension among these values themselves, for under conditions of scarcity they cannot all be realized at the same time. The first element of tension that I should mention here is in a sense the lasting echo of that great historical clash between the great emancipatory ideologies—liberalism and socialism—and traditionalism. The first two were erected around the central values of liberty and equality, respectively, and were carried by the new social classes that early capitalism had brought to life, whereas the third was the expression of an organic solidarity that had permeated preindustrial society, a solidarity in which people from all walks of life had meaningfully shared while accepting the established patterns of inequality. In its resistance to the new claims and the new views of humanity and society that the emancipation ideologies propagated, this relatively inarticulate traditionalism found the intellectual precision that turned it into an ideology in its own right: the ideology of conservatism. It gave expression to such values as tradition, the historically grown legitimacy of social inequality, or the right of elites to rule, arguing on behalf of a natural superiority that would later harden into racialist views. The central value that conservatives rose to defend, however, was an intuitive communitarianism that, as they saw it, had bound both high and low in a shared sense of forming part of a larger social whole imbued with historical sense and meaning.

The true clash here is between the worldview of a preindustrial, estate-like society, and that characteristic of class society, a clash—to use Ferdinand Tönnies's famous concepts—between a *Gemeinschaft* and a *Gesellschaft* view of society. This mental rift has survived the demise of precapitalist society; in a certain sense fraternity (or solidarity) and security are the contemporary version of this Gemeinschaft value, of this hankering after organic solidarity. Although central to conservatism, these values are not absent from other ideologies. Elements of this worldview appear both in Catholic social thought, with its views of solidarism and corporatism, and in socialism, although they are arguably more prominent and traditional in the former.

The tension between liberty and equality stems as much from the concepts themselves as from the conflicting interests of the social classes that centrally subscribed to these values in either liberalism or socialism. Historically liberalism can be seen as the ideology of the bourgeois class, economically and socially self-supporting individuals wedded to the idea of freedom of choice in planning their own careers and those of their children. Equality in their view was mostly of a formal kind, seen as an equality of rights or equality before the law. This class used individualist terms to explain the nonformal, substantive inequality between rich and poor, between the socially strong and weak, seeing it as the outcome of the free interplay of social forces, a social competition that later on would be dressed with the semblance of scientific insight. Borrowing from Darwin's views, it would become known as social Darwinism. This substantive inequality would form the central issue of socialism. As socialists saw it, the class differences in power and economic strength made the rhetoric of free negotiation between individual employers and workers or of a labor contract freely entered into nothing more than a parody of freedom. These differences forced the weaker party to sell its labor on terms that were no longer humane.

Against the individualist divide-and-rule approach of liberalism, the history of socialism traces the continuing struggle for the right of the weak to get organized: to unionize, to bargain collectively with employers, and to form their own political parties. To the extent that this last struggle has aimed at getting the right to vote, it constitutes a struggle for a right of formal equality. Here socialism fought liberalism on its own turf, in the terms that liberals were wont to use themselves. To the extent that the socialist strategy of uniting for power brought forth the socialist rhetoric of social solidarity, socialist leaders applied the value of brotherhood (or fraternity) to the cause of one class in society: the workers. Nonetheless, socialism's central motive force is equality in its substantive, distributive sense.

It should be added, however, that socialism, like liberalism, must at times choose to live with a formal rather than a substantive version of its central value. Socialism's historical attack on private property as the bastion of social inequality has for many years been inspired by the alternative of communal ownership, particularly of the means of production or at least of the "commanding heights of industry," as it was called in England during the 1960s. In practice, however, at least in democracies, this has always meant a state takeover—that is, nationalization—and the institution of a so-called public sector of the national economy. Moreover, it meant that management and labor relations practices remained unaffected. The same established patterns of subordination, division of labor, and labor conflict that the private sectors of the economy had known would repeat themselves in the public sector. State ownership therefore offers no more than formal equality; only formally can the community—or society—be seen as the owner. Every version of ideas concerning worker participation or workers' codetermination that socialists have devised forms an attempt to give this formal equality some substantive features, but none has ever become a central tenet of democratic socialism.

The great, historic compromise between both ideologies—liberalism and socialism—ushered in a period of institutionalized collaboration for parliamentary politics and government policies, as well as the economic arena. This did not mean, however, that the underlying tension between their central values never surfaced. The various attempts to give substance and institutional shape to these values repeatedly made it clear that they were at odds. The recent debates in a number of European countries concerning the shape of secondary education is a case in point. The central issue was always the possible uses of the educational system as an instrument for reducing the inequality of opportunity among children of various class backgrounds. To the extent that ideas for such reduction translated into the homogenization of secondary education and the postponement of the age at which students are selected and streamed according to their tested abilities, as have been done in the English "comprehensive schools" or the Dutch "middle school," they infringe on liberal views that prefer a plurality of types of schools and educational approaches and would leave it to parents to make their own choices. Such ideas are hard to reconcile with views in which education's function is seen as the early recognition of individual talent in order to support and foster it. Those on the side of egalitarianism rejected this view, arguing that a plurality of types of secondary education had tended to reflect and *reproduce* the prevailing social stratification. In other words, the selection of students and their assignments to various types of schools had always proceeded according to class rather than individual talent. This conflict of views does not lend itself to an easy resolution. Every attempt at enlarging the educational opportunities of lower-class children by widening access to secondary education risks curtailing those forms of education "that are only for the happy few," even if they are the more intellectually gifted. There is the risk of a downward leveling of educational standards. There is the further risk that groups of people in society will no longer subscribe to the view of government as the sole agency responsible for schooling and education. They may well push back the borderline of the public sector and set up their own educational institutions. The United States, more clearly than any European country, has throughout its history kept this particular option open. Whatever the road taken, the different priorities of both ideological camps and the relative scarcity of government resources make it clear that choices will have to be made. But they are never easy.

Open and Closed Ideologies

Despite all the differences in their views of society, all great ideologies, from conservatism to socialism, have one thing in common: they all subscribe to the democratic ideals and practices ushered in by the era of bourgeois revolutions. Each apparently recognizes in those ideals and practices the very preconditions for its own continued existence, particularly in the classic freedoms of expression, organization, and belief and opinion. Each of these ideologies carries with it the image centrally linked to the bourgeois revolutions: a public sphere of debate and discussion (e.g., in the press, in government, in public conversation), a sphere in which the various ideologies can vie among themselves while influencing one another. This common feature in a certain historical sense makes "bourgeois" ideologies of all of them, including democratic socialism. In other words, it makes them into *open* ideologies, open to counterargument, open to continued reflection on their underlying premises, yet sufficiently assured of their central values to speak up and be heard.

As such, they form a group distinct from what we might call *closed*, or totalitarian, ideologies, which may orient themselves to either the left or the right but are all equally antibourgeois. In a sad historical paradox, however, these latter ideologies are equally the product of the chain of social change and struggle occurring since the rise of industrial capitalism. They are equally inspired by the radical hope of once and for all coming to grips with rifts and conflicts in society, with social fission and fragmentation. On both the right and the left, they constitute the atavistic impulse forcibly to bring back the quiet waters of the Gemeinschaft. They have done so either by imposing the classless society, forcing the pace of history toward that promised final salvation, or by reaffirming the nation seen as a tribal covenant, the *Volk,* forcing the pace of history toward the promised "final solution." In the case of Nazism, the Holocaust was seen as the final act of exorcism of the evil of bourgeois freedoms.

There is a paradox in this outcome. We can see the connection to the "age of ideology"; we can link it to that modern stage of history in which the task of giving sense and meaning to life was thrust on human beings themselves. At the same time, however, the totalitarian worldview appears as the very antithesis of this task. It seems rather like a throwback to a world of controlled thought, censorship, manipulated information, terror, and repression in reaction to which modern ideologies had sprung up in the first place. The closed ideologies are an intellectual caricature of the image of ideologies as outlined in preceding paragraphs. Given their use of manipulated language and distorted facts, they are more like propaganda systems. The intellectual habitus of skepsis and critical self-reflection has been replaced by the dogmas of a secular church.

The closed ideology can come fully into its own only in the totalitarian state. To the extent that such ideologies occur in a context of democratic pluralism, such as the democracies of Western Europe during the cold war, membership of this self-enclosed world has always been an act of free will and has always known the option of exit. These two options, in combination with the rival presence of other ideologies, have served to keep the degree of intellectual closure relatively high. Entry is limited to those who can be tempted by the pretense of total truth and absolute certainty, and the freedom of exit or the forced expulsion of dissidents will serve to keep dissidence under control. The appeal of the closed ideology—or (to use Eric Fromm's words) the "escape from freedom" that it seems to offer—increases in times of social disruption and of an increased sense and experience of individual powerlessness vis-à-vis chaotic social forces. Intellectual skepsis then becomes a burden that people are glad to abandon in exchange for the promises of salvation or final solutions, whether from the left or right.

Europe, the Birthplace of Ideologies

The cultural forms of the open, "bourgeois" ideologies are historically specific, dependent on conditions of time and place. These ideologies resulted from a number of historical trends and developments, several of which I already mentioned: a feudal past, bourgeois revolutions, the rise of an industrial mode of production, the rise of the press and the secular order of intellectuals, the dissemination of literacy and education, and the acquisition of political rights. Only in Europe have all these developments emerged in this historical sequence over the last two to three centuries.

This balance of historical conditions is sufficiently complex and precarious that these ideologies cannot easily be transplanted elsewhere. Even in Europe, for all their rootedness there, the great ideologies have not always been immune to social disruption and economic crisis. The great mass-society theorists of the interwar period—and Karl Mannheim can certainly be ranked among them—have all tried to show that the failure of the great ideologies at precisely this time of distress was not a random event, not a historical fluke. Rather, they saw it as a failure whose causes were inherent to the system, contained in the inner logic of industrial society and in the egalitarianism of the democratic ethos. They showed how the demise of traditional frames of integration, such as regional and local communities, church denominations, and larger integrated family structures, had not brought the liberation that egalitarian enthusiasm had led many to anticipate and had not ushered in the new community of brothers and sisters. Rather, they argued, it was as if individual human beings had been expelled into the world of anonymous forces of economic life, with all its uncertainty for individuals and society alike. The mass society, in this view, is an atomized society, yet prone to herdlike collective swings of mood and movement, as Gustave Le Bon and other mass psychologists had argued.

Such views of mass society clearly do find their place in a conservative frame of mind. The much-mourned and idealized integrating frameworks are truly those of a traditional and vanished, Gemeinschaft world. Perhaps more typical of conservative critiques of mass society, however, is the general tone of an anguished jeremiad. These critics see not just a loss of integrating structures but rather a general decline of transcendental and universal cultural values. They stand in a line of cultural conservatism that goes back to Alexis de Tocqueville, continues through the cultural pessimists of the interbellum and the postwar critique of the culture of consumption as it attended mass society, and on to contemporary critics who view the mass media as producing the ultimate fake version of whatever cultural conservatives hold dear.

A related critical tradition, more political than cultural in its concerns, is of a mixed liberal-socialist parentage. As it developed, liberalism grew away from the radical individualism of its early views of society. It came to stress the new integrating frameworks that have taken the place and function of the traditional frameworks: the multitude of free associations that now fill social space and jointly constitute what came to be known as *civil society*. Again Tocqueville, in his classic study of democracy in America, is among the first to have noted this new force of social integration and stabilization.

A typically liberal concept in this connection is that of *social control,* in the sense of a social body's capacity to regulate its course collectively. Liberalism recognized the expression of such social control in the institutional structure of free associations, such as political parties, and in the institutional rules of the game, such as elections and parliamentary representation. It was a view of undeniably greater sociological sophistication than liberalism's early assumption of a social automatism, of invisible hands working for the greatest good for the greatest number. Socialism as well recognized the need for social organization but tended to conceive of social control in terms of centralized state guidance. Whereas liberalism may have tended to focus on civil society as providing for social control, socialism's view was the politicized and much more self-conscious version of it.

Whatever the precise emphasis in conservatism, liberalism, or socialism, all three found themselves faced with the breakdown of social control in the setting of mass society during the 1920s and 1930s. The democratic revolution had been completed, at least in the formal sense that the struggle for equal civil rights had ended and the general franchise had been introduced. Henceforth the entire population over a certain minimum age was free to participate in the established structures for the expression of the collective political will and for the formation and implementation of social policies. Early in the century, however, the institutions of democracy appeared incapable of coming to grips with problems of employment, price stability, social security, political stability, and most important, production of the symbolic systems needed to legitimate and give sense and meaning to citizenship. Mass society seemed afflicted by a social, ideological, and cultural deficit.

In pondering this deficit, each of the great ideological movements was forced to rethink the problems of the erosion and impotence of mass society's integrating structures. The core problem was novel and contemporary. On the one hand, the nation-state's entire population had reached political emancipation. It now formed a citizenry free to air its political demands. On the other hand, contrary developments obstructed the effective expression of the collective will and the capacity for effective social control. These contrary effects originated in autonomous processes that worked to unhinge social integration, processes such as the continued transformation of economic production or the urbanization and continued uprooting of parts of the population from their traditional settings, mobilizing them as new cohorts added to the labor force of industrial capitalism. I address the answers to this particular quandary in the section concerning the rise and problems of the social welfare state. What concerns me here is the notion that the problems of modern mass society, first acknowledged and formulated in Europe in the period leading up to World War II, have since emerged as the central challenges facing the Third World and have assumed their own characteristic ideological configurations there.

Nationalism and the Third World

The problems of mass society have appeared in novel and unanticipated forms in all those countries that shed their colonial status and acquired national independence following World War II. In most cases, there was initially a marked ideological continuity with the former European centers of empire. The indigenous elites that had led their countries on the road to formal independence were familiar with and often inspired by forms of Western thought concerning liberty and equality. More often than not they had encountered their first taste of this ideological heritage when they were students in the colonizing countries. Except for a few notable exceptions, such as India—the largest democracy in the world—the experiments with the democratic way ended in failure.

Evidently the handicaps were many. For one thing, the new nation-states hardly ever constituted actual self-conscious nations. They were often the continuation of administrative entities within borders drawn up by the previous colonial rulers, in total neglect of existing patterns of ethnic or tribal solidarity. These traditional settings often prevented any meaningful affiliation with the new nation-state. The new rulers of these states therefore had to invent from scratch the symbolic systems that could meaningfully express the new national unity. The ideology of nationalism, originating in Europe, could help them to accomplish this task, although not without some drastic recasting. In Europe nationalism, unlike the great emancipation ideologies of liberalism and socialism, had been the product not of the Enlightenment but rather of the movement following it: romanticism. Romanticism has historically served as a reaction against the abstract, and ahistorical worldview of rationalism, much as conservatism has done. Thus the nation could come to the fore as the true embodiment of feelings of belonging and affiliation that had been shaped by a shared history. Often, however, the nation was more a mythic construct, a romantic projection, than the reflection of reality. Nationalism was therefore more an ideological project than a tool of historical description. It aimed more at inventing the nation, at producing symbolic repertoires of national tradition. Nevertheless, it had to rely on historical exploration for its inventions and constructions, using bits and parcels of collective memory, local traditions, and a shared sense of "us" versus "them." The project was therefore highly dialectical: in addition to defining the nation, it had to give precision and detail to the construction of diametrically opposed "Others" so as to rally support for its views of the nation. What was offered as characteristically typifying the nation, its crucially binding elements, could widely differ. Thus, the nationalism of the Irish and the Poles became strongly centered on their Catholicism, whereas Hungarian nationalism based itself on the shared sense of forming a linguistic community. Whatever the case might be, one common impulse was to set the nation as an inspirational and historical entity against the individual, taking away the latter's alleged centrality on the stage of history. As these things go among open ideologies, however, mutual influences did occur. Thus the liberal idea of liberty inspired nationalism in many different ways in nineteenth-century Europe, as in the Greek national movement, whose fight for national emancipation from Turkish rule assumed the heroic features of a confrontation between Western civilization and the world of Islam.

In the twentieth century, a similar confluence of liberalism and nationalism occurred in President Woodrow Wilson's views of national self-determination. He in fact projected the individualist worldview of liberalism onto the world stage, conceiving of independent nations as so many individual actors subject to the same rules and conventions of collective self-regulation as the individual citizens in a democracy. Even though this Wilsonian vision played a role in legitimating processes of decolonization throughout the twentieth century—and in fact became a liberation ideology in its own right—the inescapable paradox is that many colonial entities did not represent nations in any current sense of the word. In all such cases nationalism preceded the nation. It was a conjuring trick of ruling elites, projecting views of national coherence onto the amorphous arena of the newly independent states. It became a mobilizing ideology aimed at "nation building." The endeavor was highly eclectic and could enter into different relations with, for instance, Western views of technological development or develop its own variants of socialism to legitimate the state's guiding role. Nation building thus turned into a central political responsibility. In that sense it constituted the characteristic response to the specific forms that mass society had assumed in the Third World. This crucial challenge of having to give meaningful form to the abstract principle of popular sovereignty, a principle that all modernizing elites had taken from Western tradition, was compounded in all cases by the formidable task of devising answers to problems of underdevelopment, poverty, scarce resources, and the emergence of a vast urban proletariat.

It is small wonder, then, that in the face of these problems many developing countries opted for authoritarian alternatives, with centrally imposed and enforced regulation replacing free and collective self-regulation. Too many of the preconditions for the latter model were simply lacking. *Coercive control* replaced *social control,* although it did so under the same banners of mobilization and development ideologies. We might call this authoritarian hybrid ideology national populism. It is national because national development became the central task and justification of the collective effort; it is populist to the extent that, in the absence of functioning mediating structures in society, the national leadership sought direct symbolic communion with the masses, casting itself, at least in its political rhetoric, as the sole executor of the will of the masses. This construction of a mystical and charismatic authority is enhanced by selective and propagandistic reference to fragments of precolonial history presented as an inspirational past.

In themselves these processes are nothing new: the ideological inversion turning inferiority into superiority is a tactic often used by emancipation movements. Thus, when Germany's emerging urban bourgeoisie resisted the Frenchified feudal elite in the late eighteenth-century, it prided itself on the superiority of its *Kultur* vis-à-vis the decadent *Zivilisation* of the aristocracy, opposing the inner authenticity of the former to the latter's fake exterior, a mere veneer. Later on Italian fascism referred back to the glory of the Roman Empire as a shining model for the present, whereas German National Socialism prided itself on the superiority of the German race, the *Herrenvolk*, born to lord it over other, lesser breeds. Early African nationalism came up with ideas of *négritude* to express its inalienable inner authenticity as a contrast to the dominant white worldview. In every instance we can recognize the central function of all such ideological constructs: to use the tools of the human intellect for articulating sense and meaning in particular historical settings, to arouse an inspiring sense of identity, and thus to rally support for large projects of collective improvement.

Ideology: Double Binds and Dual Connections

In a seminal article Clifford Geertz distinguishes two main approaches in the study of the social determinants of ideology: interest theories and theories of social strain.[11] We might also call them conflict theories and theories of consensus, or integration. In both variants ideologies appear as the expression, or reflection, of underlying social conditions, such as conflicting interests or weakened social cohesion. At the same time they also appear as a means toward overcoming such conditions.

Nevertheless, both theoretical approaches fall short when it comes to understanding the phenomenon of ideology itself. They blithely neglect to explore how ideologies as symbolic systems work to fulfill their functions. Too often ideologies have remained a black box, a mysterious link in the chain of functional connections. What remains in the dark is the entire area of what Geertz calls "symbolic action." Among sociologists, Geertz was the first to suggest the need for a sociology of symbolic action with a view to understanding ideology.

What he wants to explore is the connecting role that ideologies play at the interface between various functional approaches to the phenomenon. More specifically, he proposes an analysis of the ways in which ideologies use language, the characteristically human means of social communication. He wants to explore how ideologies in language make sense of the world and manage to gain a hearing. In this view ideologies are in need of an analysis on their own terms, as symbolic signifying systems that characteristically use such linguistic tools as metaphors, connotations, and allusions to persuade an audience and to rally it for purposeful action.

The rise of the so-called American studies movement at American universities beginning in the late 1930s nicely illustrates what Geertz has in mind. Perhaps surprisingly, it was not just a case of setting up another area studies program, alongside Asian studies or Soviet studies. It was rather a case of an intellectual emancipation movement. It sought not simply to explore the history of one part of the world but rather to probe the sense and meaning of that history. As such, it sought a cultural self-exploration, an interpretation of the symbolic contours of America's place in history and in the world. This urgent reflection on America's guiding mythologies was meant to demonstrate how the historical experience of uniqueness, of promise and fulfillment of what long since had been prophesied and foretold, constituted the essence of American history. This world of historical experience accorded its epical allure to something that in itself was not truly unique; the conquest of a continent, the taming of a wilderness, and the formation of one society from a large number of immigrants had occurred elsewhere and earlier. But rarely had such a process been understood in the light of predestination and election. Exploring this spiritual side of the story, its allegories as well as the symbols used for its self-expression—that was the task of the American studies movement. As a cultural emancipation movement, it was at the same time an attempt to settle scores with the Old World, which had exercised a cultural hegemony in America for too long, instilling feelings of cultural inferiority among Americans. The long series of cultural self-explorations by American studies pioneers and followers constitutes one continuing illustration of the program Clifford Geertz had in mind when he called for a study of symbolic action. Nevertheless, the word *ideology* hardly ever occurs when Americans engage in such intellectual endeavors. There is a certain ingrained aversion to the word. I will return to that topic later. The more commonly used words have included *myths, allegory,* and *symbols.* As it is, they are precisely the central ingredients of what we may well be warranted in calling a national ideology.

Ideology and the Welfare State

As I pointed out before, the great nineteenth-century ideologies entered into a "historic compromise" in all the Western democracies during the twentieth century. This compromise found its institutional shape in what is commonly known as the welfare state. Instead of emphasizing mutual incompatibility and antagonism, the ideologies have come to explore areas of compatibility and possible cooperation. Thus the institutions of the welfare state resound with historical echoes of conservatism, liberalism, and socialism, echoes that never quite merged into an identifiably new and contemporary ideology undergirding the welfare state. If we define the welfare state as a type of society characterized by a system of government care under democratic control that, while leaving the capitalist system of production in place, assumes responsibility for the collective social welfare of its citizens, the underlying compromise among the various "open" ideologies becomes clearly recognizable. Clearly, also, the borderline with the "closed," totalitarian ideologies is unambiguous: the preservation of democratic civil rights testifies to that. As for the compromise character of the system, the following comments apply.

The conservative worldview, with its predilection for organizing citizens within a multiplicity of institutional settings reflecting the social patterns of organic solidarity, a worldview averse to an image of society as made up simply of individual citizens and their state, has led to the use of mediating social settings for the implementation of welfare policies. Thus, as the state and that middle area of voluntary associations in civil society mutually coordinated these various agencies of collective social control, they produced patterns of cooperative integration. This general process has given rise to various nationally specific configurations. In the Netherlands, for example, this mutual interweaving found its characteristic expression in the Dutch *Verzuiling* system, a system of social segmentation according to the various lines of religion and class that ran through the Dutch population. Ideas concerning subsidiarity prevalent both in Calvinist circles claiming sovereignty in their own bailiwick (soevereiniteit in eigen kring)—in other words, freedom from direct state intervention in their way of life—and in Catholic circles undergirded the two groups' calls for the power to implement welfare policies for their own clienteles. Thus the actual expansion of government's responsibilities in the welfare state in fact strengthened the voluntary associations in civil society by delegating the provision of welfare-state benefits to them. In a following section I will compare this Dutch system with the one that arose in the United States. There, too, as in many other welfare-state systems, the middle ground in society has strengthened similarly. All such arrangements arose in response to deep-felt conservative concerns about the social impact of an unbridled capitalism on the one hand and the unhampered expansion of the powers of the state on the other.

The liberal worldview is reflected in various aspects of the welfare state. Views concerning individuals as responsible for their own life chances—views traditionally centered on the liberal virtue of parsimony and of the deferral of instant gratification—found expression in the idea of social insurance, essentially a collective form of saving based on the shared individual sense of collective risk. Thus people share each others' burdens. A strictly individual calculation of risk and responsibility can thus lead to social behavior, to a joint approach, to truly *social control* of collective problems. It should be added that the conservative worldview also played its part to the extent that the burden of insurance is not carried only by those immediately at risk but is shared by workers and employers as an expression of the community of interest that connects both groups. This arrangement in particular reflects views current in Calvinist and Catholic social thought. The much more dominant position of conservative and liberal thought in the United States and the lesser weight of socialism there has helped to make social insurance the prevailing way to finance the welfare state in that country. Americans tend to frown on the alternative of financing from the general tax income. More generally, however, taxes take the form of earmarked payments in the United States, a good example being the real-estate tax. In their traditional distrust of government, Americans prefer to know what they are paying for.

The liberal view persists in yet another feature of the welfare state: the preservation of a market sector in the national economy. It appears more specifically in the relations established between government and the private sector in the formation of economic policy. Liberal thought long ago moved away from the simple determinism of Adam Smith and the early utilitarians and from their belief in the natural harmony between private interest and public interest. This determinism had already been qualified by Jeremy Bentham and John Stuart Mill, who both saw the need for a socially regulating role for government. In the twentieth century, liberals such as William Henry Beveridge and John Maynard Keynes, saw an anticyclical role for government in countering the ups and downs of national economies and their effects on employment, Beveridge saying so in a scholarly address from 1906. During the 1930s Keynes in particular elaborated a macroeconomic view that held the promise of governments acting as guardians of macroeconomic equilibrium at a level of full employment and price stability. While setting macroeconomic parameters, however, government would leave private industry free to pursue its economic goals. This basic motive—to leave people free to make their own choices—also appears in the specific form given to the social security system as it applied to its individual recipients. What counted was to eliminate the chances that people would lose their sources of income by guaranteeing a minimum wage for all, leaving it to the individual beneficiaries to spend the money as they saw fit.

Finally we can recognize the heritage of socialism. After its period of revisionism, it no longer conceived of the state as the instrument solely of the capitalist class, an instrument of exploitation and ideological manipulation. Accepting the parliamentary road toward social change, socialism too was ready to translate its programmatic views into government policies. The explicit role accorded to the state, and the acceptance of government intervention across a wide range of social life, may be the most direct reflection of socialist thought. The growth of the public sector in national economies is only one indication of this. Another indication appears in the area of income inequalities, where, as the Dutch economist Jan Tinbergen has shown, governmental intervention has realized socialism's central value of equality, at least to some extent. Through socialist influence on government policies, the transfer of income that in the liberal view of social insurance proceeds mostly horizontally (from healthy workers to the diseased and from active workers to the unemployed) has also assumed a vertical direction, from high earners to low-income groups, through progressive taxation and the redistributive effects of government payments to the socially weak.

The Ideological Anemia of the Welfare State

In the foregoing I have shown the extent to which such central values as equality, liberty, solidarity, and security are each reflected in the compromise underlying contemporary welfare-state systems. Many observers agree, however, that the welfare state has not come up with its own legitimating ideology, an ideology that, as the Dutch sociologist Van Heek put it, would "offer encouragement in the face of adversity and work to unify in the case of disagreement."[12] According to him, the sheer material advances brought by the welfare state have provided a means to pacify social discontent, but that is a far cry from having an ideology to inspire its supporters.

I doubt whether this is the most promising approach to current problems of the welfare state. No single shared ideology could have outweighed the shifting configuration of social forces that gave rise to current doubts and critiques of the welfare state. Some of these changes may be explained in terms of a category that is a little out of fashion in social thought: the generation. In England and other countries, the welfare state was initially welcomed as the expression of a newfound social solidarity, promising once and for all to expel the specter of a depression that everybody then living had experienced. This historical generation—in the sense of a social cohort that shares a formative collective experience—could gratefully welcome the first signs of what it recognized as a new and more just social dispensation. The paradox here is that these feelings of gratitude and contentment were strongest in the relatively meager early years of the new system, during the fifteen or so years following World War II, and that they declined or turned into their opposite as the system expanded, both in its coverage and reach and in the means at its disposal. The paradox is only apparent, however, for two reasons. The specific historical recollections, the high hopes and expectations of a generation coming out of depression and war, have been alien to younger generations. The achievements of the welfare state are now seen as normal, as an entitlement, lacking any historical grandeur. This must be what Van Heek had in mind. In its contemporary appearance of a technical and administrative bureaucracy, the system can no longer infuse enthusiasm among later generations.

As I said, however, there is a second, equally sociological reason. The classic theory of reference group behavior and relative deprivation, elaborated by a host of sociologists, makes it clear how, given a continuing rise in the benefits distributed within a social setting, the level of general satisfaction initially goes up only to decline later. The common explanation for this is that the awareness of these benefits, such as promotions or pay raises, creates hope and expectations for all. A larger distribution of such benefits, however, leads to the jealous and disgruntled reassessment of each individual's position relative to that of others. Groups that have been overtaken are disgruntled, as are groups that stayed behind, whereas those that did benefit see their advance diminished by the fact that others have moved up as well. Processes of a similar nature have occurred on a large scale in the context of the welfare state. Given the general and marked rise in income positions, partly due to welfare-state policies, people tended to focus more on their poor position relative to others than on their advances made in absolute terms. With the distribution of welfare-state benefits—the field of action of the welfare state in a more narrow sense—similar envious comparisons have become the name of the game.

A necessary condition for this phenomenon is, of course, the availability of information concerning the state of others and of society as a whole. It happens that the contemporary welfare state, with its wealth of statistics, meets this condition perfectly, albeit with many unforeseen consequences. These are due to the fact that statistical data, such as inflation figures, are no more than approximations, educated constructs, for the analysis of social trends. When making judgments in terms of reference groups, however, people often take such data at face value. Thus, for example, labor unions use inflation figures as the basis for their wage claims. In addition, levels of social security benefits are linked to them. Thus the statistical data harden into objective facts, becoming a self-fulfilling prophecy. Furthermore, figures such as an overall price index may be based on specific price movements that do not affect certain groups in society, as, for example, in the case of mortgage rates. In the United States as well as in other countries, these rates are included in the overall index of prices and the cost of living, affecting a number of benefits, such as cost-of-living allowances. Any rapid rise in mortgage rates may thus, through the overall price index, create an impression of inflation affecting everyone. Nothing is further from the truth, of course. In fact, people with fixed interest rates need no compensating payments, nor do people in rented housing. According to the logic of indexing, only those with recent mortgages would qualify for compensation. This example illustrates two more general problems: the intrinsic effects of statistical information on economic life and the problem of determining how governments should target groups of welfare beneficiaries. More often than not, in the latter case, one has the general impression of targeting a mosquito with a shotgun.

In the study of welfare-state policies, known as "social administration," which in England is connected with the name of Richard Titmuss, this problem is presented as the more general dilemma of universalism versus selectivism. Here is one example: should all families with children receive children's benefits if the underlying motive is truly to support the income of the poorer families? As Titmuss and others see it, the alternative of a selective approach that would focus only on less well-off individuals has a sociological drawback. A selective approach may lead to stigmatizing the recipients, setting them apart in the eyes of others as socially dependent if not deficient. Titmuss and his followers, all of a social-democratic bent, constantly focus on determining how the welfare state can avoid the profligacy of universalism and more effectively provide assistance and support as an expression of social solidarity supported by tax payers and recipients of benefits alike. The general attitude of people in contemporary welfare states, however, seems far removed from this lofty inspiration. It is an attitude of group and individual self-interest rather than of a shared solidarity.

The Crisis of the Welfare State

In a sense, the welfare state has succeeded beyond all expectation, yet it has worked to undermine its own legitimacy. We may follow the American political scientist David Apter in distinguishing two main functions of ideology, a function for solidarity and a function for identity: the welfare state has run into trouble on both counts.[13] As I indicated in the foregoing discussion, the welfare state has had unforeseen negative effects on a living sense of social solidarity. Moreover, despite all its efforts to bring about a greater measure of individual social security, the welfare state has not helped to create a strong, self-confident sense of identity among its individual citizens. To the extent that people benefit from the blessings of the welfare state, it is always from a position of weakness, when they are unemployed workers or bankrupt employers, if not simply diseased and disabled. But there is more. As the welfare state evolved, an inner logic appeared to lead toward ever more positions of dependency and weakness, creating a need for government support and guidance. In its social-work approach of guiding and counseling its clientele, the system judged ever more people as being in need of its support and thus called for state-funded programs to extend its reach. The cultural critic Christopher Lasch, among others, has pointed to this therapeutic approach as undermining the social competence of individual citizens. Over the years the institutional shape of a large welfare bureaucracy that this therapeutic approach assumed in and of itself tended to alienate the welfare state from its beneficiaries, inculcating ever more deeply among them a sense of incompetence and impotence. If the outcome is alienation from the welfare-state structures, not identification with them as a meaningful expression of social solidarity, we may well see it as just another unforeseen and unintended consequence of the system's expansion. We can also choose to look at it, as did Daniel Moynihan with almost Swiftean venom, as a willful masquerade, hiding the interests of welfare workers as an occupational group from public view. "The ideology of compassion," as he put it, "serves the class of the post-industrial surplus of functionaries who, in the manner of industrialists who earlier turned to advertising, induce demand for their own products."[14]

As it is, economic constraints may well put a limit to such trends. Gigantic increases in the cost of welfare-state programs can no longer be covered by the surplus that the national economy generates. The government increasingly covers them through deficit financing, making welfare a source of inflation and social strain in its own right. But other, less "objective" reactions are beginning to appear. The ideologies that jointly entered into the compromise underlying the welfare state are beginning to part ways again, each taking a critical position from its own characteristic perspective.

The critique from what is sometimes called the neoconservative angle points to the overload of the government apparatus and to government's overreaching itself in its social intervention. It even recognizes a totalitarian potential in these trends. Ironically, in this respect, it finds itself in agreement with critical views coming from neo-Marxist corners. Neoconservatives' skeptical analyses of the inability of parliaments or similar such representative bodies to fulfill their central role of collective social self-regulation all point up the logical paradoxes that seem to preclude any consensual ordering of social priorities through majority votes.

Left-wing critics perceive a similar drift but see no reason for political skepticism. Quite the opposite: as the true voluntarists that they have historically been, they see a failure of will among the democratic parties in their collective task to reduce social problems to clear-cut programmatic priorities. In their view, parties too often conceive of the motley array of social interests and demands as the stuff of electoral gains. Despite all skepsis on the political right, moreover, socialist economists such as Hans van den Doel, a student of Tinbergen's, see parliament as the agency entrusted with the task of giving expression both to the collective political will and to an economically optimal welfare function. In this context, however, the word *function* refers to the realm of pure economic theory rather than to any recognizable way in which social processes work themselves out. Every approach that tends to ignore the rough and tumble of practical political life appears doomed to remain a fiction.

The liberal critique takes aim at the undercutting of independent, mature citizenship and argues on behalf of a reduction of government intervention or a decentralization of government functions. The United States in particular seem to have come up with a number of interesting approaches in this connection. The liberal critique further aims at the economic dysfunctions of the welfare state and the drag it exerts on economic growth. According to this view, in trying to establish social security while pursuing full employment, the welfare state tends financially to support stagnating, if not declining, sectors of the economy, trying to save jobs in a short-term administrative reflex that endangers long-term growth.

This ideological discussion is in a sense the perfect reflection of the bureaucratic institutions of the welfare state; the two are equally technical and equally the terrain solely of the expert and the initiate. What the discussion forsakes is the classic task of ideologies: to come up with clear and symbolically felicitous accounts of the great dilemmas of our age. Perhaps those dilemmas have become too complex for that. Perhaps, therefore, we do face the end of the era of ideologies. That would be a historic loss.

Health Care and Welfare: The United States and the Netherlands Compared

Welfare-state programs have run into dire straits everywhere in the industrialized world. As much as these programs may have differed within the various nations in their reach, coverage, and the ways they were financed and implemented, they were similar in the strains they began to exert on government budgets. Ever since the 1970s, the industrialized world has entertained a debate concerning the containment of the burgeoning cost of welfare-state provisions. Economists tended to emphasize the public-finance side of the issue, highlighting the problems of controlling the quasi-autonomous growth in the expenditures for social programs. They were keenly aware of the economic paradox involved. On the one hand, they perceived the growing welfare-state deficit's negative effect on such leading indicators as the competitiveness, growth, and productivity of the various national economies. On the other, it was precisely such macroeconomic tensions that tended to swell the ranks of the clientele for welfare-state provisions. Sociologists and political scientists joined the critique of the welfare state in their analyses of social policy's impact on the political process. They, too, emphasized an implied paradox in their explorations of the ways in which existing welfare-state programs have limited the degrees of freedom that governments have had in effectively controlling public finances. From that perspective, the problem concerns the viability of parliamentary regimes. A third approach, and one most typical of the time's changing mood as it moved toward political and cultural conservatism, focused on the unintended consequences of welfare-state provisions. In this view, such provisions are not so much a safety net, guaranteeing its beneficiaries a life of minimal decency, but rather a trap leading the recipients into lives of dependency outside the social and cultural mainstream. A similar conservative critique focused on the rise of a culture of entitlements and the accompanying erosion of a sense of social duty; the welfare chiseler was the favorite culprit in this view of the malfunctioning of the welfare state.

Of the many studies that began to appear in the 1970s, one in particular deserves mention: Morris Janowitz's seminal *Social Control of the Welfare State*, published in 1976. In a masterly sweep of the various approaches, Janowitz gave central place to what he called "the old-fashioned concept of 'social control.'" As defined by the pioneer generation of American sociologists around the turn of the century, this concept referred to the capacity of a society or any other social group to regulate its collective life, pursuing a set of higher moral values. Janowitz's concern was with the quality and effectiveness of mass welfare institutions and their political consequences in advanced industrialized societies that have competitive election systems. Janowitz explored the following central paradox: the growth in social welfare expenditures tends to threaten the central democratic capacity for social control, for the collective self-regulation of social life. Therefore, he argued, "there is a point at which the extension of the state weakens the viability of the competitive parliamentary regime; as a result, there are limits to the enlargement of the welfare system."[15] Taking his cue from the economists, he saw the increased social welfare expenditures as one potent factor contributing to a chronic deficit in the public sector. The resulting internal political conflict derives in part from the decline of an effective surplus for social welfare and the profound escalation of demand for social welfare. The system of social control therefore comes under fundamental strain. At the same time, the democratic collectivity has lost its self-regulating capacity to the extent that existing welfare provisions have affected its political rationality. Therein lies the central paradox for Janowitz. The democratic electorate has become caught between two rival but equally rational considerations. The broad mass of the electorate has become increasingly dependent on the institutions of the welfare state, which they have collectively willed into existence. At the same time, however, there are still wide areas where individual families see themselves as the ultimate masters of their own life chances and those of their children. Thus they tend to husband their own private resources to the point where they become reluctant to pay increasingly large amounts to fund welfare-state institutions. Caught between these conflicting rationales, their electoral behavior tends increasingly to produce weak political regimes lacking clear mandates for action.

As Janowitz saw it, such is the predicament that welfare-state systems must confront. It is a situation they all must face, irrespective of the many historical differences among the institutional shapes of contemporary welfare states. His analysis applied equally to advanced welfare states in Europe and to such relative laggards as Canada or the United States. In the following two decades, however, many authors have looked into the specific options and impediments that specific welfare-state systems have experienced over the courses of their evolutions. In fact, it may well be the case that various democratic regimes are faced with crucially different options when it comes to the social control of the welfare state. In the remainder of this section, I will focus on two cases: the United States and the Netherlands.

There is a time-honored tradition of accounting for America's peculiar institution of welfare-state provisions, particularly as regards its reluctance to institute a system of national health coverage, in terms of an American exceptionalism. The American unwillingness to follow the examples of European welfare states whole hog is explained in terms of its prevailing liberalism and voluntarism, its antistatist inclinations, or in related terms, the absence of a strong working-class or socialist movement. As Theda Skocpol has shown in her *Protecting Mothers and Soldiers*,[16] however, such ideological attitudes have never prevented the federal government from playing an active role in the social protection of the needy, nor have they made the larger population unwilling to grant it that role. The social security legislation of the 1930s, then, stands in a perhaps unexpectedly long line of gestation and readiness. Nevertheless, Europe still served as the model for the United States to emulate, particularly for the great Roosevelt legislation.

That balance of pioneer nations serving as models and of other nations following their example did change after the war, however. In evolving its system of welfare provisions, America instituted a system peculiarly its own. Indeed, it can even be argued that America rather than European countries began to serve as a model beginning in the 1970s—this time showing not how to expand the welfare state but rather how to contain its unintended outcomes. As Edward Berkowitz has pointed out: "What strikes me as unusual in the current debate is the degree of influence that American ideas have had over it."[17] As one indication of this trend, the definition of disability in the Dutch social insurance program changed in 1993 to resemble more closely the definition used in the American social security program. The Dutch have also expressed interest in the American method of reviewing disability claims, in the workings of the American workers' compensation system, or more generally in ideas concerning workfare, coaxing welfare recipients back to work with a variety of pressures and training programs.

Nonetheless, whatever the various positions of leaders and followers in the contemporary debates about the predicament of the welfare state, critical differences among the various welfare states affect their present freedom in tackling the problems of their provisions. These differences centrally concern the political configuration of the constituencies that have emerged as welfare-state institutions and programs evolved. A comparative look at the way that health-care provisions have developed in various nations may provide a particularly enlightening illustration.

Despite individual variations, European nation-states as a group have created health insurance systems that emphasize access to health care over its supply. Various gatekeeping devices, such as a preference for general practitioners over medical specialists, have tended to contain the cost of medical services. Access to medical services for all who need them has been Europe's driving rationale behind the design of health-care institutions. This principle was widely supported by an alliance of interest groups, such as employers and workers, the medical profession, insurance agencies, and political parties, and always led to the wide acceptance of a central coordinating role for the state. The United States was different, even at the time when policy elites oriented themselves toward the European example. The configuration of forces involved in institutionalizing health care was always much more conflict-ridden there because of views of corporate interests and more ideological views about the virtue of keeping the realms of civil society and the state separate. Given this configuration, Roosevelt chose to keep health insurance out of his plans for social security legislation, for he feared that the conflicts around health-care provisions might otherwise spill over into the area of social security. As Edward Berkowitz and Lawrence Jacobs, among others, have shown, America then set about developing its own checkered pattern of health-care provision, focusing centrally on employer-provided health-care insurance.[18] To the extent that the federal government did step in as a provider and lawgiver, it was to supplement this system, based in civil society, for those who fell outside the sway of regular employment. It did other things as well, however, putting its money into the supply of medical services rather than in access to it. Unlike European countries, the United States emphasized medical specialists rather than general practitioners and the construction of hospitals and the provision of other costly medical hardware rather than considerations of gatekeeping. Thus, while over 40 million Americans are underinsured or not insured at all—and the number is going up—the United States leads all other industrialized nations in the percentage of national income spent on health care. The typical American problem, then, is the combined one of controlling cost while extending coverage, a problem crucially different from the one European nations are facing. As recent analyses of the failure of the Clinton health-care proposal make clear, the historically unified configuration of interests entrenched around America's health-care system could again be mobilized in opposition. Ironically, it is once again in the sphere of civil society, outside the reach of government plans or government interference, that a new system of health insurance has sprung up: the burgeoning health maintenance organizations, commonly referred to as HMOs.

It would be wrong, however, to see this as America's multifarious configuration of conflicting interest groups contrasted to a European model wherein interest groups fall harmoniously into line. In fact, the Dutch case offers an interesting example of collaboration between state agencies and civil society. The Dutch have a strong tradition of antistatist sentiment, emphasizing the autonomy and self-regulation of the various cultural compartments of society. One consideration that may have helped cooperation between the political sphere and civil society was the fact that the Dutch segmentation of society, commonly known (even in English) as *Verzuiling* (or pillarization), found its perfect reflection in the party system. As it has developed since the late nineteenth century, this system has allowed the central government to cede the implementation of social welfare plans to the lower level of non-governmental agencies that had sprung up in civil society. The result, ironically, was not one of greater cost efficiency. In fact, totally inefficient duplications arose because each of the constituent forces in Dutch *Verzuiling* insisted on having its own apparatus for welfare provisions. It was not until *Verzuiling* lost its hold on Dutch society in the mid-1960s, that the Dutch welfare system came fully into its own with the landmark Social Assistance Act, guaranteeing a minimum income to all citizens. This time central government implemented the program. In a further irony, the Netherlands soon faced the problems of exploding welfare costs. It thus joined the ranks of welfare states everywhere and like those states began taking its cues from the United States.

Ideology in Europe

One earlier statement bears repetition here. In its historical genesis and evolution, the concept of ideology displays a peculiarly European character. It arose as one outcome of specifically European intellectual history. Undoubtedly, much writing of history does have an unspoken Eurocentric slant to it and can duly be criticized on that ground. One should not move all the way to the other extreme, however, and rob processes that do have European features of their historical face simply because later on they have reached other parts of the globe. Of course, the word *ideology* has become common coin and has lost its historical specificity, yet that is insufficient reason to omit its historical features from an analysis of its intellectual origins. Only by recognizing them can one begin to fathom the extent to which the concept has changed following its international adoption, coming to reflect intellectual molds different from the European one it initially received.

A telling case is the adoption of the word by Americans. They long looked askance at it, treating it as a word not quite suitable for American conditions. Until after World War II the great American dictionaries defined it either in the old, literal sense used by Destutt de Tracy—as the study of ideas—or, referring to European examples, as propaganda and intellectual fallacy. The word did gain currency in the United States during the postwar years, but with a similar loss of specific resonance and connotation, as in the case of the American adoption of the concept of "class." In much the same way that *class* in America came to represent a relatively open and changing structure of social stratification, *ideology* came to refer to the shifting and unstable set of views that people held in their various social roles and positions. The unsettling implications of the typically European connection between ideology and class as undermining the status of knowledge never found resonance or recognition in the more optimistic intellectual climate of the United States. The prevailing attitude toward ideas there was too practical, if not pragmatic, geared too much toward the practicability and utility of ideas to dwell on the feeble foundations of human knowledge. "The truth is what works," as that great American philosopher of pragmatism William James put it. Equally, indigenous forms of American socialism and like-minded protest movements around the turn of the last century expressed an optimistic belief in a universe of discourse, in a fundamental agreement concerning America's ideals, that they felt they shared with their opponents in social conflicts. This stands in marked contrast to imported versions of European socialism, with its disillusioned views of the unbridgeable gap separating social classes and their outlooks on the world. Whereas European left-wing circles, particularly of an anarchistic or syndicalist bent, urgently called for workers to turn their backs on the bourgeois world in order to preserve a pristine and untainted working-class consciousness, Americans mostly saw such an attitude as alien, if not un-American. It is no coincidence, therefore, that American confrontations with this imported concept never explored more than one form of the basic dilemma between ideology and truth, a dilemma that early in this chapter I argued can take at least three main forms. In America we see mostly the continuation of Durkheim's discussion of the tension between ideology and science. Given the enduring, if somewhat archaic, Enlightenment optimism in the United States, it need not surprise us that in this discussion ideology has been seen mostly as bad science and untenable knowledge, inspired more by emotion than by rational thought. Only much later would this perspective give way to the more subtle and nuanced approach by people such as Clifford Geertz and others whom I mentioned earlier.

In this context of the migration of ideas and the changes they undergo while traveling, it is of interest to point to the changing face of ideology as Lenin used the notion. In his approach we can recognize a new form of the basic dilemma between ideology and truth; it now appears as the tension between ideology and action. This constitutes one of many surprising analogies that one might see between America's cast of mind and that of Lenin's missionary and revolutionary Russia: Lenin's view that a superior ideology will bear itself out in revolutionary action parallels James's pragmatic dictum that the truth is what works. The rivalry between America and Russia later in this century, for all its rhetorical flourishes, has proceeded on the basis of a remarkable agreement of outlook: each was pragmatic rather than ideological and sought the measure of its success in such tangible achievements as economic leaps forward. Overtaking America in such respects had truly become the secular version of the communist ideal.

Nation-State and Ideology

My focus on Europe in this section is prompted by more than the European origin of the concept of ideology. Europe may well serve as the larger geographic backdrop to more abstract discussions of ideology. All too often writers on the subject tend to conceive of it, tacitly or explicitly, in the political context of the state. It seems like a lasting heritage of Marx's analysis of the bourgeois state. In his approach the state appears as the political instrument by which the capitalist bourgeoisie maintains its class rule, either through the state monopoly of the means of violence, or—subtler and more disguised—through the dissemination of ideological views legitimating bourgeois preeminence. According to this view, such liberal ideals as public education or a free press are no more than channels for the indoctrination of the citizenry. The more recent neo-Marxist critique of late capitalist society still emphasizes the closed front for the manipulation of public consciousness via the media, advertising, and education, assuming a remarkable unity of purpose and interest on the part of the manipulators. In this view, our consumption society is a modern, worldly system fulfilling what to Marx had been the function of religion: to serve as an opiate for the people. The image of the enslaved and addicted consumer serves to prove the point. The French communist philosopher Louis Althusser has taken this view of a united front of manipulation to extremes: all media of communication in modern capitalist societies are media of manipulation. He calls them ideological instruments of the state, the pillars of a rigid and unchanging world.

A similar petrified view appears in the work of ideologues in former communist Eastern Europe, in their analyses of what they termed *StaMoKap*, or *Staats Monopol Kapitalismus* (state monopoly capitalism). The petrification even affected their language. This kind of approach seems like a throwback to the intellectual Stone Age of reification (*Verdinglichung*) against which Marx himself had inveighed with such force. These later communist authors must have believed themselves really to be describing something without, however, describing something real. Once again it turns out that the master polemicist Marx wielded a two-edged sword. In the hands of lesser followers it cut right through their work and the hardened forms of their doctrinaire world.

There is a further reason to connect the concepts of ideology and the state. Nationalism as a driving force of modern European history has worked to bring them together. We can repeatedly see the effects of this force. Thus, during World War I the doctrine of the internationalism of the working class—and, for that matter, of the inherent internationalism of capitalism itself—succumbed to nationalist fervor in all the countries engaged in that war. Similarly, during World War II the Soviet Union chose to tap the reservoir of indigenous nationalism in its struggle against Nazi Germany, using images, symbols, and patent references to a precommunist Russia that it had tried to root out before the war.

* * *

In my preceding discussion of the welfare-state's problems, however, I drew a picture of ideological anemia and divided views concerning the plight of that form of society, a picture rather of ideological fragmentation and of feelings of impotence and anomie in the face of global trends beyond the reach of individual states. American sociologist Daniel Bell once claimed that the modern state is too big for the small problems and too small for the big ones. Government bureaucracies have grown too unwieldy, too slow and impersonal, to be able to respond efficiently to the individual problems of the citizenry. I discussed this in the preceding section. On the other hand, individual states are too small to cope with such international problems as inflation and unemployment, problems of resources and the environment, or issues of technological innovation. For many of these problems, the state is no longer the appropriate agency for redress. Here lies a further reason for the alienation that people may feel toward politics and the state.

Of course, behind all expressions of a sense of crisis and impending doom, there is often a world whose tone is entirely different. It is a world of a remarkable unity of outlook, a world of unproblematic certainties. People do tend to see many things in a remarkably similar light. If anything becomes clear from a close reading of the ideologically coded messages circulating in society, it is the way they reflect this unity of outlook. Entire areas of social life appear to many in the light of a natural and self-evident order. Of course, one may propose a different account. For example, neo-Marxists would see this unity of view as resulting from a coordinated manipulation of thought controlled by the reigning alliance of interests in the late capitalist, or neo-corporatist, state. Perhaps so, but I for one have not seen any convincing evidence corroborating this point of view. I would rather follow a different line of reasoning.

Complex social interaction is feasible only on the basis of assumptions taken as self-evident. For ages people have taken even the vagaries and vicissitudes of fate as natural, as part of the natural order of things. Nevertheless, one of the outcomes of the long process of secularization and demystification described early in this chapter was the novel view of human beings as the masters of their own destinies. Indeed, this new view of humankind and the human condition has led to an expansion of human control and mastery across large areas of life that had hitherto seemed subject to blind fate. Surely people in the industrialized West live in a world that is far more certain and predictable, more under control, than any previous one has been. Even in our present-day world, however, this existential experience is the prerogative of a minority of people only; it is still exceptional. Nonetheless, even though *actual* dependence and a submission to outside and alien control may still be the experience of most people, the modern *image* of humankind—the secular belief in the capacity of human societies collectively to control their destinies and conditions of life—has gained worldwide currency. Adversity and crisis are no longer "natural," beyond human responsibility, but can be attributed to human agency through omission or commission. All ideological accounts of the continuing misery and inequality in the world, in theories concerning neocolonialism and imperialism, testify to this view of human agency in history. The wrath of the gods of old now appears in the secular garb of "capital," the "multinationals," or "imperialism." In a certain sense, despite their radical intent, all such accounts have something reassuring in the eyes of those who accept them. They all reduce problems as people experience them to human proportions. Nothing goes so much against the grain of this modern cast of mind as having to confront anonymous forces without any sign of human agency. People are no longer ready to accept adversity as part of the natural order of things. If there is human agency, however, what are we to do in the case of unintended outcomes and unanticipated consequences? What are we to make of situations of poverty and injustice that produce victims we can all see on our TV screens but no clear guilty parties? The webs of interconnectedness of human actions may well be the contemporary version of blind fate, instilling a sense of impotence and alienation among those adversely affected. They are the ready clientele for demagogues of any stripe, individuals who have all the easy answers and appeal to people's need for an account of their conditions in terms of the patent self-evidence that guides much of our lives.

National and Supranational

In the industrial West, bulwark of the modern belief in human agency and the scene of much successful social control, some of these more ominous trends have occurred. Europe offers many examples. It may seem like a paradox: so much success, yet so much alienation. The driving forces behind the postwar project of a supranational Europe were all inspired by the quest for collective control and a reduction of external dependence. Whether the issue was one of laying to rest the ghost of French-German animosity or of self-sufficiency in Europe's agricultural production, the basic motive was always the control of the blind forces of history that for centuries had held Europe in their sway. For too long the old Carolingian dream of a unity of European governance had taken the self-destructive form of dominance through national hegemony. It had seemed like the blind nemesis of European history. Among the fathers of present-day Europe, such as Paul Henri Spaak, Jean Monnet, and Winston Churchill, the old dream still held its fascination. The ideological innovation in their perspective and endeavors, however, lay in their views of supranationality, of the design of forms of organization in which national interests would henceforth be interwoven.

Much of this dream has been realized. Nonetheless, an attempt to articulate the balance of achievements so far faces a number of paradoxes. For many "citizens" of the new Europe, their national state is still the natural framework for political affiliation. It is one of those natural and self-evident facts that I mentioned before. This situation in itself harbors a paradox. A second one is closely related to the first. Despite all the transfer of political decision making to European levels and the concomitant loss of national powers of self-determination, most citizens still see national states as the final resort for the expression of their political will and their demands of political accountability. This paradox in particular underlies much political disillusionment, giving rise to feelings of political impotence and anomie. Even though the larger European space may have filled with agencies forming policies and issuing regulations, on balance the situation has produced an image of a diffusion of power and authority. People have lost their usual address for their grievances, demands, and expectations of an efficient response. In terms of a psychology of political experience, matters are radically different in the United States, with its clearly structured pyramid of centers of power and that one person at the top who can ultimately be held accountable and sent packing. As a description of political reality, this picture may be found wanting in many respects, yet on the experiential level the situation certainly works to maintain a sense of political efficacy among individual citizens.

By contrast, the situation in Europe is almost classically Durkheimian. There, an intricate web of structural interdependence expressive of (as Durkheim would have it) mechanical solidarity interweaves political authority, economic activity, and social groups to an extent that is radically out of joint with the individual citizens' senses of belonging and of collective control. Never mind the rapid economic advances that Europe has known; it has lagged behind in producing a legitimating view, a European ideology, allowing each and all to see their places as meaningfully related to a larger system of conscious and collective control. The sense of a historic mission, of forming part of a "Great Experiment," which in the United States has provided citizens with the collective inspiration to weather adversity and crisis, is sadly lacking in Europe.

There is a third paradox. European integration may have enlarged the space for collective action and its freedom for independent policy—and statistics are there to prove the point—yet at the same time Europe finds itself confronted with novel constraints. This time the constraints come from outside, set by the vicissitudes of an expanding world economy that Europe cannot independently master.

So far, Europeans' ideological responses to this situation have all exhibited aspects of crisis ideologies, pessimism and irrationalism, if not nihilism. At times these ideologies go hand in hand with forms of action, exemplified by the urban guerrillas of the Rote Armee Faktion in Germany, the Brigata Rossa in Italy, the political terror of the Basque independence movement (Euskadì Ta Askatasuna, or ETA), in Spain, or the Irish Republican Army in Northern Ireland. They all mimicked the romanticized lifestyle of Cuban revolutionaries turned into an international T-shirt iconography. They all acted on the spur of fake diagnoses of society's ills, whether an alleged fascism in Germany, capitalist oppression in Italy, or state violence in Spain or Northern Ireland. Later on other patterns of ideological reaction came to the fore. The absence of larger frameworks for meaningful political affiliation fostered the contrived revival of primordial, prenational entities such as the region, elevating them to the status of true communities bound together by history, language, and local culture. What the Basques, Bretons, Scots, and Corsicans share in their activism and ideological zeal is this quest for a meaningful framework for collective action. It is a response to what in the final analysis is a shared individual sense of deprivation and powerlessness. The new and evolving Europe, in its appearance as an impersonal bureaucratic and technological project, is simply too much at a distance and too anonymous to make for meaningful affiliation on the part of its "citizens." Ironically, Europe's common policy of regional development, transferring money from richer to poorer regions, may in its implementation be perceived as a policy coming from on high, never as a response to the demands of regions meaningfully organized as political entities.

Still another pattern of ideological reflection of inarticulate feelings of alienation can be discerned. It has no clear shape yet, but even so, it is ominously reminiscent of earlier periods of cultural doom and gloom in both Europe and the United States. This trend may be most clearly apparent in France in the emerging Nouvelle Droite (New Right), centered on a group of erudite intellectuals, such as François Pauwels and others, who see Europe's malfunctioning, if not impotence, as signs of a larger crisis of culture, a loss of cultural vitality due to immigration and the erosive impact ideas of egalitarianism have on social hierarchies based on talent and the cultural capital of elites. From there the indictment tends to fan out toward other forces undermining a vital Western civilization, such as the forces of Christianity or its secular variant, Marxism, or the force of ideas concerning the miscegenation of "higher" and "lower" races. Underlying all this is a view of the true French nation in an eclectic concoction that appears as little more than an intellectualized version of the comic-book France of Asterix. As an organized political force it appears as the ultra-right-wing party of Le Pen. Averse to intellectualizing its views, it condenses its diagnosis into a tactic of scapegoating, blaming the immigrant contingent in French society for all the country's problems. It is all reminiscent of earlier periods of cultural pessimism and of the critique of the social and cultural leveling wrought by mass society.

In this context, the United States may provide an interesting parallel. Around the turn of the last century, established upper-class circles saw their cultural heritage threatened by forces of industrialization and urbanization, most visibly apparent in the influx of immigrants of "lower" racial caliber. Doomsday ideas concerning the racial suicide of the "superior" Anglo-Saxon part of the population, based on demographic data concerning the differential birth rates of immigrants and the older American stock, merged with fashionable views of a quasi-scientific nature concerning heredity and eugenics. Cultural decline, in this view, was a matter of racial hybridization. Such ideas came to undergird a long campaign for the restriction of immigration to America and resulted in the racially based quota legislation of the 1920s. Similar trends have occurred in Europe since the mid-1960s. Large-scale immigration from the Mediterranean basin, or from parts of the former colonial empires of France, Belgium, Portugal, the Netherlands, and Britain, toward the new centers of economic growth in Europe have caused tension and conflict in most receiving countries. Particularly at times of slow or no economic growth, the situation has seemed to be an ideal breeding ground for the kind of ideas developed by the French New Right or for those of populist or neo-Nazi groups in a number of European countries, most recently in Austria. The latter may be less intellectually articulate, yet they are remarkably astute in rallying support for their causes through such new-fangled technologies as the Internet.

A climate of cultural pessimism, of the loss of economic security and individual self-confidence, has often led to a sense of the imminent end of time, of an *Untergang des Abendlandes* (decline of the West), as Oswald Spengler called it. Time and time again, however, such gloomy views have been contradicted by actual developments, most recently in the United States. Not more than ten years ago the analysis of American decline and the end of its empire was a flourishing cottage industry. Today, in an America that has regained its technological prowess and economic leadership, these voices of doom have fallen silent. Here, as in many similar cases, the end of time turned out to be a period of transition, a radical and unsettling overhaul of the global economy. In all such cases the pessimist party was faced with a party of progress, of daring optimists summoning their imaginative powers in a forecast of change and innovation rather than decline and demise. In recent history we may recognize those two camps in debates centering on problems of the environment, of the information revolution, or of nuclear energy. The jumble of points of view, action groups, and political movements clustering around these issues is always the manifold manifestation of simpler underlying worldviews. One view is held by those who cling to conditions as they know them. Another view welcomes new technologies in the hope that they will bring more of the same, such as employment opportunities and economic growth. Yet another view favors radical changes away from the established conventions, away from globalization, growth, and technology. The key to all such ideological views may, in musical terms, always be minor versus major, opposing pessimism to optimism. It may also be a matter, as I have shown, of rationalism confronting irrationalism.

Both contrasts find representation among the supporters and opponents of the new technologies. Action groups and government agencies may exchange solid data, statistics, and thorough reports to support their positions, but they also use arguments of a more emotional sort. Some of the proponents of technological revolutions see them as a last chance for staving off stagnation and decline. They are willing blithely to accept the cost of change. This position includes an element of defeatist optimism, a sense of there being no other way to go. Others, with daring and imagination, join these revolutions, taking command of their organization and direction. There is a clear generational aspect to this, although the pace of some technological changes tends to make generations ever shorter. Among groups intuitively opposing these continuing revolutions, there is an inarticulate, if not irrational, fear of technological change. Clearly, then, to keep all such views within the band-width of democratic debate and discussion, democratic government must reinvent itself. It should never try to force the pace of change, imposing decisions that are precooked by inner circles of technical and bureaucratic experts. If it wants to remain the central instrument of collective control in contemporary society, it needs to provide for the coordinated expression of public views, accommodating action groups and other extraparliamentary organizations, thus increasing and improving its own responsiveness. The future will come anyway, but under whose auspices? To maintain more than the semblance of democratic control, Europe's most urgent challenge is to prove itself as the "natural" framework for the collective control and change of the life of European citizens.

7. Neopopulism and Neoconservatism in the United States: Social Drift and Sociological Dilemmas

American historiography has given two faces to populism, one left-wing, or progressive, and the other right-wing, if not reactionary. The same applies to neopopulism. The right-wing variety of populism has enjoyed a resurgence as a political style. Ever since the civil rights movement ushered in a period of bipartisan support for affirmative action, neopopulists from George Wallace to David Duke have directed appeals to the white voter. In fact, if we can still speak of a rallying appeal to "the people" (as one would expect populists to make), it is one that narrowly defines "the people" as white. It is therefore inherently racist. As it happens, political candidates within the mainstream of representative politics occasionally draw on this populist repertoire (consider, e.g., the role that black convict Willy Horton was made to play during George Bush's first presidential campaign). Populism in this instance is harnessed as an electioneering tool, undercutting the existing bipartisan support for affirmative-action policies.

This, as I said, is the reactionary, right-wing face of neopopulism. At the same time a liberal, emancipatory neopopulism can be recognized in a movement that is more cultural than political: multiculturalism. Under its banner, both inside and outside academia, as well as in cultural products such as novels and even Hollywood films (e.g., *Places of the Heart, Heartland,* and other neopopulist movies of the mid-1980s), there have been attempts to present "the people" not in any narrow, homogenized version but in manifold forms, exploring the many "forgotten others"—women, indigenous peoples, blacks, immigrants, and ethnic minorities—who together can be seen as making up "the American people" yet whose voices and places have been ignored in the mainstream, canonized narrative of the history of the American people and the American "self." The current debate about the

"canon of American culture" has in turn caused a reaction in neoconservative circles. As they see it, multiculturalism is bound to break up the cohesion of American culture, the continuity of its past, the legitimacy of its claim
of having its roots in Western, Judeo-Christian civilization.

Neopopulism wears two faces, then, and bears various links to neoconservatism as it has arisen since the early 1970s. Among neoconservatism's early
targets were affirmative action and the policies of an interventionist judiciary that had begun to tamper with the workings of society, for example, by ordering the busing of black and white children and imposing school-district
lines. More recent neoconservative themes have included the preservation of
an established mainstream reading of American culture, for example, by protecting English as the one official U.S. language, opposing the hardening of
multiculturalism into a new orthodoxy of "political correctness," and more
generally defending a reading of American culture as standing squarely in a
line of development that ties it firmly to the history of Western civilization.

This chapter focuses on the tensions between these clamoring voices from
left and right; at the same time it tries to listen to the quieter voices of a number of academicians who try to steer clear of the ready answers that ideologues
in both camps keep bandying about.

* * *

I am not an economist, yet economics forces itself on any observer of America's recent history. The early Reagan years saw a two-pronged economic
approach, with America reducing its taxes and hiking up its defense budget.
In the campaign leading up to the presidential election of 1980, George Bush
had already referred to the hopes of supply-side economists as "voodoo-
economics," but unwisely no one, including Bush himself, chose to read his
lips then. Budget deficits of an unprecedented scale began piling up, forcing
the U.S. government to borrow massively. The already low savings rate in the
United States and the debt born by its nongovernmental sector, producers
and consumers alike, forced the country to borrow abroad. From a net lender
the United States turned into a net debtor nation. In the unavoidable competition for scarce financial resources, it drove up interest rates, which again
affected every individual American's life chances and every American production firm's prospects for profitable investment. To put matters in the language of economists, these massive opportunity costs go a long way to account for American society's drift in directions that no government had
planned or anticipated. For most of the 1990s average Americans were no
better off than they were a generation before. They began to realize that they
might be nearing the end of the American dream, wherein each generation
could look forward to better life chances for its children in terms of income,
housing, and education. In addition, after years of decline, poverty was again

on the rise, afflicting segments of America's black population and some of its more recent immigrant groups with particular harshness.

Admittedly trends other than (though not unrelated to) government deficits have had their own separate impact. Changes in the structure of employment, the shift from an industrial to a service economy, with its different career prospects, different scales of pay, and different educational requirements, have affected the individual American's opportunities, especially for those on the lower rungs of the social ladder. According to left-wing observers, labor has undergone a deskilling that has made for an increasingly rigid dual labor market and an attendant bifurcation of American society into an underclass and an established mainstream. If this is the unintended outcome of the free play of social forces, as proponents of free-market capitalism would have it, or of social drift, as I would prefer to put it, government retrenchment from social intervention is all the more regrettable.

Of course, there are always those who prefer not to live with the idea of unintended consequences, either seeing things as welcome and intended the way they are or arguing that the unintended consequences are caused by too much government intervention, not too little. After all, the reigning ideology undergirding the Reagan revolution and similar developments in Europe was precisely the view of government as a dead weight on society's creative potential. In an ironic contradiction that I have never been able to resolve, those who criticize the welfare state as being unwieldy, inefficient, and counterproductive are at the same time unblushing advocates of the "warfare state." No reports of wasteful spending, cost overruns, two-hundred-dollar toilet seats, or what have you have ever shaken their faith in government as provider for "the common defense."

Clearly, as the case of Western Europe may illustrate, the welfare state would have run into financial trouble even without a massive increase in defense spending. Factions across the political spectrum, from socialists to conservatives, have been debating the financial quandary that the various social support programs of the welfare state have encountered. Voices from the left to the right are discussing remedies of varying degrees of realism or harshness—depending on your point of view—that formerly one tended to associate only with right-wing critics of the welfare state. Today, however, the new harshness and stringency are imposed by hard facts of government finance, particularly in countries, such as Sweden and the Netherlands, whose elaborate welfare systems have made for historically high levels of taxation.

This is markedly different from the case of critics who would have attacked the welfare state regardless of the health of government finances. With varying degrees of prima facie cogency, a number of critics in America have analyzed the "poverty trap," and more generally the plight of welfare recipients, in what we might call a game of blaming the victim. Charles Murray's *Los-*

ing Ground is only one invidious example of a critique of the "culture of welfare dependency," of a culture of "entitlements" insufficiently balanced by a sense of social obligation on the part of the recipients, a critique with the allegedly disinterested motive of wishing "to help those who help themselves." Of course, this argument goes back further than the 1980s. It was a minority view in the liberal 1960s, angrily seen as "blaming the victim"—in language that is definitely 1960s coinage—but as Michael Katz has argued recently, there are even older echoes dating back to the time of the Poor Laws and the search for the "deserving poor."[1] In that respect the 1980s have shown only one characteristic configuration of the interplay of contending ideological cross-currents; whether the pattern of alternation is cyclical, as Arthur Schlesinger Jr. has argued, with the relatively precise temporal rhythm the term suggests, I am not quite sure. Certainly there are periods where either a liberal or a conservative discourse seems to command the arena of public debate. The 1980s, then, can be summarized as a period of relatively greater social drift and less political command and guidance, accompanied by the rise of a neoconservative, if not neo–social Darwinist, view that broadly justified both the social drift and the retrenchment of government. This may seem an overly voluntarist way of putting things, but as I have taken care to point out, autonomous forces were at work both on the level of social drift and change and on the level of government intervention (on the former level, e.g., a socioeconomic transformation with shifts in the international division of labor, trade patterns, relative competitive advantages, and so on; on the latter, financial problems), forces that have worked independently to give the 1980s and much of the 1990s their characteristic face.

I should make a more general point about the neoconservatives. We have to look back further than a mere decade to get the proper perspective on their program as well as on their sense of a counterrevolution that has succeeded, at least in part. If we follow their arguments through the 1970s and 1980s, we are tracing only one-half of a dialogue that connects them to the prevailing liberal, if not libertarian, discourse of the 1960s. In that sense the 1980s and 1990s are dialogically—or for that matter, dialectically—connected to the 1960s. The neoconservatives are still trying to exorcise evil spirits that were then let out of the bottle, doing so on at least three levels. First, at the level of social policies that sought to intervene in areas of social inequality, affirmative action has since the early 1970s been a favorite culprit in neoconservative writing, for example, in work by Nathan Glazer and others in the pages of *Commentary*. Culture was a second area of neoconservative action. When Susan Sontag tried to break through the established hierarchies of cultural values, most notably in her essay on camp, she made herself the favorite bête noire of cultural disciplinarians such as Hilton Kramer and his journal *New Criterion*. Finally, whereas established values such as the family, the nation,

and the flag had all been cause for derision in the 1960s, the neoconservatives struck back with a vengeance. The neo-conservative reaction, setting in
during the 1970s, came into full bloom in the 1980s.

Nevertheless, I do not mean to cover these various ideological swings here.
Rather, I want to argue that the prevailing social drift of the 1980s has presented sociologists—or more generally, students of American society—with
characteristic dilemmas. They are dilemmas of two different kinds. The first
could be called dilemmas of sociology proper; the second, dilemmas of sociologists. As to the first, it is a matter of choosing between contending sociological approaches and explanations. Working on the level of social change
and drift, sociologists discussing the bifurcation of American society must
choose among a number of rival approaches. There are those, such as Thomas
Sowell, who focus on the role of different ethnic subcultures, considering the
markedly different histories of ethnic groups in their economic success, social cohesion, educational performance, and the like. There are those, such
as Ira Katznelson, who focus on theories of internal colonialism, racism, and
discrimination. There are others, such as Stuart Butler and Anna Kondratas,
who follow a vein that has been worked by Daniel Patrick Moynihan since
the 1960s by focusing on the central role of the family.[2] Still others try to assess the effects of over twenty years of government support programs. The
choice always involves policy implications, not surprisingly so in view of
sociology's long-time social engineering hopes. Probably the most pragmatic
policy advice coming from social scientists is the "workfare" version of social welfare, combining government support with a requirement to join the
labor force. It is pragmatic to the extent that it tries to address problems both
of social drift and of limited government resources as these have appeared
during the 1980s.

Characteristically, social scientists have failed to reach a consensus. They
are still caught up in the dilemmas that are intrinsic to sociology as a disparate body of knowledge about our contemporary world. As I said before,
however, they are faced with a different dilemma as well. Working as they are
in an area that has been noisily preempted by the big guns, if not the rival
"canons," of contending ideological camps, there is the constant danger that
whatever approach or position they take as professional sociologists will leave
them exposed to the slur of being mere ideologues. Scholarly argument on
the merits of one or another sociological approach has often been compounded with the invective of ideological polemics. A telling case in point is
Daniel Patrick Moynihan's early work on the role of the black family as a
central factor in the plight of America's black population. In the heated debate following the publication of the *Moynihan Report* in the 1960s, much
liberal comment accused him of "blaming the victim," when clearly—or so
it was argued—white racism was to blame. Now that the disorganization of

the black family has become an accepted issue for research and policy studies even among the black community, Moynihan had a moment of wry triumph when he published *Family and Nation,* his Godkin Lectures at Harvard University, in 1986. His case illustrates a wider problem as well as a more recent trend in the social sciences. Whenever sociologists feel pressure to gear their insights and public statements on current social issues to the prevailing ideological fashion, there is an unacceptable narrowing of the range of academic speculation and research. It takes a measure of individual guts and gusto—and Moynihan has plenty of both—to go against the established fads. Recently, however, it seems that there has been a more general trend among social scientists that leaves them relatively immune to the dangers of ideological cooptation or excommunication.

Thus we find black social scientists who are not afraid to argue a case that the Reagan administration might have liked. We find liberals who no longer shrink from analyzing problems of American ethnic and racial minorities in terms of causes that lie inside these communities. A good example is the black sociologist William J. Wilson, who effortlessly moves across the political spectrum with books such as his *Declining Significance of Race* (1978) and *The Truly Disadvantaged* (1987).[3] In the first of these books Wilson stresses the emergence of class stratification among blacks. No longer constrained by discrimination, a black middle class had moved into better jobs and neighborhoods, its upward mobility no longer hampered by race. The situation of blacks left behind in inner cities, however, had worsened. Wilson's thesis provoked a major controversy that centered on his description of improvements in the circumstances of the black middle class and neglected his argument about the "deteriorating conditions of the black underclass." Incorrectly labeled a conservative, Wilson, who thought of himself as a social democrat, decided to focus on the ghetto underclass and spell out the policy implications of this thesis. The result was *The Truly Disadvantaged.* His work shows how wider trends of a bifurcation of American society run right through the black population. It also shows how a spatial dimension in the formation of America's underclass makes for a geographical concentration of this class in inner-city ghettos not seen in Europe, a phenomenon that adds to the problem of reaching out toward this problem group. Wilson may still be caught in sociological dilemmas about the best way to tackle the problem of the underclass, yet he seems to have transcended the dilemmas implied in the ideological reading and reception of his work.

Other recent examples of the kind of writing that goes against the grain include works by Shelby Steele, a black author who in *The Content of Our Character* offers "a new vision of race in America,"[4] as the subtitle of his book puts it, and by Jim Sleeper, an old-fashioned yet fairly young liberal who, amid the fray of racial confrontation in New York, calmly makes the point that "a purely symbolic politics" (by black leaders) "of communal and personal posturing only dooms its practitioners to impotence and to others' condescension." It is a kind of politics that, as he argues, has already resulted in "the waning of black moral influence upon the larger society."[5]

Problems of poverty, unemployment, social disorganization, and bifurcation do not constitute the only area of autonomous social drift that social scientists have to confront. Another such area is that of large-scale immigration during the 1970s and 1980s and the attendant increase in the heterogeneity of American society. Again, as in the previous instance of social drift, a noisy social debate accompanies the issue. In a sense we have seen it all before in earlier peak periods of immigration, the tendency to close the gate, to patrol the border, to narrow the reigning definitions of Americanism. With the spread of foreign-language enclaves, mainly but not only Spanish-speaking communities, across the United States, there are vociferous groups rallying to the cause of English as the national language. One such group, called "U.S. English" (which to the nearsighted reads "US English"), campaigns for the statutory status of English as the sole official language of the United States. Its advisory board includes such Anglo-Saxon scions as Charlton Heston and Arnold Schwarzenegger, but in fairness I should acknowledge that the board joins ubiquitous neoconservatives such as Norman Podhoretz and Nathan Glazer with Eugene J. McCarthy and Saul Bellow. Apparently the call to hold up the national tradition, if only linguistically, strikes many a responsive chord.

A parallel but wider and probably more vicious ideological debate about the defining boundaries of the national identity and heritage focuses on higher education and its role in transmitting the national culture. The liberal response to the nation's increased cultural heterogeneity had been to widen America's established cultural canon, which viewed the culture as essentially originating within a long line of Western civilization, and to pay homage to the cultural heritage of many of America's new immigrants. Not surprisingly, neoconservatives gladly added the defense of the established canon of American culture to their agenda. With all the apocalyptic fervor they are wont to bring to their cause, they see the demise of Western culture at the hands of guilt-ridden, weak-hearted, and alienated liberals.

Again, the question is how academic students are behaving in the midst of their society's massive and unplanned drift and the ideological cacophony that it has provoked. Essentially two intellectual paradigms are developing, one among social scientists and social historians and the other among a number of American studies people. Both developments are taking place within the relative quiet of academia, at one remove from the tumult outside the walls. To the extent that the schools and perspectives clash, however, academia may have reproduced the outside tumult, more often than not mistaking its own noise for the real thing. But I am being facetious too soon.

First let us look at recent trends in thinking about ethnicity and multiculturalism. Book titles alone make it clear that we have moved well "beyond
the melting pot" and perhaps even "beyond ethnicity." As recent work on
the subject has shown, ethnicity is never a matter of simply blending cultural elements, some of which can be traced back to the old country, while others have been selectively adopted from the new American environment.
Immigrant groups have always experienced complex processes of cultural
struggle over their collective identity and its proper definition. With the recent debate about the canon of mainstream American culture, the argument
among academic students of the subject has shifted toward a greater understanding of the strategies of cultural self-definition that individuals and
groups employ, drawing on various cultural repertoires while subtly changing the webs of significance that had held groups of immigrants together.
Recent work has begun to look at ethnicity as a process of continual change.
Perspectives of the historian, the cultural anthropologist, and the sociologist
have become intertwined in these recent developments. More often than not,
ethnicity is seen as a cultural construct, an invention, that has less to do with
the conscious motive to preserve a cultural tradition that goes back to the
homeland than with the problems of making sense of life in America. And
"making sense" in this context may well read as "fabricating meaning."

There is much to be gained intellectually from these new approaches to
multiculturalism and ethnicity in America. Confronted with the stark dichotomy of homeland traditions as relatively immutable entities and an equally
reified view of American culture, these new approaches dialectically transcend the dilemma and see process and flux as equally affecting the view of
both American culture generally and its many transplanted immigrant cultures. They thus undercut the entrenched positions that the ideologues outside the gates of academia have taken, yet they may be far too subtle to be of
any relevance there.

This seems to be even more strongly the case for the newfangled American studies paradigm. Multiculturalism there reflects not only the area of
ethnic diversity and the problems it poses for scholarly reflection but also,
and more widely, the many emancipist stirrings born in the 1960s. In language
usually indebted to European writers, often of a deconstructionist bent, much
new work in American studies explores the cultural space of neglected minorities, ethnic minorities, racial groups, indigenous peoples, and women in
American history or American literature. They are acts of justice and at the
same time acts of emancipation, for much of the new research and writing
comes from members of those forgotten groups. While exploring their own
space, and reporting on it to the outside world, they at the same time establish their space, extending the reach of American history, culture, and life.

Emancipist as it may be, however, it is also highly esoteric if not solipsistic. Enclosed within the enclave of academia, many of the rituals of emancipation take place before the converted, in the small world of conferences and conventions. It may echo emancipist strivings and stirrings in the wider society, yet I wonder whether it really affects them. Part of the problem—and a dilemma in its own right—may be the language used to communicate to an outside world whose attention these forgotten groups may wish to draw. It is truly ironic that all these feverish presentations of the Other—mostly with the deferential capital O—use an alienating language that can only perpetuate the status of being Other. There is a strange amnesia about this whole recent trend. All the recent work exploring the forgotten Others in American history and society that I have seen totally forgets one potent indigenous tradition in American social thought. The kind of sociology that came out of Chicago, inspired by James and Dewey and developed by thinkers as diverse as Mead, Thomas, and Park, has been one long exploration of the Other in American society. From the early figures to such later writers as Blumer, Goffman, and Becker, Chicago sociologists have focused on the outsider, the marginal individual, and the stranger in their explorations of the cosmopolitanism, variety, and complexity of American society. They developed a language by Americans and for Americans from which much work in American studies today could benefit.[6]

More important, much of the work in the Chicago tradition, despite its focus on deviancy and subcultures, always exhibited a sense of context, an attempt to relate an understanding of the many divergent fragments of American society to the wider culture and, vice versa, to find an interpretive view of the wider society as meaningfully related to the pluralism of its parts. That sense of context, that search for the wider framework of American culture, is missing from much recent work, least so in sociological reflections on, e.g., the bifurcation of society and most so in recent trends in the field of American studies. Centrifugal forces dominate the latter field. American studies has become a many-splintered thing, incapable, it seems, of transcending the particularist impulse to restore an untold number of forgotten groups to their rightful places in American history. What happened to the old urge to find the unifying discourse and the factors of integration that have made for an American culture as much as for the rise of American studies itself? Have American studies people become so deafened by the hectoring voices of the neoconservatives outside their safe little preserve, have they become so averse to any language that might be construed as a new hegemonic discourse, that deconstruction is the only decent option left? Then, I am afraid, American studies, along with the multiculturalist impulse itself, will self-deconstruct before too long.

What impact would such a development have on society at large, in terms of the wider configurations of cultural affinities and political affiliation among the citizenry? Scholarly clashes may well be confined inside the walls of academia, but they do reflect stirrings and concerns among the general population. The metaphor of "culture wars" only slightly exaggerates the present state of American studies in the United States, whose debates are only the mild, verbal version of the more vicious confrontations going on in society. There we find real battle lines that have a real impact on the civil status of real people, ejecting entire categories such as unregistered aliens and their children from political safety net structures providing education, health care, and income supports. Lines of cultural affinity are being redrawn in society at large, pitting projects for inclusion against projects for exclusion, the result of which may well affect the reigning views on citizenship and political affiliation. Against that backdrop there seems to be all the more reason for American studies scholars to get their act together and return to the larger mission and inspiration of their country's American studies tradition as a wide-ranging exploration of what citizenship in the United States has come to mean in terms of its cultural affinities and political affiliations.

That, certainly, has been an inspiration to their non-American colleagues, who are engaged in the same endeavor of gauging the continuing yet ever-changing dimensions of American citizenship. To non-American students of this subject, American studies has always had this added significance of a civics lesson, an exploration of citizenship in action that has helped to determine their views of citizenship in their own national settings. American studies abroad has therefore always added to the cultural affinities and political affiliations underlying people's reflections on citizenship in their own countries. If American studies has this larger existential relevance, for Americans and non-Americans alike, it may be worthwhile to explore the relevance in its different settings more systematically. In the following chapter I propose to do this, comparing the relevance and practice of American studies in the United States with ways this relevance and practice may be translated for countries in Europe.

8. National American Studies in Europe, Transnational American Studies in America?

Among the buzzwords in American studies today, two are linked together like Hegelian twins. They are a quarrelsome pair, thesis and antithesis. Their names are "canon" and "multiculturalism." Both are cult figures. Both have their cult, if not multicult, following. First there was "canon," and the world was still in one piece. Then came "multicult," and the world would never be the same again.

If canon was the thesis, then in the great Hegelian fashion it was also a synthesis. It offered a view of American culture and the American national identity that in a unifying discourse using overarching metaphors and concepts managed to synthesize such contradictory forces as fusion and fragmentation, unity and diversity, continuity and rupture, high culture and low culture, and consensus and conflict. To the extent that the American studies movement was once characterized by a unity of purpose and a sense of collective enterprise, it was a movement of emancipation, freeing American culture from all remaining servitude to foreign dominion. The canon as it then emerged had been a long shadow before, stretching back all the way to the *E Pluribus Unum* of the early republic. Its cosmopolitanism as a potential world culture, in a romantic, almost Goethean sense, had been implied in Emerson's and Whitman's transcendentalism, as well as in later views of the *Seven Arts* generation, most notably in Randolph Bourne's concept of transnationalism. America's cultural nationalism has long had this dual face, defining America as quintessentially a non-Europe while at the same time transcending the implied binary opposition. If American culture could be seen as sui generis, as different from European cultures, it was different in a different way, an exceptional way, a new way. Back in the days when language was not yet free of gender bias, Crèvecoeur could refer to the American as "this New Man." As a Turner *avant la lettre,* he could conceive of America as a fountain of youth, a regenerative force that would make European immigrants undergo a new birth. "Here they are become men."

Americans may never have been quite so sure. They might have shaken off the European dominion politically, but many of them felt left out in the cold culturally. There is a characteristic sense of disenchantment in Herman Melville's lines in *Clarel:* "Columbus ended earth's romance: / No new world to mankind remains!"[1] No longer was there an America of the mind, the uncharted territory that a collective European imagination could fill. No new world in the sense of a utopian invention remained. Disenchantment could translate into a sense of loss. If America was a non-Europe, if it was a tabula rasa, it could leave Americans empty-handed. Lacking Europe's rich repertoire of cultural traditions and forms, America confronted its creative minds with a "poverty of material," as James Fenimore Cooper plaintively put it. This awareness developed into the litany of absences that would be repeated over and over again. Here is Theodore Dreiser, writing in the *Seven Arts* in 1917: "It is a thing for laughter, if not for tears: one hundred million Americans, rich . . . beyond the dreams of avarice, and scarcely a sculptor, a poet, a singer, a novelist, an actor, a musician, worthy of the name."[2] Similar statements, in haunting self-deprecation, run through Americans' assessments of their compatriots' cultural achievements. We find it in Sinclair Lewis's acceptance speech for the 1930 Nobel Prize in literature; more recently, in 1981, we find it in a facetious piece by George Steiner in *Salmagundi.*[3] The longevity of the lament need not surprise us. After all, it had been the work of early cultural nationalists such as the poet John Trumbull, one of the "Connecticut Wits," to announce the coming of an American Shakespeare, thus raising a standard and a banner essentially European. It was a counterblast to disparaging European views proffered by such as Jean-Louis Buffon, Corneille de Pauw, and the Abbé Raynal. Indeed, Raynal wrote the following in 1770: "It is amazing that America has not yet produced a good poet, a capable mathematician, or a man of genius in a single art or a single science."[4] Since the challenge came from Europeans, Americans may have felt compelled to meet the challenge on European terms. Formulated thus, however, the criterion is asinine and has blinded Americans to a cultural production that could claim to be genuinely American. In fact, it was not until the 1930s— that decade of feverish self-discovery—that Americans began to recognize the creative riches of a truly American culture and to take it on its own terms. Only then did a true emancipation from Europe's cultural pantheon begin. Only then did a canon of American culture begin to take shape.

Constructing a canon always involves selective appropriation. No matter how explicit or self-evident the criteria of selection—and they may have the quasi-objective compelling force of standards of literary quality or structural complexity—any corpus of works or consensual reading of history that truly constitutes a canon is always at the same time a reflection of submerged assumptions, of nonexplicit cultural conventions. When Crèvecoeur spoke of the American as "this New Man," he in all likelihood "naturally" tended to think of white males only, however well that limited sample may have illustrated the more general dynamic forces of unity and diversity characteristic of American society. When Turner referred to the "frontier" as the geographic locus where Crèvecoeur's interplay of forces could fully come into its own, he "naturally" conceived of the frontier as the forward line of settlement encroaching on a space that the logic of his view could see only as empty. He may have seen the frontier as a meeting ground of cultures, the true locus of the American "melting pot"; in that sense it may have served him to highlight processes that more generally characterized the cultural cast of American society, yet he never truly viewed it as a meeting ground between cultures on opposite sides of the line. Every canonical reading of the quintessential forces used in making a national culture and a national identity, no matter how complex, no matter how open to contradictions and dialectics, remains only a partial story.

Nonetheless, however partial such a canonical reading may be, it can sway an audience only if it can convince those who in one way or another are outsiders to the story. Many of the later immigrants willingly adopted the Pilgrim Fathers and Founding Fathers as their new foster parents, meaningfully related to them by the sheer force of shared hopes and aspirations. It is an act of voluntarism on the part of the outsiders who chose to place themselves in a line of history even if their parents had never formed part of it. They elevated consent over descent, affirming the universalism implied in the story of America as a nation of nations. When, during his more populist period of the late 1930s and early 1940s, the composer Aaron Copland celebrated the American heritage, he selectively drew on a repertoire of vernacular music that could be traced back to the British Isles, setting Carl Sandberg's *Lincoln Portrait* to music that added to the soaring quality of Lincoln's Gettysburg Address. The son of Jewish immigrants, Copland may have sung a song of himself as part of that great ringing tradition, yet at the same time he cast the tradition in a remarkably homogenizing, almost Anglo-Saxon mold. It is almost as if through his music we see shimmering the rugged features not only of Lincoln and Carl Sandberg but also of all those Anglo-Saxon faces that Walker Evans portrayed at the same time. Much like Evans and Agee, when Copland praised famous men, he placed himself, like an adopted son, in the longest line of descent within the American nation.

Similar acts of voluntary affiliation with the canonized reading of "America" have occurred outside America's national borders. One need not be an immigrant, or even a would-be immigrant, to sense an affinity with the

American dream. More than a century ago, at the time of the Second Empire in France, America could serve to keep dreams of republicanism and democracy alive in France; it was a French initiative to turn those dreams into that classic icon of Americanism: the Statue of Liberty, of "Liberté éclairant le monde." Clearly, the dream in this case symbolically expressed political ideals, but it could also be a dream of abundance and secular opportunity. It could refer to a democracy of citizens or to a democracy of goods. Whatever its precise contents, the dream has been kept alive by Americans and non-Americans alike.

As a shorthand reference to the wider repertoire of canonized versions of America's mission and meaning, the American dream has never been without its critics. Americans and non-Americans alike have developed critical repertoires that constitute one sustained attempt at the "deconstruction," the ideological critique, of the American canon. Such repertoires have always been inspired by the sense of a gap between the realm of American ideals and the reality of American life. Such critical awareness can arise only if people find themselves at a distance from consensual communities that control the production and flow of legitimating language in society. The sense of distance has taken many forms: the alienation of an intelligentsia that no longer felt itself to be a meaningful part of what it saw as the drift of society; the estrangement of people such as Henry James or Henry Adams, who saw America slipping away from their assumed right of consensual control; or the alienation of younger generations of cultural rebels, such as Van Wyck Brooks or Randolph Bourne, who could still hope to gain control of the social production of meaning. There are, however, other structural varieties of distance that can turn people into critics rather than advocates of the American canon.

Travelers and immigrants are two groups that always find themselves at a distance from America as a consensual community. Not only do they always bring their own cultural repertoires from their home countries, but as relative outsiders they also tend to have a keener eye for the rift between dream and reality. In *Martin Chuzzlewit* Charles Dickens set the tone for a long line of caustic comments on American hypocrisy, which could vaunt liberty and justify slavery and which was never below reducing intrinsic value to exchange value. Later on Sigmund Freud would lift this repertoire of anti-Americanism to new heights with his tirades against American gullibility and "dollaromania." He saw America as the country where quality had been completely replaced by quantity. Hundreds of variations on these themes appear in the reports that European intellectuals published in Europe following their visits to the New World.

Immigrants form another category of people who typically find themselves at the margin of American society. Many never gave up their sense of affiliation with canonized versions of America as the land of promise (or at least

the promise of land), the land of opportunity, the land of freedom and justice. To students of the immigrant experience, however, the letters they sent
home, the memoirs they wrote, offer many illustrations of a rude disenchantment, a crude awakening from the American dream. There is the classic story that tells us of the three sobering discoveries of the immigrants: not only
did they find out that American streets were not paved with gold, but they
also discovered that most of the streets were not paved at all and that they
were expected to do the paving. There is also the beautiful vignette in Louis
Adamic's *Laughing in the Jungle* (1932), to which I referred in chapter 4. It is
the story of an immigrant who has returned to the Balkans, where he was
born. Looking at a photograph that he brought home with him, a picture of
New York, the old man realizes that he has left much of his strength "frozen
in the greatness of America." Walking the streets before boarding his ship,
he felt that, although he was going home, he was leaving himself in America. The alienation from America that had made him go home again had
turned into a tragic self-alienation. America had robbed him of his true self.

What is only a budding insight here, the recollection of a wasted life that
begins to turn into a wider reflection on life in America, assumed the full force
of an ideological critique of alienation in the case of people who were neither immigrants nor travelers. They were "émigrés," forced into exile by the
disasters of European history. People like Theodor Adorno, Max Horkheimer,
Erich Fromm, and Herbert Marcuse had alienation forced on them. Intellectually uprooted and displaced, they turned their critique of capitalism into
a critique of America as the country most typically representing the conditions of life under advanced capitalism. They may have been projecting their
subjective sense of alienation more than they would have cared to admit, but
they were only repeating, perhaps more radically, what many European critics
of culture had said before them. They, too, conceived of America as an image of Europe's future. From Alexis de Tocqueville to H. G. Wells, from
George Duhamel to Jean Baudrillard, from Johan Huizinga to Hermann
Keyserling, America showed the ugly face of a mass society and a mass culture that would eventually threaten European civilization on its own turf. The
intellectual émigrés of the Frankfurt school may have been more inclined
than most to translate the evil force of Americanism into the underlying
rationale of capitalism, yet their indictment of American conformism, com-
mercialism, and standardization found its place in a repertoire that was not
exclusively Marxist.

Nor was it exclusively European. From the late 1930s through the 1940s and
1950s, American mass culture was a recurrent concern for American intellectuals. The tone of analysis may have ranged from the picaresque, as in
Riesman's view in *The Lonely Crowd,* to the more directly Marxist, as in the
pages of the *Partisan Review,* yet their common concern was with the con-

formism of American mass culture as a pervasive form of "false conscious-ness." They had a keen eye for the falseness of the dominant canonical con-sensus. To use the newly coined buzzword of the 1950s, they all saw it as a matter of a manipulated *image*. As Daniel Boorstin put it in his book that he aptly entitled *The Image:* "Now the language of images is everywhere. Every-where it has displaced the language of ideals. If the right 'image' will elect a President, or sell an automobile, a religion, a cigarette, or a suit of clothes, why can it not make America herself—or the American Way of Life—a sale-able commodity all over the earth?"[5]

In fact, the critique has never truly abated. From the days of the New Left to John Kenneth Galbraith's recent indictment of the "culture of content-ment," or Robert Hughes's *Culture of Complaint,* we find one continuing il-lustration of that characteristic American genre the jeremiad, always weigh-ing the reality of American life against the demanding "language of its ideals." As Sacvan Bercovitch has convincingly argued, the jeremiad is always a two-pronged rhetorical device. Like a true disciplinarian instrument, it sternly points to society's straying from its ideal course while at the same time reaf-firming the course and the destiny. In that sense I may have misspoken ear-lier when I used terms such as *deconstruction* and *ideological critique.* What is remarkable about American intellectual critiques of U.S. society, politics, and culture is the underlying unity of the discourse. Even critics who dismiss "the language of ideals" as mere cant aim less at the deconstruction of the ideals than at the critique of convential praxis. Their anger appears to have been inspired by what the practice of American life has done to the avowed universalism of its ideals. Time and time again their aim has truly been to remind America of its high calling.

That brings us back to the twin pair of contemporary buzzwords that I introduced earlier, *canon* and *multicult.* At first their continuing quarrel may seem to show a new fault line appearing, as if for the first time the American canon is truly subject to "radical deconstruction" (to coin a phrase). Indeed, it may seem as if for the first time the very universalism of the American ideals is exposed as no more than mere cant, an oppressive, hegemonic discourse masking the reality of segments of society whose stories are suppressed, their places ignored. They are literally misfits who have always led a life of bor-rowed identities, imposed from outside. Now for the first time, in an accu-mulated movement building up from the emancipatory enthusiasms of the 1960s, they not only knock on the door, screaming for equal time and equal rights—which would still have meant relying on an American unity of dis-course—but now draw on foreign repertoires of critical language, mostly imported from France, in an attempt to explode precisely such unity of dis-course. Against an assumed universalism of Americanness and American ideals, they have set the many particularisms of the forgotten Others as so many voices from beyond the pale of the American canon. Under their impact American studies in the United States has splintered, preferring the plural over the singular form, constructing, if not inventing, American histories rather than American history, American literatures rather than an American literature.

Looked at more closely, however, is not the onslaught of multiculturalism a mere dialectical swing whose very force illustrates the continuing strength of an overarching American universalism? Is not the rhetorical hyperbole, setting out to deconstruct the entrenched version of American universalism, merely a reflection of the heat of battle? Is not their violent shakeup of the American kaleidoscope truly an attempt to reach more sophisticated patterns? Is it not a matter of instilling an awareness that every reading of history and collective identity is always a matter of cultural invention and creation? In their crusade the multiculturalists may have veered toward a polemical extreme of creating particularisms unheedful of the greater challenge eventually to pick up the pieces and put them together again. At the same time, this very effort to fragment what seemed to be whole and of a piece strikes the outsider as characteristically American, reminiscent of a fragmenting freedom, a modularizing cast of mind, that has always amazed foreign observers. Americans have a keener eye for the parts that make up a whole; they feel less inhibited in taking apart what to Europeans may have seemed an untouchable organic whole, a metaphysical unity. There is a radical Whitmanesque, democratic enthusiasm that recognizes the essential equality of the tiniest parts and ingredients. There is the playfulness of the tinkerer, the curiosity of the inventor. Americans may have an inclination to take things apart, to decontextualize, but they always reassemble and recontextualize. When asked what he did to recordings that disc jockeys had previously simply played from beginning to end, MC Grandmaster Flash, the American inventor of "scratching," once said: "I take it apart and put it together again."

American multiculturalists are busy taking apart the canon of their national culture. Thus, they are acting very much in an American cultural vein. At the same time, they may be abiding by the language of American ideals rather than deconstructing it. They may have felt left out of the universalism of its ideals, but they still are taking their cue from those ideals. They may be overstating the particularism of their claims, yet in the end they will have added to the qualities of a Hegelian synthesis that American universalism has always possessed. It has always been an American hybrid, a universalism that could accommodate particularisms. During World War I, when Europe gave free rein to its suicidal instincts, the French writer Romain Rolland, in his introduction to the first issue of *The Seven Arts,* could call on the Americans to transcend European nationalisms and to turn all the voices of Europe's immigrants "into one Symphony." Similarly, and with equal urgency, Ran-

dolph Bourne sought the final emancipation from the British cultural dominion in the same reservoir of America's immigrant population. The transcendence that he foresaw was of a transnationalism, of Europe's cultures
taken apart and put together again in a spirit of democratic equality, acknowl-
edging the many particular voices yet merging them into one transnational
culture. If America is a nation of nations, its culture could be a culture of
cultures. Present-day multiculturalists have not reached that stage yet. Their
sense of urgency still takes them in a direction of ever further particulariza-
tion, away from the canon of the great white whale and the dead white males.
But the quest for a larger framework of meaningful "transnationalism" cannot be far away.

* * *

Whereas some form of transnationalism should perhaps be next on the agenda of American studies in the United States, in Europe there may a case for a
greater emphasis on nationally specific approaches to American studies. Not
surprisingly, in many European countries the work done in American studies has normally followed the reigning paradigms of the field in the United
States. Most students may have even been unaware of the many indigenous
traditions of intellectual reflection on American history, society, and culture.
As far back as the late 1950s, one of the fathers of American studies in Europe, Sigmund Skard, had already made the case for writing a separate history of the European study of America as an intellectual endeavor. Many
motifs and motives would underlie such work. There is the intellectual curiosity of trying to fathom the specificity of American culture, seen as an
intriguing variant within a wider framework of Western civilization. There
are the many attempts to read Europe's future in the contemporary contours
of America. There is the anguished or exhilarated exploration of America as
a cultural presence in Europe, where American culture has appeared as an
outside force, influencing Europe's various national cultures.

The European Association for American Studies has long sought to work
in this vein, organizing its biennial conferences around themes that would
at least allow for comparative work. Nevertheless, a survey of European work
on American literature and American history would show that the large
majority of it has no marked European dimension. In recent times, however, a trend toward a Europeanization of American studies seems to have
emerged. Everywhere one sees conferences and volumes on such themes as
the European reception of forms of American culture or the Americanization of European cultures. The sources for this change in perspective are
many, mostly European. There is the impact of work done in Great Britain
in cultural studies, focusing on the analysis of mass culture and the mass
media. A central concept in such analyses is that of cultural mediation and

the degrees of freedom involved in the reception of mass culture. There is a paradigm shift among cultural anthropologists who try to fathom the impact of cultural centers—America foremost among them—on the periphery of what they have come to conceive of as a world-system of interdependent cultures. Concepts and metaphors central to this approach include the creolization and hybridization of cultures. The work of French and Italian semioticians provides another reservoir of sensitizing concepts.

Nonetheless, we cannot begin to do justice to America as a cultural presence in Europe without thoroughly exploring the history of images of America in Europe within their various national contexts. There is a strange alchemy at work whenever Europeans try to cope with the otherness of America. Time and again, regardless of whether they were concerned with cultural survival and resistance against the encroachment of America, trying to preserve public domains of meaningful citizenship, Europeans have conjured up an image of "Europe" rather than of their own national cultures. The image of "America" has always tended to evoke the counterimage of an invented "Europe." America in that sense may have worked to instill an overarching sense of Europeanness among European intellectuals. Even when they rallied to the cause of Europe, however, their choice of words was often tellingly national. The "Europe" that we see emerging in texts by French authors, such as André Siegfried or Georges Duhamel, or in German texts, by authors such as Oswald Spengler, Adolf Halfeld, or Hermann Keyserling, is often portrayed in a characteristically French or German light. French authors were inclined to project typically French concerns with traditions of creative individualism and craftmanship onto a larger European canvass to highlight the contrast with an American culture seen as catering to the average tastes of the masses through the standardization and uniformity of its production. German authors tended to argue in terms of the collective "soul" of the *"Kulturvolk"* seen as the font of culture of the *"Abendland,"* the West. Such were the terms of contrast to "Americanism" as they conceived it.

Not only was the image of "Europe" often cast in characteristically national terms; more generally, "Europe" often served as no more than a flimsy rhetorical veneer. Typically it could hardly paper over the fault lines between the various national cultures. André Siegfried's writings provide an amusing example of this. In 1927 he wrote the preface to André Philip's study of labor conditions in America, *Le problème ouvrier aux Etats-Unis.* The book investigates the place of the worker in an industry that had become organized around the tenets of Fordism, Taylorism, standardization, mass production, and above all, *"le machinisme."* Siegfried lauds Philip as a "bon européen" (a good European) who had set out to measure American labor conditions by a European yardstick of humanist values. He remembers how only in America had he himself become aware of "le monde européen comme un ensemble" (the

European world as a whole). It is only in America that "on prend conscience d'une réalité qui nous échappe ici, c'est qu'il existe un esprit européen, dont l'esprit américain est souvent la parfaite antithèse [one becomes aware of a reality that escapes us here, namely that a European spirit does exist, to which the American spirit often stands as the perfect opposite]." From a moral point of view, America, new as it is, has been cut off from Europe's twenty-centuries-old traditions by the hiatus of immigration across the ocean; it no longer shares much with the old Europe that is still in direct communion with Rome, Greece, and even India. Clearly up to this point Siegfried conceives of Europe "comme un ensemble," as a integral whole. Nonetheless, he soon begins to add individual detail to his picture: "Parmi les peuples européens, le français est celui qui a eu, le plus, la conscience de ce qu'est un individu, un homme [among the European peoples, the Frenchman is the one who has had the clearest sense of what it means to be an individual, a man]." France clearly takes pride of place in the European ensemble, embodying some of the core values of Europeanism, but Siegfried does not leave it at that. He goes on to single out one other country from the European whole, describing it as an America in Europe: Germany. "Les Allemands, si semblables à tant d'égards aux Américains modernes, se sont jetés dans la standardisation avec une sorte de passion, comme ils font toutes choses. Il n'est point d'Allemand, aujourd'hui, qui ne chante avec conviction l'hymne de la 'rationalisation'; celle-ci répond évidemment à leur génie de discipline, avouons-le aussi, à leur manque de personnalité [The Germans, so similar in so many ways to the modern Americans, have hurled themselves onto a course of standardization with a kind of passion, as they do everything. There is no German, today, who does not with conviction sing the praise of 'rationalization'; this clearly accords with their mind for discipline, and, let us admit it, their lack of personality]." So much for the European ensemble.[6]

Pursuing American studies in this vein will tell us, as well as Americans, at least as much about European cultural and intellectual history as about America. Nevertheless, part of the life that America has led ever since its inception—and let us not forget that it was already invented by the European imagination before it was actually discovered—has been lived under foreign auspices, as an image and a phantasm far beyond any manipulative control of Americans. Non-Americans, too, may claim America as theirs. That life—America as conceived in the minds of people elsewhere who have tried to make sense of their own cultural and political situations by contrasting them to America—cries out for systematic exploration. The following two chapters are offered as illustrations of this larger project. As I hope they will make clear, there may be inventions and discoveries on the way. There certainly is a European Columbiad to be composed by American studies scholars working in their various national settings.

PART 3

Transnational Affinities
and Affiliations

9. Traveling Theories, Traveling Theorists: French Views of American Modernity

I might flippantly call this essay a study in occidentalism. Taking my cue from Edward Said's seminal exploration of orientalism as a repertoire of European representations concerning "the Orient," I propose to look at "America" as similarly an object of the European imagination. Much like the Orient, the Occident was a European invention devised long before the historical discovery of the Americas. It has served as the screen for the projection of a wide range of European dreams, utopian as well as dystopian. Among the many repertoires in which "America" figured as the quintessential counterpoint to Europe, representing everything that Europe was not or had not yet become, would never be or want to be, modernity was one important point of reference. Although European constructions of America, irrespective of national setting, have been congruent in many ways, there have also been characteristically national discourses concerning America. In the following I look at one national setting, exploring French views of America seen as the site of the politically and culturally modern.

Establishing a Repertoire

Recently an unpublished manuscript by Jules Verne was discovered. It is a futuristic novel, rejected by his publisher in 1863 and now published as *Paris au XXe siècle*.[1] In an uncharacteristic gloomy mood, Verne conjures up a technological nightmare that has made human life subservient to the utilitarian logic of technological progress, industrial production, and commerce. High culture has been leveled down to mass culture, industrially produced, endlessly recombining team-made ingredients to render soap operas and sitcoms, in much the same way that replaceable parts make up a machine tool. For his apocalyptic projection Verne used the future, choosing Paris as his illustrative case. Rather than project across time, however, he might as well have projected across space, using America as the site of a dystopian modernity, for what appears here is the repertoire of much rejectionist writing about America as Europeans have chosen to envisage it.

When used in conjunction, the words *America* and *modernity* will most likely conjure up images of twentieth-century America in its heyday as an industrial power, ushering in a new era of mass production and mass consumption. To the European gaze such images have offered the distant mirage of a Promethean technical prowess, of energy unleashed in many different directions, going skyward in its high-rise architecture, going westward in its unbridled conquest of open space, and going global through its penetration into new markets for mass entertainment. Nor, in the end, was this America only distant; in the twentieth century it became a presence in Europe, seen as either threatening or liberating, opening vistas of a new world as versions of "the New World." The sense of "the modern," strongly centered on Europe's bourgeois societies in the late nineteenth century, now found its favorite site in America. In a Promethean act of cultural robbery, America had taken over Europe's leadership role in defining what modernity was all about. To many Europeans this must have appeared to be a latter-day installment of the long-running saga of the Westward Course of Empire, which—as an inspirational myth—Americans had already made their own in the nineteenth century.[2]

Yet the association of modernity with America as an advanced technical civilization is not the only one that Europeans have tended to make. There are earlier views that cast America in the light of the modern, contrasting it to Europe seen as mired in the past. Partly this was a matter of European dreams of the future being projected onto America, but not only so. There was a sufficient continuity of discourse across the Atlantic for Americans themselves to share these visions of the collective endeavor in which they as a new nation were engaged. Metaphors of America as having moved beyond Europe, having entered a new plane of history, may be traced back to the early Puritans' use of biblical prophecy, yet in their secular versions made at the time of the revolution and of the early republic, these metaphors clearly echoed the Enlightenment hopes of the day in Europe. Again, however, despite the continuity, there was at the same time—much as in the case of the Puritans—a widespread sense, voiced loudly, that it was for Americans to realize these hopes.

From early on the choir of voices has always included French ones. They contributed to a discourse that has conceived of America as a counterpoint to Europe. The contrasts on which I will focus always played on underlying dimensions of new versus old, the future versus the past, the modern versus the antiquated. In these contrasts America appeared in essentially three different constructions. One was humanist, focusing on "the American" as a "new man"; the second was political, focusing on America as a successful republican experiment; and the third was what for want of a better term we might call existential, focusing on America as empty space.

An early French voice, heard widely at the time in many European countries and then forgotten until Americans rediscovered it more than a century later, turning it into one of their canonical definitions of American nationhood, was that of Michel-Guillaume Jean de Crèvecoeur, who wrote as Hector St. John. Born into the *petite noblesse* in Normandy, he had fought the British in North America under Montcalm and after the defeat of the French had moved south to take up farming in the province of New York. In his *Letters from an American Farmer,* published in 1782, he asked the now famous question: "What, then, is the American, this New Man?" The very choice of words is telling. The American is seen not simply as representing yet another different nationality, adding to a European pattern of national differences. He is new in the sense of transcending the European pattern. The transcendence is of two kinds. Americans may be of European descent, as Crèvecoeur argues, yet they have left Europe's internecine differences of nationality behind them: "From this promiscuous breed, that race now called Americans have arisen." And he continues: "*He* is an American, who, leaving behind him all his ancient prejudices and manners, receives new ones from the new mode he has embraced, the new government he obeys, and the new rank he holds. He becomes an American by being received in the broad lap of our great Alma Mater. Here individuals of all nations are melted into a new race of men, whose labours and posterity will one day cause great changes in the world." In a vein of historical predestination, echoing the old repertoire of the westward course of empires, he goes on to say: "Americans are the western pilgrims, who are carrying along with them that great mass of arts, sciences, vigour, and industry which began long ago in the East; *they will finish the great circle.*"[3]

As I said, however, there was a second sense in which Americans were new. They had overcome other European differences that worked to keep Europe divided against itself. Religious difference and strife had resolved themselves into a pluralism of coequal denominations happily coexisting on American soil. Even more important, they had overcome European social inequality. "Europe," Crèvecoeur argues, "contains hardly any other distinctions but lords and tenants," whereas American society does not consist "of great lords who possess everything, and of a herd of people who have nothing." Crèvecoeur continues by giving one of those rhetorical enumerations that would echo in the work of later American authors such as Nathaniel Hawthorne and Henry James: "Here are no aristocratic families, no courts, no kings, no bishops, no ecclesiastical dominion, no invisible power giving to a few a very visible one."[4] Not only does America tend to level such differences, but in the act it elevates all those involved. America, "this great asylum," has accepted the poverty stricken from all across Europe and turned them into citizens. Crèvecoeur speaks of a metamorphosis worked by America's intrinsic regenerative power: "Everything has tended to regenerate them; new laws, a new mode of living, a new social system; here they are become men."[5]

Crèvecoeur's is thus an amazing early statement of America's being modern in the sense of offering to fulfill that essentially Renaissance humanist dream that saw individuals as their own free agents, capable of taking charge of their own lives, molding their private and collective destinies as they saw fit. America, rather than Europe, was the historical stage for this humanist transformation. Crèvecoeur had daringly chosen to make the point by posing as an American farmer himself, the proud yeoman-citizen that typified the new social order of free and equal human beings.

* * *

A second variety of modernity projected onto America was linked to its great experiment in republicanism. That was how Alexis de Tocqueville and a younger generation of French liberals during the Second Empire chose to look at America. In the preface to his *Democracy in America* Tocqueville had already admitted to the act of projection, to conceiving of America as showing what the future might have in store for Europe: "I admit that in America I have looked for more than America; I have been in search of an image of democracy itself . . . if only to know at least what we might have to hope or fear from it."[6] Tocqueville's approach foreshadows later Weberian methodology. He turns America into an ideal type of democracy with a view to gaining more general insights into the workings of democracy, irrespective of its precise historical setting. As we know, his final view of democracy was never one of total civic bliss. He found grounds for both hope and fear, as he had set out to do. His insights into democracy in America were always keenly aware of rival forces kept in tenuous balance, such as liberty and equality, individualism and conformism, political participation and civic apathy. His single most important contribution may have been to the theory of republicanism. The inherent instability of republics, a form of political order that critically hinges on politics of disinterestedness, of civic virtue, had engaged political philosophers ever since Greek antiquity. Tocqueville was aware of the American answer to this quandary. He knew the Enlightenment views of the American federalists, who had sought to rein in human self-interest through the countervailing arrangements of constitutional checks and balances. As Tocqueville saw it, however, the true American genius responsible for the stability of its republican order was not political; it was social. The

pluralism of the nation's social life, the citizens' freedom to engage in manifold associations, was the key to understanding America's political stability. This view made Tocqueville a father of modern political sociology. At the
same time, it made clear what was truly modern about America: Tocqueville
saw it as a society whose central organizational vectors were freedom and
equality.

This view in particular would be taken up by a younger generation of
French liberals at the time of the Second Empire. Their republican hopes were
kept alive by the distant republic in the West and would find grateful expression, after the demise of Napoléon III's regime, in the iconic Statue of Liberty, a French gift to the American nation symbolizing "Liberté éclairant le
monde." In the dark days of the Second Empire, one of these liberals, Ed-
ouard Laboulaye, could express his admiration for America only indirectly.
He used Swiftean satire, as well as a writer's alias—le docteur René Lefèbvre—to hold up the democratic virtues of America as a mirror to his French
readers. In his *Paris en Amérique,* published in 1862, he describes how a mir-
acle concoction provided by a traveling American trickster and con man,
Jonathan Dream, magically transplants a French bourgeois family from Paris
to America. The narrator, head of this transplanted family, is the only one to
keep his French perspective. The others, his wife and his daughter, have mi-
raculously become Americans, naturally falling into American ways of life
that are shown in their greater informality, their greater equality between the
sexes and more generally between people of different rank. It is a narrative
ploy that allows the author seemingly to criticize the American way, in Pari-
sian disdain, while at the same time showing it as a liberating counterpoint
to established French social forms. At the end of the book we are informed
that the poor doctor, following his return to France, has gone insane. "Folie
d'amour, on en guérit quand on est jeune, les vieux en meurent; folie
d'ambition cède quelquefois à l'âge et au mépris des hommes; folie de liberté, on n'en guérit jamais [One recovers from the enchantment of love when
one is young, while the old die of it; the enchantment of ambition at times
passes with time or due to the disdain of others; one never recovers from the
enchantment of liberty.]"[7]

* * *

The third view of American modernity focuses on America as empty space
providing an exhilarating contrast to a Europe that had reached the Malthu-
sian limits of marginal existence. Again, the view was central to the American celebration of its manifest destiny, but visitors could not escape sharing
in this prevailing mood. New techniques of mechanical reproduction, such
as the chromolithograph, were powerful mediators in transmitting the iconography of an American civilization vibrantly engaged in its westward

march. The imagery of a never-ending renewal of life in America's endless western expanse fired the imagination of Americans and foreigners alike. Fanny Palmer's 1868 painting *Across the Continent,* published as a Currier and Ives print that tellingly changed the name to *Westward the Course of Empire,* has all the iconic ingredients: an endless space of prairie, lakes, and mountain scenery; a train diagonally cutting across the image, belching smoke that almost obliterates two Indians on horseback as an ominous reference to the "vanishing race"; and, to the left, a bustling frontier settlement, its public school featured prominently. It is only one among many representations of America's daring westward venture. Probably the most popular example was John Gast's 1872 painting *Westward Ho, American Progress,* displayed at the Philadelphia World's Fair of 1876 and widely distributed as a chromo reproduction. Again it shows the restless process of social renewal and individual regeneration in the westward march. Covered wagons take pioneers into a space that will soon be emptied of the last remaining buffalo and Indians. Above, blessing the enterprise, hovers a scantily clad goddess Columbia pointing the way west with one hand, while the other holds a roll of telegraph wire. Both this painting and Fanny Palmer's merge different visions of modernity into one: beckoning empty space wedded to the modern technologies of communication, provided by the railroad and the telegraph. It was not long before this iconic repertoire would be made to serve yet another version of American modernity, if not postmodernity: America's advertising wizardry. In its endless capacity to resemanticize reality, advertising early on transformed the West into an imaginary realm to be vicariously experienced by anyone who bought a particular product. As early as the 1870s and 1880s posters for tobacco brands such as Westward Ho used the same repertoire of the West as empty space where anyone could be a pioneer for as long as it took to smoke a pipe or cigarette. Such images are early versions of what we now know as "Marlboro Country" and the "Marlboro Man." This commercial appropriation of the repertoire of the West as the site of human self-reinvention has now become so well known that effective Marlboro advertising need do no more than show gorgeous western scenery with the slogan of *Come to Marlboro Country.* Although there is no cigarette in sight, we get the message.

French liberals traveling to America at the time of the Second Empire gave us occasional glimpses of this infatuating cultural climate. Visitors such as Jean-Jacques Ampère, Adolphe de Chambrun, Oscar Comettant, Ernest Duverger de Hauranne, and Xavier Eyma commented on a wide range of aspects of life in the American republic, but in one way or another, they all connected the energy and dynamism, "le goût du progrès," to the grand project of civilizing a continent while conquering its empty space, spreading the values of liberty, democracy, and hard work.[8] Ampère and Eyma, for instance, point to the American people's spirit of mobility and independence. Unlike the French, the Americans never get attached to a single place. They are constantly on the move, ever ready to adopt new ways and adapt to new conditions. In the open space of the West there is no room for social envy and class resentment. Fortune is open to all. Rich and poor can change roles and costumes in a matter of a single day. It is a condition of life that tends to instill a sense of brotherhood and equality, according to Duverger de Hauranne.

The French travelers were not without criticism. They noted the rapaciousness and greed, the coarseness of manners, and the rape of the land attending the westward march, yet at the same time they appreciated the boundless energy, the technological feats, and most of all, the democratic quality of life emerging on the western frontier. America, they found, was in a state of endless transition. As Ampère put it, the poetic quality of American life lies precisely in this motion. The America of Atala no longer exists, he concluded; it had made way for an America propelled by grandiose visions of its future.

* * *

American modernity thus has faces other than that of a Promethean technical civilization, but it is still clear that the technical dimension is already present even in the earlier views. It inspired awe among travelers in the nineteenth century as much as it would later in the twentieth. In particular, the view of America as empty space, offering room to modern dreams of individual transfiguration and regeneration, was wedded to a sense of the organizational acumen and technical prowess that Americans invested in this process. Observers of American modernity, however, whether American or European, did not arrive at this sense only by implication. By the mid-nineteenth century there was already an astute awareness that America was assuming the features of a technical civilization. World's fairs on both sides of the Atlantic were powerful transmitters of this new face of America. They could inspire panegyrics, as in Walt Whitman's case, or a more brooding sense of spiritual loss, as in the case of Henry Adams. Abroad, the impact would be equally dual. Modernizing entrepreneurial elites would see America as involved in a project parallel to theirs. There were others, however, for whom the view of America as a technical civilization provided the ingredients for a discourse of cultural anti-Americanism. The French word *américanisation* dates from those times. It was Baudelaire who, on the occasion of the 1855 Exposition Universelle de Paris, spoke of modern man, set on a course of technical materialism, as "tellement américanisé . . . qu'il a perdu la notion des différences qui caractérisent les phénomènes du monde physique et du monde moral, du naturel et du surnaturel [so americanized . . . that he has lost the sense of differences characterizing the phenomena of the physical and the moral world, of the natural and the supernatural]."⁹ The Goncourt brothers' *Journal,* from the time of the second exposition, in 1867, states: "L'exposition universelle, le dernier coup à ce qui est l'américanisation de la France [the universal exposition, the last blow in what is the americanization of France]."¹⁰ As these critics saw it, industrial progress ushered in an era where quantity would replace quality and where a mass culture feeding on standardization would erode established taste hierarchies. There are echoes of Tocqueville here, yet the eroding factor is no longer the egalitarian logic of a mass democracy but the logic of industrial progress. In both cases, however, whatever the precise link and evaluating angle, America had become a metonym for modernity.

Postwar French Views of American Modernity

If my interest is in "traveling theories," in the question of what happens to systems of critical analysis once they start functioning in a different intellectual setting, my approach may seem a little off.¹¹ After all, I have so far focused on "traveling theorists," trying to fathom what happened to their theoretical concerns once they had set foot in America. With the exception of Crèvecoeur, who was an expatriate, and Laboulaye, who never went to America, the other French observers of the American scene whom I will discuss were all visitors whose central interest was in the tenuous relation between democracy and modernization. America as a civilization that managed to combine political and economic liberalism served as a counterpoint to the France of their days, which was engaged on a course of economic modernization under the guidance of a tutelary autocracy. Their explorations of American life were always geared to assessing how their newly gained insights might apply to France. Their perspectives were always critical; they may have been liberals, yet their cultural standards in particular were cast in an aristocratic mold that led them to beware of mass democracy's erosive effects on the quality of cultural and intellectual life. To the extent that they published their views—and with the exception of Chambrun, they all did—they addressed a French audience with a view to informing a public debate concerning politics in France. America mostly served as an illustrative case that allowed them to make points of more general relevance.

In the post–World War II period, however, there is one clear case of a traveling theorist whose views have taken on a life of their own as a traveling theory. The case, of course, is that of Tocqueville. After a long period of decline, his reputation revived in the late 1930s. In 1938 the historian George W. Pierson retraced Tocqueville's steps in *Tocqueville and Beaumont in America.* In 1945 Knopf reprinted Tocqueville's classic text. Only then did he reach canonical status in America. In intellectual debate, in sociology, and in political science, his work would time and again serve as a treasure trove for insights that were recognized as highly topical. Thus in the 1950s, both consensus historians and social science theorists of pluralism returned to Tocqueville's discussions of the associative habits of Americans as a politically stabilizing factor; in the darker intellectual mood of the 1970s, Tocqueville's analysis of voter apathy and withdrawal from political life informed such American social critics of the day as Christopher Lasch and Richard Sennett.

More recently, Tocqueville—and Crèvecoeur—have appeared as key witnesses for the defense of the *E Pluribus Unum* view of American nationhood. In his spirited polemical treatise *The Disuniting of America*, Arthur Schlesinger Jr. joins the debate about multiculturalism and ethnicity in America.[12] According to Schlesinger, "a cult of ethnicity has arisen both among non-Anglo whites and among nonwhite minorities to denounce the idea of a melting pot, to challenge the concept of 'one people,' and to protect, promote, and perpetuate separate ethnic and racial communities."[13] In a world torn by ethnic conflict, Schlesinger cannot but see atavism in America's return to viewing ethnic roots as the defining criterion of its national existence. Crèvecoeur and Tocqueville, to Schlesinger, are the early authoritative voices affirming the very cosmopolitanism and modernity of America's project in nation building.

But Tocqueville and Crèvecoeur are the exceptions to my story. In the preceding I traced the emergence of a French discourse concerning modernity in America; I will continue that approach, now focusing on postwar French visitors, including one French expatriate. The focus, in other words, will be on traveling theorists rather than on traveling theories.

Of course, the global context in which France and the United States found themselves in the postwar era had changed drastically, affecting the sense of psychological distance that French intellectuals experienced toward the United States. From a distant fledgling civilization, intriguing precisely because it was remote, America had become the new hegemon on the world stage and a little too close for comfort in the eyes of many Europeans. With America's rise as an economic, cultural, and political force in the first half of the twentieth century, the interbellum writings—for instance, those of Georges Duhamel and André Siegfried in France and of like-minded cultural conservatives in other European countries—began to exhibit a new shrillness in their critical views about America, the urgency of a call to arms in defense of European cultural values. The reaction in their case was antimodern, directed against modernity as it presented itself in its American guise. They set a tone that would continue into the post–World War II era.

Through its victorious presence in Europe, America confronted Europeans with its mercurial modernity more strongly than ever before. Europeans now had to respond to the American challenge in more than one area. The response could move between rejection and reception, but it was never solely cultural. To a Europe in search of new directions, America held out the example and provided guidance in the economic field, emphasizing economic growth and industrial efficiency and weaning Europe away from its protectionist instincts and old-fashioned managerial traditions. Politically it sponsored the idea of a larger Atlantic community whose universe of discourse centered on democratic values and civil liberties. Militarily, in terms of collective security, it willingly entered into an "entangling alliance" under its hegemonic leadership, establishing a "Pax Americana" that—at least within its sphere of dominance—also worked to transcend age-old European rivalries. Finally, to return to the cultural domain, through its physical presence in Europe as much as through cultural artifacts such as Hollywood films, consumption goods, records, and advertising, America transmitted to Europe the tempting image of a mass-consumption society, the image of a "democracy of goods."

Given the plethora of options, people were often of more than two minds about the impact of American modernity. In search of cultural renewal, they could enthusiastically endorse the freedom they found in American mass culture or envy the informality and mobility of American social life while at the same time begrudging America's political dominance. Others could welcome American leadership in political and economic life while deploring the impact that American mass culture had on European societies. In addition, over time these positions could change and sometimes merge. A rejection of America in one area could then lead to a more general anti-Americanism.

An interesting case is that of Jean-Paul Sartre and Simone de Beauvoir. Both had visited the United States in the immediate postwar years, before the dividing line of the cold war had hardened. Both were on the political left, in a rather anarchist vein: they were as yet unaffiliated to a political party, and they did not vote. They were antiauthoritarian and anticapitalist. Yet both were fascinated by America. They loved jazz, Hollywood movies, and the great American modernists in literature. Both loved the metropolitanism of New York. Time and time again, however, the censorial voice of their left-wing conscience reined in their enthusiasm. There is an ambivalence to their early views about America that is often reminiscent of the older repertoire that I explored previously.

Thus Beauvoir, having established her left-wing credentials by saying that America is the country where capitalist oppression has most odiously triumphed, goes on in this vein: "Néanmoins, par-delà le bien et le mal, la vie avait là-bas quelque chose de gigantesque et de déchaîné qui nous fascinait [Nonetheless, beyond the good and the bad, life over there has something gigantic and unfettered, which fascinated us]."[14] In her choice of metaphors, using words such as *gigantic* and *unfettered,* she clearly evokes two faces of American modernity: the towering one of a technical civilization, proudly representing itself in its sky-scraping architecture (corporate as its auspices may be), and the one of America as empty space, sucking in Europeans while at the same time liberating them from the fetters of their home cultures.

Ever the dialectician, Sartre returns to old Tocquevillean ground when he tries to fathom how Americans manage to reconcile conformism and individualism: "Conditionné par une propagande qui n'est pas le fait de l'Etat mais de la société tout entière, encadré par une collectivité qui l'éduque constamment à être un Américain pur, l'individu agit naturellement comme tout le monde [Conditioned by a propaganda which emanates not from the state but from society as a whole, cast in the framework of a collectivity that educates him constantly in being a pure American, the individual acts naturally like all the others]." It allows the American to feel "à la fois le plus raisonnable et le plus national, c'est en se montrant le plus conformiste qu'il se sent le plus libre [to feel at the same time the most rational and the most national; in showing himself at his most conformist, he feels most free]."[15] This is not a totalitarian condition; rather, Sartre emphasizes the universalism of it all, open to everyone of whatever background and nationality. It is a "homeless" rationalism, reinforced and further universalized by the mobility of a mechanized society. Thus to Sartre, the Americans are "conformistes par la liberté, dépersonnalisés par rationalisme, identifiant dans un même culte la Raison universelle et leur Nation particulière [the Americans are conformists in liberty, depersonalized by rationalism, merging into one cult universal Reason and their particular Nation]."[16] Money and success, in this context, are not the mere product of cupidity. They are the symbolic means that let individuals "se poser, en face de la foule[,] comme une personne [present themselves, when faced with the others, as an individual person]."[17] Thus Americans can always hope to regain their autonomy and to reach an "individualisme presque nietzschéen que symbolisent les gratte-ciel dans le ciel clair de New York [an almost Nietzschean individualism symbolized by the skyscrapers in the clear sky of New York]."[18] This may not be exactly Crèvecoeur, yet there are similarities in the sense that individual autonomy is seen as a daring modernist endeavor.

At the same time, although Sartre here echoes Tocqueville's explorations of the tyranny of a majority in mass democracies, reflecting Tocqueville's darker, more critical passages, he also presents observations that are more in line with Tocqueville's positive views. Tocqueville once told John Stuart Mill that his true subject was the leveling of ranks and distinctions as a new principle of social order, and Sartre again shares his perspective. Thus he notes that the "signes extérieurs de la classe sont inexistants [the exterior signs of class are nonexistant]" and that there exists a "gentillesse vraiment humaine qui préside aux rapports entre les classes [a truly humane kindness that presides over the relations among classes]."[19]

Whereas in these early writings about America Sartre manages to keep a sense of distance and balance, Beauvoir, in her *L'Amérique au jour le jour,* tends more clearly toward criticism. Her attitude may be due to the fact that she came to America a year later, in 1947, when a climate of anticommunist repression was building. Her book contains many moments of rapture where the pace and energy of American life draw her along, yet throughout a censorial voice calls her back, a voice equally reminiscent of Marx and Tocqueville:

> Dans cette profusion de robes, de blouses, de jupes, de manteaux une Française aurait peine à faire un choix qui ne choquât pas son goût. Et puis on s'aperçoit bientôt que sous les papiers multicolores qui les enrobent, tous les chocolats ont le même goût de cacahuète, tous les best-sellers racontent la même histoire. Et pourquoi choisir un dentifrice plutôt qu'un autre? Il y a dans cette profusion inutile un arrière-goût de mystification. Voici mille possibilités ouvertes: mais c'est la même. Mille choix permis: mais tous équivalents. Ainsi le citoyen américain pourra consommer sa liberté à l'intérieur de la vie qui lui est imposée sans s'apercevoir que cette vie même n'est pas libre.

> [In this profusion of dresses, blouses, skirts, and coats, a French woman would be hard put to make a choice and not offend her taste. And then one begins to notice that underneath their multicolored wrappers all chocolates have the same taste of peanut, all bestsellers tell the same story. And why choose one toothpaste rather than another? There is an aftertaste of mystification in all this useless profusion. A thousand possibilities are open: yet they care all the same. A thousand choices allowed: all equivalent. Thus the American citizen will be able to consume his liberty inside the life that is imposed on him without so much as noticing that such a life itself is not free.][20]

Her critique of American conformism denounces America's vaunted republican liberty as a sham, its individual consumers as so many dupes of capitalism, and its industrial production as capable of producing nothing but spurious variety.

For Sartre, Beauvoir, and the French left-wing intelligentsia more generally, however, not until the 1950s would America assume its place in a Manichaean world as an empire of evil. Interestingly, from the point of view of traveling theories, Tocqueville returned to France with a vengeance. The rediscovery of his work in the United States had not only inspired the consensus view of a benign pluralism. His work had also influenced the social critic David Riesman, who, in *The Lonely Crowd,* returned to Tocqueville's theme of American conformism and presented the Americans of his day as "other-directed," as subordinate to peer-group guidance. Work by Riesman and other American critics, such as C. Wright Mills and William H. Whyte, led

Beauvoir to reject Americans as a "peuple de moutons" (a nation of sheep), conformist, and "extéro-conditionnés" (other-directed).[21]

* * *

It was not all Manichaeanism on the French left, however. Michel Crozier, a self-described "pro-American leftist," first visited the United States in 1946. A sociologist working mostly in the area of industrial sociology and human relations, he was well-connected with the American academic world. He, too, would return to Tocquevillean concerns with the working of the American republic. In 1980 he published *Le mal américain*.[22] Among his observations on the plight of America following its many setbacks, from the Kennedy assassination to the Tehran hostage crisis, several concern the role of interest groups. For Tocqueville, they fulfilled a crucial function for the preservation of republican order. As Crozier sees it, the United States today is no longer the America Tocqueville described. "Its voluntary associations have ceased to be a mainstay of a democracy constantly on the move but are now simply a means of self-defense for various interests. . . . This breakdown of community structures is what has made America a country full of anxiety."[23]

Published when it was, Crozier's gloomy analysis stands rather as an exception. Since the 1970s, views of America among the French intelligentsia had undergone a remarkable change for the better. Not only had one pole of intellectual attraction—Soviet Russia—lost its force, but America had redeemed itself through the way it handled its many torments. It had shown remarkable regenerative power as a republican order at the time of the Watergate crisis, and it also stood clearly as a model for international emulation in the 1980s, when it could claim renewed success in combining political and economic liberalism. Having shed their infatuation with the closed world of ideological thinking, French intellectuals were ready to appreciate the Americans' unideological cast of mind. America had regained its power to exhilarate culturally, politically, and economically.

In 1978, as almost a Crèvecoeur redivivus, another French aristocrat who had chosen to become an American published a personal memoir, *On Becoming American*.[24] Born Sanche de Gramont, he adopted the American alias of "Ted Morgan" (an anagram of de Gramont). It is an act of voluntary affiliation that illustrates the main theme of his book. American modernity in its humanist version, promising individual regeneration, is central to Morgan's narrative. "Americans are the true existentialists. An American is the sum of his undertakings. . . . He makes himself and is responsible for himself." Morgan asserts that "in old societies, people knew who they were, they were given cards of identity at birth, and they were expected to remain in their allotted compartments. In a new society, people asked themselves who they were and what they might become. It was a matter of finding one's natural place rather than an assigned place." Morgan is impressed by the eagerness with which Americans still join voluntary associations. Unlike Tocqueville, however, who had chosen to see these associations as a stabilizing force amid the buzzing energy of America, Morgan sees "pure process; it is an open-ended system. . . . We are a people in transit." Morgan thus appears to merge two older varieties of American modernity into one: its promise of individual regeneration and its existential qualities of being open-ended, empty space ever to be filled by new projects.[25]

The rediscovery of America as an existential counterpoint to Europe inspired more French authors. Edgar Morin may have set the tone in his *Journal de Californie,* published in 1970. Californian pop culture and 1960s counterculture are the background to a rapturous existential travelogue:

> Je ressens une grande félicité d'être en Californie . . . c'est aussi l'exaltation de me savoir et me sentir à l'intérieur de la tête chercheuse du vaisseau spatial terre, de vivre en témoin ce hic et nunc décisif de l'aventure anthropologique . . . me voici en mon milieu: là où se forgent des mondes nouveaux possibles, là où jaillissent les forces trophiques de l'humanité, là où fermente ce que dans l'exaltation je pourrais nommer le Génie biologique ou l'Etre-en-devenir-du-monde.
>
> [I feel great bliss being in California . . . it is also the exaltation of being inside the reconnaissance center of spaceship earth, of witnessing the decisive here-and-now of Man's adventure . . . here I am at home: here where new possible worlds take shape, where the guiding forces of humanity spring forth, where what in exaltation I might call the biological Genius is fermenting, a world in gestation.][26]

America as the command post of spaceship Earth: it is the ultimate version of America seen as the gateway to empty space. Morin's exalted views verge on the postmodern, where *Star Trek* and similar space imagery are more evocative of "America" than anything "real" and down to earth.

If there is such a thing as a postmodern rendition of America as the site of the modern, Jean Baudrillard's book *Amérique* comes close to filling that bill. In an era that has announced the death of the author, America has no more Founding Fathers. In an era of deconstructionism that has announced the reader's total freedom, "America" has become a text that anyone is free to read at will. Baudrillard uses this freedom to the fullest possible extent. America has become pure space, sidereal, a realm in which the imagination can roam free.

America may still offer a visiting European intellectual a shocking sense of alienation, but Baudrillard now appraises it as a fountain of youth, a sacred fount. To him, Europe has become mired in its heritage of intellectual rituals, caught in rigid conceptual frames, decadent, incapable of an unmediated, direct confrontation with reality. America offers the liberation from that conceptual imprisonment.

> What we lack is the inspiration and courage for what one might call the zero degree of culture, for the power of non-culture. . . . We will always remain nostalgic utopians, torn between the ideal and our reluctance to realize it. We declare everything to be possible, while never proclaiming its realization. Precisely the latter is what America claims to have achieved.

> It is we who think that everything culminates in its transcendence and that nothing exists without first having been thought through as concept. Not only do they [the Americans] hardly care for that at all, but they see the relationship in reverse. They want not to conceptualize reality but to realize the concept and to implement the ideas.[27]

Old echoes resound in this statement. Baudrillard, after all, is not the first to hold that America has had the audacity to implement what had been thought out and dreamed of in Europe. It has shed off the old Europe, burdened by history, caught up in unreal structures of thought. Thus, America could have become the authentic expression of modernity, while Europe, in Baudrillard's words, will never be more than its dubbed or subtitled version. But there is more to Baudrillard's argument than this. In a sense he seems to return to the 1960s, hankering for the libertarian rapture, the sense of instant gratification unmediated by the intellect that many at the time saw as the appeal of the counterculture. Even though he was on the left himself, as an ideologue he had missed out on the excitement of the moment. It took the disenchantment of the French left during the 1970s, their sense of ideological bankruptcy, for Baudrillard to become susceptible to the lure of American culture.

And once again, before our eyes, a romance unfolds, a game of cultural adultery in which many French intellectuals have indulged. They have a keen eye for all that is banal and vulgar in America, yet at the same time they more than anyone else are tempted by the vital élan, the shameless authenticity of American culture. These romances always have one basic plot. It is always a case of a tired, elderly European turning toward America in the hope of regeneration, if not rejuvenation. America is unspoiled, primitive, youthful. It is unaware of itself. It is just there. It is Eden before the fall. Europeans have tasted the forbidden fruit—they are obsessed by knowledge and reflection—yet hope to lose themselves in America. Baudrillard is in a sense a twentieth-century Crèvecoeur, reaffirming America's regenerative potential.

Both Baudrillard's book and Umberto Eco's *Travels in Hyperreality* put a remarkable twist to every argument made by the many critics of American mass culture. Whereas critics from Henry Adams on have deplored America's forsaking its historical spirituality, whereas they have seen the signs of a fall from grace precisely in the mindless entropy of consumerism, Baudrillard and Eco testify to a sense of exhilaration. Cities, traffic, highways—they are all as meaningless as America's deserts, but their impact is equally liberating. It is all utterly devoid of significance. It is just there, but in a rather complex way. Both Baudrillard and Eco speak of hyperreality. Reality has spawned its own replicas. Surrounded by phantom images of reality, one can no longer tell which is the real thing. America is just like Disneyland. Whether it is vulgar or sublime no longer matters. Those are European categories best left behind. One should undergo America as it presents itself, the only truly primitive society of our age, a utopia become reality.

Eco at one point refers to America as the "last beach" of European culture.[28] It will all still be there after the real heritage has crumbled to dust in its countries of origin. For America to fulfill this salvage mission, it has to treat Europe's culture in a highly (post?) modernist fashion, treating all of it as one large *objet trouvé,* recasting, duplicating, multiplying, cross-breeding, and mass-marketing it. On the whole, Eco's tone and choice of words are slightly more critical; for example, he quotes Luis Marin on Disneyland as degenerate utopia: in this world of the fake, "what is falsified is our will to buy, which we take as real, and in this sense Disneyland is really the quintessence of consumer ideology."[29] Baudrillard is well beyond such criticism and seems to revel in alienation. Freely floating through America's universe, an escapee from European gravity, he offers a reader's guide to America's phantom images. He moves from image to image with great metaphorical virtuosity. At one point he calls America "a special effect." It leaves the reader slightly puzzled. Who is behind the effect? The French book cover does not help. It gives us two names: "Amérique" and "Jean Baudrillard." Is it Baudrillard who allows us to perceive America in its many phantom images, or is it the other way around? I tend toward the latter option. America becomes one wide projection screen for Baudrillard's fantasies of self-liberation. In one ongoing stream of aphoristic, often highly imaginative, but totally noncommittal snippets, he takes us on his psychological journey. Strangely, however, he still seems to be trapped in habits he tells us he has quit. With all his metaphors and associations, he is still busy weaving America into an argument and a structure of concepts. He is still quintessentially the European, involving America into a world of preoccupations that are typically those of a French intellectual.

America: The Web Site of Modernity

In our present age of globalization, with communication systems such as the Internet spanning the globe, national borders have become increasingly porous. They no longer serve as cultural barriers that one can raise at will to fend off cultural intrusions from abroad. It is increasingly hard to erect them as a cultural "Imaginot" line in defense of a national cultural identity. Yet old instincts die hard. In a typically preemptive move, France modernized its telephone system in the 1980s, introducing a communication network (the Minitel) that allowed people to browse and shop around. It was a network much like the later World Wide Web. The French system was national, however, and stopped at the border. At the time it was a bold step forward, but it put France at a disadvantage later on, when the global communications revolution got under way. The French were slower than most of their European neighbors to connect to the Internet. And that may have been precisely the point.

At every moment in the recent past when the liberalization of trade and flows of communication was being discussed in international meetings, the French raised the issue of cultural protection. They have repeatedly insisted on exempting cultural goods, such as film and television, from the logic of free trade. They insist on protective quotas for trade in this area and on the sovereign right of national governments to set national content criteria for television and cinema programming and to subsidize its production. The subtext for these defensive strategies is not so much the fear of opening France's borders to the world but rather fear of letting American culture wash across the country. Given America's dominant role in world markets for popular culture, as well as its quasi-imperial place in the communications web of the Internet, globalization appears to many French people as a Trojan horse. For many of them, globalization means Americanization.

With the recent attempts at starting a new round for the further liberalization of world trade, France was up in arms again. The French minister of culture published a piece in the French daily newspaper *Le Monde,* again making the French case for a cultural exemption from free trade rule. A week later one of France's leading intellectual lights, Pierre Bourdieu, joined the fray in a piece also published in *Le Monde.*[30] It was the text of an address delivered on October 11, 1999, to the International Council of the Museum of Television and Radio in Paris. He chose to address his audience as representing the "true masters of the world," those whose control of global communication networks provides them not political or economic power but what Bourdieu calls "symbolic power," that is, power over people's minds and imaginations gained through cultural artifacts—books, films, and television programs—that they produce and disseminate. This power is increasingly globalized through international market control, mergers and consolidations, and a revolution in communications technology. Bourdieu briefly considers the fashionable claim that the newly emerging structures, aided by the digital revolution, will bring endless cultural diversity, catering to the cultural demands of specific niche markets. Bourdieu rejects this out of hand; what he sees is an increasing homogenization and vulgarization of cultural supply driven by a logic that is purely commercial, not cultural. Aiming at profit maximization, market control, and ever larger audiences, the "true masters of the world" gear their products to the largest common denominator that defines their audience. What the world gets is more soap operas, expensive blockbuster movies organized around special effects, and books whose success is measured by sales, not by intrinsic cultural merit.

It is a Manichaean world that Bourdieu conjures up. True culture, as he sees it, is the work of individual artists who view their audience as being posterity, not the throngs at the box office. In the cultural resistance that artists have over centuries put up against the purely commercial view of their work, they have managed to carve out a social and cultural domain whose organizing logic is at right angles to that of the economic market. As Bourdieu puts it: "Reintroducing the sway of the 'commercial' in realms that have been set up, step by step, against it means endangering the highest works of mankind." Quoting Ernst Gombrich, Bourdieu says that when the "ecological prerequisites" for art are destroyed, art and culture will not be long in dying. After voicing a litany of cultural demise in film industries in a number of European counties, he laments the fate of a cultural radio station about to be liquidated "in the name of modernity," a victim to Nielson ratings and the profit motive.

In the name of modernity: never in his address does Bourdieu rail against an America as the site of such dismal modernity, yet the logic of his argument is reminiscent of many earlier French views of American culture, a culture emanating from a country that never shied from merging the cultural and the commercial (or, for that matter, the cultural and the democratic). Culture, as Bourdieu defends it, is typically high culture. Interestingly, though, unlike many earlier French criticisms of an American culture that reached Europe under commercial auspices, Bourdieu's defense is not of national cultures, more specifically the French national identity, threatened by globalization. As he argues, the choice is between "the kitsch products of commercial globalization" and those of an international world of creative artists in literature, visual arts, and cinematography, a world that knows many constantly shifting centers.

Yet blood runs thicker than water. Great artists, and Bourdieu lists several writers and filmmakers, "would not exist the way they do without this literary, artistic, and cinematographic international whose seat is [present tense] situated in Paris. No doubt because there, for strictly historical reasons, the microcosm of producers, critics, and informed audiences, necessary for its survival, has long since taken shape and has managed to survive."[31] Bourdieu manages to have his cake and eat it, too, arrogating a place for Paris as the true seat of a modernity in high culture. In his construction of a global cultural dichotomy lurks an established French parti pris. More than that, how-

ever, his reading of globalization as Americanization by stealth blinds him
to more subtle interpretations of the way French intellectuals and artists
before him have discovered, adapted, and adopted forms of American commercial culture, such as Hollywood movies.

In his description of the social universe that sustains a cultural international in Paris, he mentions the infrastructure of art-film houses, of a *cinémathèque,* of eager audiences and informed critics, such as those writing for
the *Cahiers du cinéma.* He seems oblivious to the fact that in the 1950s precisely this potent ambience for cultural reception led to the French discovery of Hollywood movies as true examples of the "cinéma d'auteur," of true
film art showing the hand of individual makers, now acclaimed masters in
the pantheon of film history. Their works are held and regularly shown in
Bourdieu's vaunted *Cinémathèque* and his art-film houses. They were made
to work, like much other despised commercial culture coming from America, within frameworks of cultural appropriation more typically French, or
European, than American. They may have been misread in the process as
works of individual "auteurs" more than as products of the Hollywood studio system. That they were the products of a cultural infrastructure totally
at variance with the one Bourdieu deems essential may have escaped French
fans at the time. It certainly escapes Bourdieu now. This should only make
us more intellectually cautious before we jump to a facile reading of commercial culture as necessarily a threat to things we hold dear.

10. America and the European Sense of History

The ways in which Europeans have tried to make sense of America constitute a special chapter in the European history of ideas. What first strikes us in the bewildering variety of European readings of America is the recurring attempt to formulate the critical differences that set America apart from European nations in terms of historical experience and cultural conventions. America is never seen as purely sui generis, as constituting an alien entity to be fathomed in terms of an inner logic wholly its own. There is always the sense of America as a stray member of a larger family, a descendant from Europe. If it belongs to the *genus proximum* of Western civilization, the point then is to define the *differentia specifica* according to an almost Linnaean taxonomy. European conventions have always served as the yardstick, implied or explicit, in European attempts to uncover the rules of transformation that had cut America adrift from the European mainstream. This intellectual quest for the crucial difference is hardly ever entirely disinterested, however. More than merely an academic exercise, the exploration of the American difference typically involves an existential urgency. Europe serves as the standard for measuring difference, so that the outcome of such measurement is always geared to a discussion of its potential impact on Europe. In other words, there is always a triangulation going on, in the sense that the reflection on America as a counterpoint to European conventions functions within a larger reflection on Europe's history and destiny.

This claim may seem to intellectualize the repertoire of European views of America unduly, so I hasten to add that vernacular, or popular, versions exist alongside the more intellectually articulate versions. Widely shared and informing everyday conversations, they may seem more like unreflected stereotypes, providing ready answers to those trying to make sense of the many

Americas that reach them in their daily lives through modern mass-communication media. Yet we should not exaggerate the difference between the intellectual and vernacular views of America. Both levels effect a triangulation, and though the vernacular view is less articulate than the intellectual, the two are similar insofar as they reflect people making sense of America in ways that are meaningful to their own lives. Their constructions of America, shared with peer groups, focus on American counterpoints that then help them to develop individual and group identities different from models and standards prevailing in their home setting.

There are yet other ways in which we can explore similarities underlying the European views of America. If we look at them as so many narrative accounts of perceived differences, they appear as repertoires of metaphors. Again, the metaphors are many, yet a much simpler deep structure underlies them. In a recent publication I proposed reducing these repertoires to essentially three underlying dimensions that are remarkably stable irrespective of time, national culture, or class.[1] These three main dimensions have repeatedly served to structure a discourse of cultural difference, of "us" (people in Europe) versus "them" (the Americans). One of these three main dimensions is spatial, portraying America as flat, as reducing European verticality, hierarchy, and sense of high versus low, cultural heights, and depth to purely horizontal vectors playing themselves out on the surface, exteriorizing what to Europeans is the inner life of the soul. The second dimension is temporal; it involves a contrast that casts Americans as lacking the European sense of the past as a living presence. The third dimension represents all those views that portray American culture as lacking the European sense of holism, of organic cohesion; Americans in this view are never loath to take the European cultural heritage apart, dissecting it into component parts and recombining them in total irreverence to what has grown in historical and spatial specificity. These three dimensions form the discursive formation of Europe's "occidentalism," the underlying structure of meanings, as Raymond Williams called it, capable of spawning an endless number of meaningful sentences and individual utterances ranging from the highly subtle and nuanced to the coarsely stereotypical. Nonetheless, despite all variation at the level of explicit statements, the motifs they use echo repertoires that are widely shared among the larger public and are of remarkable historical stability.

Three further points should be made here. The metaphorical repertoires of European occidentalism were often used to reject America and its culture, but not always. When European intellectuals elevated America as an example for Europeans to emulate, the same metaphors could serve their expressions of praise. Similarly, at the vernacular level, readings of American culture as a counterpoint to established European cultural modes have used the same metaphorical dimensions to represent America, yet the general appreciation changed from rejection to reception. Developments in cultural studies during the last fifteen years or so have helped to shed light on processes of popular or mass-culture transmission and reception and on the way that American culture has influenced the processes of identity formation among younger generations elsewhere. During the twentieth century these generations have chosen not simply to reproduce their national cultures—or at least parental cultures as imposed on them; rather, they have often selectively appropriated American popular culture for acts of cultural rebellion and resistance. What needs further exploration in this context is the way in which European constructions of America have been a dialectical exercise in which the real discussion was about the national identity of their home countries in the larger context of a debate about Europe. When national elites or non-elite groups use references to "America"—or to "Europe," for that matter—we have to see them in the light of infranational discussions concerning the contours of a national identity, whether French, German, or British.

Concerning the second point, I should remind the reader that given my focus on Europe in this chapter, I may seem to imply that Europeans' narrative constructions of America are in some way typically European. This is certainly not the point of my exercise in exploring the deep structure underlying views of outsiders who find themselves confronted with the challenges posed by an expansive American civilization. As I have argued at greater length elsewhere,[2] the three-dimensional underlying structure of meanings seems to hold for any views of rival cultures seen as overbearing yet alien. All defensive explorations of the authentic core values of cultures threatened by vigorous rivals have a logic to them that casts the rival civilization as lacking depth and authenticity, as being an exterior veneer without historical rootedness and legitimacy. The same deep structure of cultural defense and indictment plays its role whether the case is that of an emerging German bourgeoisie fending off the appeal of French civilization in the late eighteenth century; African intellectuals exploring their Africanness, their *négritude,* in the face of an overbearing European mode of civilization; or Latin Americans confronted with the inroads of an American civilization radiating from the United States. The defensive quest for authenticity seems always to hinge on a diagnosis of the rival culture as lacking depth and soul, as being devoid of a sense of historical growth and organic wholeness and integrity. I should also point out that the Europe emerging in my text is a Europe as imagined by intellectuals in countries that I have studied in relative depth, countries such as France, Italy, Germany, England, and the Netherlands. I am insufficiently knowledgeable about Europes dreamed up by intellectuals in Eastern European settings in their reflections on the American difference. It may well be the case, however, that Western Europe has been more directly confronted with the American challenge and has felt more directly urged to respond to it.

Third, I should emphasize that however stable the discursive formation of European views concerning America may be, it is a dormant resource. In the continuing European-American encounter, some moments are more likely to trigger a European interpretative response than others. Thus, for instance, the 1920s were not just like any other preceding decade in the way that America forced itself on the European consciousness. In the wake of World War I the United States had literally, even physically, become a presence in Europe, inducing Europeans to a renewed and urgent reflection on the American identity. America's intervention in the war, the presence of its armies in Europe, and the massive advent of its mass culture in following years allow us to look at World War I as a watershed. The war forced Europeans to reconsider their traditions, their economic, social, and political plight—in short, their collective destinies—but they could no longer do this without reflecting on America as well. There may be continuities in the ways that Europeans have made sense of America, but history has also known abrupt leaps in the relative distance that Europeans have felt toward America, like floodgates opening.

In the following I take this argument further and highlight the intricate interrelations between these distinct levels of response to the cultural difference presented by America but perceived and given meaning by Europeans. I will do this first by focusing on the critical period of the interbellum, analyzing ways in which European intellectuals used America in their critical reflections on the plight of Europe and their nation-states. I will then change perspective, moving toward the post–World War II period, focusing not on the elite but on the way in which America affected nonelite groups in their senses of self and of history.

The Interbellum: Anguished European Intellectuals and Their Views of America

"I confess that in America I have wished to see more than just America. I wanted to find an image there of democracy itself, of its inclinations, its character, its prejudices, its passions; I wanted to get to know it, if only at least to find out what hopes or fears it holds for us." These words from Tocqueville's preface to *Democracy in America* aptly summarize an attitude that is more generally characteristic of European observers of the American scene. Whether their interest was cultural, political, economic, or social, their observations more often than not were inspired by a sense, anguished or hopeful, that America could provide Europeans with a view of their own future. This sense was made more acute by the intimation not only that America offered a glimpse of Europe's future, to be perceived by merely juxtaposing American settings to conditions in Europe, but also that it would be the historical agent of Europe's future. In their more lucid and detached moments, some observers were willing to grant that the United States and Europe were set on a parallel course of social and cultural transformation, with the former being further advanced along that road, but even these writers often assumed that America would have already left its typical imprint on the forms of the future before they reached Europe. All the more reason, then, for those of this cast of mind to watch American developments closely: it would leave them better equipped to fend off the threat of Europe's Americanization and to prepare strategies of cultural resistance.

During the interwar years many voices in Europe called for a defense of Europe's cultural heritage, defined in terms either of national identities or of a larger entity called "Europe." As I have argued elsewhere,[3] the line dividing the two levels of argument was never neat. Responding to a challenge as massive as the one posed by America clearly called for a canvass equally large: Europe. In that sense European critics of American culture may ironically have had much for which to thank the Americans. The American challenge led them to argue their defensive case in terms of a larger construct, called Europe, so that their idea of Europe and Europeanism formed the dialectical mirror image of their views of America and reinforced their observations on the contours of their own larger frame of identification and affiliation. Nevertheless, even when European intellectuals did not argue their case in terms of clearly national contours, rising to the defense of national cultures and national identities, a discourse cast in terms of national concerns and modes of reflection was never far below the surface. Their arguments thus invoked various Europes, each a thinly veiled version of a hallowed national identity. Whereas French critics of American culture and civilization elevated a view of Europe that showed the typically French preoccupations with individual creativity and craftsmanship, German critics tended to favor a view of Europe in a more collectivist vein, of the *Volk* seen as the carrier of a collective *Kultur*.

In a previous chapter I referred to André Siegfried, who evoked a larger European canvass as typically represented by France but at the same time deconstructed his view by conceiving of Germany as truly a country and a culture more like America. Unsubtle as Siegfried may have been in this passage, it is a good example of the kind of triangulation that I am exploring. Gauging the nature of American culture with a view to resisting it more successfully, European critics were torn between defensive positions centering on their national cultural setting and those appealing to a larger European frame of reference. In smaller European countries, such as the Netherlands, the latter point of orientation may have come more naturally to the minds of critics of American culture, yet even in their case the plight of their national culture was always at least an implied concern. The Dutch historian

Johan Huizinga may be a good case in point. For one thing, in his reflections on America, he was never solely the historian in an Olympian role of detached observer. He was rather a historian in the role of intellectual, aware of his public calling to probe and make sense of historical trends as they affected the lives of his contemporaries. In addition, and this is a point of direct relevance to my argument, he was a man who throughout his work performed a continuing triangulation. When he wrote about Dutch culture, he explored it as a variant of European culture, trying to define its specificity. When he evoked life in Europe on the eve of the Renaissance, he did so with a view to producing a picture of a European culture that European countries had abandoned under the impact of larger forces of modernization. When he wrote about America, either as a historian or as an astute observer of its contemporary scene, he did so with European or Dutch culture at the back of his mind. Finally, in his later, darker musings on contemporary history's losing form, America is the unnamed site where he had earlier seen these forces of entropy at work. In the following paragraphs I explore a little more deeply the uses that Huizinga made of America in what were truly reflections on the plight of European culture in the interwar years.

Huizinga's Triangulations

On his return from his only visit to the United States, Huizinga expressed himself thus: "Strange: among us Europeans who were travelling together in America . . . there rose up repeatedly this pharisaical feeling: we all have something that you lack; we admire your strength but we do not envy you. Your instrument of civilisation and progress, your big cities and your perfect organisation, only make us nostalgic for what is old and quiet, and sometimes your life seems hardly to be worth living, not to speak of your future."[4] The statement resonates with the ominous foreboding that "your future" might well read as "our future," and indeed, what is only implied here would come out more clearly in Huizinga's more pessimistic later writings, when America became a mere piece of evidence in his case against contemporary history's loss of form. Thus his book *In the Shadows of Tomorrow* (1935) contains the following sweeping indictment: "The number, so it was said, washed across the individual; the mass dragged the individual along, defenseless, and lowered him to a level that always was the largest common denominator of the more simple and coarser features, while leveling and washing away the more complex and 'higher' expressions of the individual. New regimes could stimulate these coarsening trends and use for their own purposes such negative feelings like rancor, vengefulness, and cruelty."[5] Still later, in an essay written when World War II already raged across Europe, he would once again connect this more general sense of cultural decline to America: "The modern world is becoming more and more accustomed to thinking in numbers. America has hitherto been more addicted to this, perhaps, than Europe. . . . Only the number counts, only the number expresses thought."[6]

Huizinga may have inveighed against an obnoxious Americanism, against an "America" in quotation marks, yet he could not be mistaken as a mouthpiece for a vulgar anti-Americanism. He was too subtle minded for that, forever aware of the counterargument, of ambiguity; he was also too open to the real America as a historical given to relinquish the mental reserve of the quotation mark. The Huizinga quotation from his book of travel observations, which was already full of ambivalence, continues: "And yet, it is *we* that have to be the Pharisees, for theirs is the love and the confidence. Things must be different than we think." What is striking in this rejection of what Europe was wont to call Americanism is the intellectual sense of wonder, even admiration, and of an affinity with and appreciation for another variety of Americanism, that heritage of high-minded ideals that had inspired much of American history. Thus, in his 1935 essay on the Dutch cast of mind, Huizinga did ponder the onslaught of ominous trends of a machinelike organization of social and political life—the mechanization of life, he called it— trends that he had earlier seen as typifying life in America.[7] At the same time, however, he saw a countervailing force in Dutch virtues of tolerance and a sense of liberty, which had formed the Dutch nation around its myth of origin in a historic struggle for freedom and independence. It had set the nation apart as a "noble part of Western Europe," finding its center of gravitation across the sea. The Netherlands found its partners in the Atlantic world, where freedom was still preserved. In its westward orientation "lay the strength and *raison d'être* of our existence," as Huizinga saw it.[8]

Nonetheless, Huizinga's attempts at triangulation, casting America as the pure type representing more general forces of social transformation, clearly employ the repertoire of metaphors that were current among critics of American culture during the interbellum. He did in fact use language that others put in the service of a more facile anti-Americanism. The previous quotations already provide clear examples of the metaphoric deep structure of a European discourse casting America as the counterpoint to European cultural traditions. When in America Huizinga longed for "things old and quiet," the triangulation may well have implied the monastic, medieval Europe with which Huizinga strongly affiliated. He may well have felt similarly estranged from the Europe of his time, yet there was more of a living past, a sense of connection to the forms of earlier European history that America could never provide. His 1926 collection of travel observations relates one such moment of epiphany, reminiscent—ironically—of Henry Adams's affiliation with the European Middle Ages. While ranting about the banality of the cultural forms that Americans used to shape their cultural consumption, Huizinga pauses to reminisce on a few hours spent in Cologne, between trains. Contemporary Cologne aggravated him. The holy city on the Rhine had become ugly and banal (not unlike, Huizinga seems to imply, the America of his day). Leaving the indifferent street life behind him, however, in the semidarkness of a church where mass was being celebrated, Huizinga suddenly realized what a true ritual is, what it represents as a cultural value and a cultural form. It is like an act of communion with a past in which these things were the essence of life to all.[9]

Observations such as these fall among a repertoire of metaphors that involve time, casting an America that critically lacks a sense of the past as the antithesis to a Europe where the present is meaningfully related to life in the past. Huizinga's other remarks quoted previously illustrate a second metaphorical dimension, one that contrasts America and Europe in terms of spatial images. America is typically seen as the country eroding European cultural heights and sense of depth. It typically does so by reducing quality to quantity, intrinsic value to exchange value, or individual difference to the uniformity of numbers. Huizinga's observation that, in America and increasingly in the Old World as well, only the number is seen as capable of expressing thought is in a sense a mild form of the more pejorative European view that Americans reduce everything to dollars. Other variations in this second, spatial repertoire point to the exteriority of life in America, a life literally on the surface, shallow, lacking depth, and devoid of the European sense of the tragic.

Huizinga's contemporary, Oswald Spengler, in his *Jahre der Entscheidung* (Years of decision), argued along similar lines, but with greater dramatic emphasis. Highlighting the European sense of *Tiefe* (depth) and *Seele* (soul), as well as the element of true historical tragedy, he actually merged two metaphorical dimensions, the spatial and the temporal, into one: he connected the shallowness of life in America to its lacking a sense of true *historical* tragedy. Others, following a later world war, would have a similar hunch. Albert Camus, following his 1946 visit to the United States, had this observation: "The afternoon with students. They don't feel the real problem; however their nostalgia is evident. In this country where everything is done to prove that life isn't tragic, they feel something is missing. The great effort is pathetic, but one must reject the tragic *after* having looked at it, not before."[10] At about the same time Jean-Paul Sartre made similar observations on the absence of a tragic sense of life in America. The country, for all its blithe optimism, struck him as tragic in a rather pathetic way precisely because of this absence. In his early postwar study of European views of America, André Visson, an expatriate Frenchman, already commented on the ironies of this peculiar complaint by European intellectuals. There is indeed a strange psychological mechanism at work among European intellectuals who tend to pride themselves on their tragic sense of life rather than admit to feelings of collective guilt about Europe's suicidal orgies in two world wars. They turned feelings of envy and inferiority toward America, the country that had twice saved Europe from its worst excesses, into a sense of intellectual superiority. The contrast between the splendor of life in a victorious America and the miseries of war-torn Europe may have been too much to confront directly. Only rarely do we come across an unmediated expression of this contrast. Camus comes close to putting it into words: "I am literally stupefied by the circus of lights. I am just coming out of five years of night, and this orgy of violent lights gives me for the first time the impression of a new continent. An enormous, 50-foot-high Camel billboard: a G.I. with his mouth wide open blows enormous puffs of *real* smoke."[11] According to Visson, Sartre, like many other European intellectuals, seems to have been convinced that Americans are fundamentally unhappy. Sartre—and Visson quotes him—met Americans who, "though conventionally happy, suffer from an obscure *malaise* to which no name can be given, who are tragic through fear of being so, through that local absence of the tragic in them and around them."[12] Clearly, however, the perception of Americans as being essentially unhappy because they are unable to rise above their collective mad dash for happiness is as old as Tocqueville's observations on "the sentiments of Americans."[13] Equally clearly, observers of cultural difference—outsiders trying to look in—can scarcely help but translate their experience of outsidership into the language of quasi-inside reports. It is small wonder, then, that never having been on the inside, they tend to report on voids and absences. Never having probed much beyond the surface, all they find worth mentioning is that the "other" culture has nothing but surface to offer. In all such cases, observations *from* the outside are no more than observations *of* the outside.

At times Huizinga seemed to be aware of the metaphorical quality of his exercise in measuring the difference between America and Europe along dimensions of polar opposites. Thus, the diary he kept while traveling in the Unites States, published posthumously, contains this observation, made almost literally in passing: "In the morning from Philadelphia to Baltimore. The landscape has something light, something *ingénu, sans conséquence,* lacking depth, *as if one dimension were missing.* At times everything here makes that impression. As if, orbiting in a sphere around the essence of things, one is suddenly moved out to a more distant, wider sphere, at higher speed but more remote."[14] Simply watching a landscape from a train, he must have become aware of the deeper logic underlying his attempts to order his observations of critical differences and contrasts between America and Europe. Otherwise, taken literally, his hunch that American landscapes lack a vertical dimension does not make much sense. Nevertheless, he was never fully aware of the full range of dimensions he used in making sense of the American difference.

So far I have uncovered two dimensions in Huizinga's order of observations, the spatial and the temporal. These dimensions are probably the two most commonly found in European constructions of America, triggered much in the way that stereotypes are, like ready-made categories of observation and interpretation. As I argued previously, they are more an indication of the facile leap made by outsiders posing as vicarious insiders than the result of any imaginative attempt at interpreting differences in terms of the inner logic of the other society, the one under intrigued scrutiny. Things may well be different with the third dimension of metaphors, which conceive of America as lacking the European sense of the organic cohesion of cultural forms and styles. Not only do Americans tend to discard the established European hierarchies, which rank cultural forms in terms of high versus low; not only do they irreverently recycle the European repertoires in their production, distribution, appreciation, and consumption of culture, merging high culture and mass culture while doing so. In addition, every level of their culture, whether in their adoptions of European forms and styles of high art or in more technical areas of production for the market, displays a spirit of blithe and irreverent bricolage that does not shrink from taking things apart and putting them together again in different forms put to different purposes.

Huizinga may have been at his most astute in exploring this difference in the mental and cultural habitus of the Americans. At times his appreciation of the difference could be highly positive, as in his attempts to account for the radically American nature of authors he liked, such as Emerson and Whitman. As he argued, they *had* to differ from European standards; there was no way they could hope to rival European authors by trying to emulate the artistic forms developed in Europe. These forms had grown in Europe, in temporal and spatial specificity, and could be of no use for expressing American thought and creativity. Innovating American authors had to experiment with formlessness. At other moments, however, similar perceptions led Huizinga to make more critical judgments inspired by an overall sense of a cultural degeneration, a sense that America had lost things valued highly in Europe. Huizinga was never solely the detached observer, particularly not in his more anguished perceptions. Europe was always foremost on his mind as the cultural domain likely to be tainted by trends observed in America.

These concerns were more central to his second book about America than to his first. Examples abound. American journalism, for instance, typified this fragmenting approach to the news, cutting its meaningful links to a larger history unfolding. As he saw it, the fragmentation of the news, the separation of current events from their historical context, and the reduction of the news to, as Huizinga put it, "slogan, the brief, catchy phrase," all constituted "a regression of culture." They all resulted from America's being a mass democracy and would therefore, in due course, come to other mass democra-

cies as well, a clear case of parallel developments, with Europe following closely on the heels of America. Interestingly, however, Huizinga also connected
these trends as observed in America to a strictly American background factor, the "anti-metaphysical cast of mind" prevalent there. This mentality was
the lasting heritage of Enlightenment rationalism, which had entrenched
itself more firmly in America than anywhere else. "Do we not feel as if placed
back in the eighteenth century?" Huizinga wondered. He continued: "The
anti-metaphysical cast of mind naturally implies an anti-historical one. In
spite of a flourishing and superbly organized practice of history (as an academic endeavor) America's mind is thoroughly anti-historical. A historiography that in the march of humankind wants to see purely the theodicy of
progress is not the true kind."[15] As he put it elsewhere, the American is too
much directed toward the present and the future to be open to the mystery
of the past.[16]

Anyone who lives totally in the present has no sense of historical meaning and context. Nor will such a person have a sense of organic cohesion.
Indeed, anything that can be conceived in terms of internal coherence has a
historical dimension, a historicist specificity in its configuration of constituent elements. This takes us to the third metaphorical repertoire Europeans
used to express American cultural defects as they saw them. Once again
Huizinga provides us with a telling example. When introduced to the Dewey Decimal System, the system for organizing library holdings then recently
adopted in America, he recognized a quintessentially American impulse at
work. As he saw it, time and time again living organic connections in the body
of human knowledge were sacrificed to the need for classification. The human mind had been made subservient to the tyranny of the decimal system.
It confirmed his intimations concerning the antimetaphysical bent of the
Americans and their inclination toward subjecting the spiritual realm to the
dictates of technical organization.[17]

* * *

Clearly, then, in his attempts to make sense of America as a cultural counterpoint to Europe, Huizinga used the repertoire of Europe's language of
"occidentalism." His reflections were geared in part toward gauging the inner logic, the cultural modus operandi, of a civilization intriguingly at odds
with European conventions and habits of mind. His more central concern,
however, particularly in his later writings, was American culture's portent for
Europe's destiny. In his musings on American civilization, Huizinga typically
takes this larger view. He perceives in America the first signs of a general
process of civilization: "Organization becomes mechanization; that is the fatal
moment of the modern history of civilization."[18] His broader view does not
make his mood of cultural demise any less acute, yet he is aware that with-

out mechanization there will be no civilization at all: "The process of refining culture is inseparable from that of instrumentalization."[19] The process, however, has two distinct effects. It has a power to bind and a power to liberate, and ("taking America as the most perfect example") the balance appears to lean too much toward the first, toward subservience and bondage rather than toward freedom.[20] Huizinga goes on to ponder whether the instrumentalization of life might not work out differently in America and in Europe: "Organization in the sense of standardization means the establishing of a uniform and well-defined technical nomenclature. . . . to the American it constitutes not only an individual need rather than a necessary evil, it also constitutes a cultural ideal. . . . Everyone familiar with their sense of conformity and collective identity will realize this. The American *wants* to be equal to his neighbor. He feels spiritually safe only in the normatively ordained, not to mention the fact that the latter also implies 'efficiency.'"[21] Huizinga is typically wavering here between two modes of interpretation. He uses a distancing strategy when he tries to link the more ominous implications of the trend toward mechanization to character traits that he deems typically American. At the same time, however, he reminds the reader that he is taking America "as the most perfect example," implying that his cultural critique applies more generally.

There is a similar ambivalence in Huizinga's reading of another ominous cultural trend perceived in America, yet another of more general portent: the shift away from a culture centering on the word toward one centering on the image. Huizinga's views on film are a good case in point. They reflect the mixed feelings he had about America. At one point in his 1927 collection of travel impressions, he accepts film as an art form for which a new muse or patron saint would have to be found. He instantly qualifies this position, however, pointing out that the "movies" (as he put it in his Dutch text) are a mere illustration, albeit the most important, of our civilization's ominous shift from reading to watching, from the printed word toward "ideographic" information. Yet again Huizinga was ambivalent. Pondering the impact of film as he had witnessed it in America, he was aware of its democratic potential. Film is Whitmanesque in its capacity to restore a democratic vista, allowing people a comprehensive, if vicarious, view of the variety of life in their society. At the same time, however, Huizinga's more pessimistic views of the mechanization of contemporary culture qualified these high hopes. As one of the new mass media, film, like radio, aims at a mass audience, catering to its average taste. Film tends to simplify and stereotype its message. It might widen people's views of society, but only spuriously so, through a flattening of the social and cultural landscape. Film "habituates the nation from high to low to one common view of life. Due to its limited means of expression, its highlighting of what is external, and the need to appeal to a general audience, film shuts off entire areas of spiritual activity. It imposes a limited number of standard views of life that will eventually become the mass view."[22] Thus, film was one of the contemporary forces of cultural erosion at work in America. As an art form, visual though it might be, it would never create lasting, self-contained forms, such as sculpture or painting. Given its narrative flow Huizinga saw film more like literature or drama. Again, however, geared as it is to a mass market, film, like radio, can capture its audience compellingly yet only transiently, for fleeting moments. Unlike drama or literature, it can never cause the audience to pause and reflect.

As mixed as Huizinga's feelings about film may have been, he managed to define the inner force of the medium in a way that inspires critical reflection on film until the present day. Even today the academic study of film is centrally involved with the intriguing exchange between the imaginary world of the silver screen and the sense of identity of the individuals watching it. A process of identification with the shadows on the screen leads viewers to step outside themselves. Huizinga made the following perceptive observation:

> [Film] shows the urban dweller country life, or at least an image of it, it shows the countryman urban life, it gives the poor a view of luxury and the rich one of misery, all highly stylized so as to make it easy to appropriate. Thus film rather works to conciliate than to sharpen class resentment. The repeated illusion of the life of the rich affords the poor a certain communion with luxury and refinement; its fantasy image becomes a part of their daily existence. In the hero the audience exalts itself, and, beyond this, film stars off the screen offer it a new model for emulation, a novel assurance of options open to everyone.[23]

Interestingly, in these musings concerning film as a modern medium for the mechanical reproduction of culture, and thus as an illustration of the wider trend of the mechanization of contemporary civilization, we can see Huizinga noting a tension between the promise of a democratic art and its fake realization as mass culture. Not only is he torn between two modes of appreciating American culture, or two forms of Americanism, experimenting with new forms of a democratic culture while at the same time subverting them through a subservience to the dictates of a mass market for cultural consumption. In addition, passages such as these on film show an awareness of the media through which American cultural influences are transmitted to audiences elsewhere. It is one thing to declare in writing that America holds forth an image of Europe's future, as so many of Huizinga's fellow critics of America's culture argued; it is quite a different intellectual challenge to explore the ways in which America's culture would work its effects on Europe.

Huizinga had a keen and open eye for the ways in which the early forms of American mass culture produced virtual fantasy worlds. In addition to recognizing film's effects, he was aware of the role that advertising began to play in the 1920s. His travel notes, which formed the basis for his 1926 collection of essays, include this observation from the streets of Chicago:

> Looked at the advertisements. Rosy-cheeked boy with a smile and three packets of cereal: For that million dollar boy of *yours*. Puffed wheat.—Speculation on the love for children, health and the sense of dollars.—The advertisements, taken together, very clearly show an ideal, an ideal of no great reach.—Girls being offered a camel by an enamored boy, surf-riding girls with sun blisters. The girl on the telephone. Remember! Keep that schoolgirl complexion. Palmolive. Always the half-sentimental type, presented as pure and healthy, a variation and refinement of what Ch. Dana Gibson launched thirty years ago. The public constantly sees a model of refinement far beyond its purse, ken and heart. Does it imitate this? Does it adapt itself to this?[24]

Apposite questions indeed. As he is in his reflections on processes of identification among film audiences, Huizinga is again aware of the problem of reception of the virtual worlds constantly spewed forth by a relentless commercial mass culture. More generally, these musings touch on the effect that media of cultural transmission, such as film and advertising, would have on audiences not just in America but elsewhere as well. In these more general terms, the problem then becomes how non-American audiences would read the American-born fantasy worlds that displayed all the characteristics of the American way with culture vehemently indicted by European critics.

In conclusion to this section, let me point out one irony. Although in his later writings Huizinga dwelt on the problem of contemporary history's changing, if not actually losing, form under the combined impact of forces of mechanization, industrialization, and the advent of mass society, he may, despite his sophistication and open-mindedness, have missed one crucial way in which people's senses of history were changing. Under the impact of mass-communication media—the very media that Huizinga had explored subtly, refusing to ignore or reject them out of hand, as many of his fellow cultural critics were wont to do—most of his contemporaries were beginning to furnish their historical imaginations with the ingredients of virtual fantasy worlds rather than the stuff of which history used to be made. What to Huizinga and other like-minded intellectuals may have been a mere epiphenomenon, hiding real historical forces from view, would provide the markers of history to generations growing up in the second half of the twentieth century.

American Mass Culture and Our Changing Sense of History

Three vignettes set the stage for my discussion. All three are taken from European films, and each represents a formative moment, if not an epiphany, in the lives of its protagonists. In each, it is America that provides the ingredients for these moments of revelation. Dramatically these moments serve as epic concentrations, condensing into a single moment what normally is a continuing process of identity formation. The first example is from Jacques Tati's *Jour de fête,* released in 1949; the second, from Alan Parker's 1991 film *The Commitments;* and the third, from Bernard Tavernier's *Round Midnight,* which came out in 1986.

In *Jour de fête* Tati satirizes the modern obsession with speed, presenting it as an obsession peculiarly American but highly contagious. In later work, such as *Mon oncle,* he would satirize other American infatuations, including the love of gadgets, labor-saving devices, automation, and remote control. The later films show these phenomena as they had already invaded France, providing French appetites for a life of ostentation and invidious distinction with the snob value of American contraptions. Interestingly, in *Jour de fête* Tati reveals the moment of contagion. At one point the film's protagonist, a French provincial postman, peeks through an opening in a big tent to watch a film dealing with speedy American postal techniques involving virtuoso time-saving feats. The feats themselves are satirically transformed into nonsensical daredevil acts of motorized mail carriers jumping through hoops of fire and airplanes dropping mailbags that are picked up by carriers riding motorbikes at full speed. Many of the propaganda films shown in Europe under Marshall Plan auspices and meant to give Europeans a sense of American efficiency may well have been perceived and remembered as equally fantastic. In fact, the viewers see the images almost vicariously, as if through the eyes of the astounded postman. The images may well be the product of his eager imagination rather than anything in the documentary film. Later hilarious sequences then show how Tati's postman creatively adopts the American model, adapting his bicycle delivery act while experiencing a new mail (male?) identity.

The other two film vignettes are variations on this theme of Europeans looking in from the outside, undergoing a culture shock while experiencing it as a moment of conversion. In Tavernier's film the moment occurs in a young Frenchman's encounter with American jazz in the late 1940s. Unable to afford the price of admission to a Paris jazz club where one of his cultural heroes is playing, he hunches outside a window, literally eavesdropping on a world of meaningful sounds, coded messages from an enticing but faraway culture. As it happens, he manages to get in touch with the revered musician, recasting his own life into a mission of supporting and protecting the drug-ravaged career of his tragic hero. In Parker's *Commitments* another musical encounter makes for a moment of epiphany. Several poor Irish youths are casting about for a musical form that will allow them to express their working-class sense of themselves. They critically reject most of the American pop music that blares from radios, seeing it as irrelevant to their quest. Early in the story, however, they watch James Brown do his trademark soul act on a television show. When the show is over, the leader of this small group translates the experience into terms relevant to the lives they lead in Ireland. "We have to become like him. He is like us. The Irish are the blacks of Europe, the Dubliners are the blacks of Ireland, and we Northenders are the blacks of Dublin. Say it once and say it loud: we are black and we are proud." In disbelief his friends silently repeat the last words, their lips moving to form the words of the punch line. "We are black and we are proud." Slowly the message sinks in. Yet another appropriation of American culture has taken place, affecting these youngsters' senses of identity. They are cast in the role of celebrants in a ritual of cultural conversion.

These moments of voluntary affiliation with American lifestyles and cultural models are a recurring feature of postwar European cultural production in film, on television, and in literature. My three examples constitute only a small sample of this larger body. A more comprehensive study would be of interest for two reasons. First, these moments provide a sense of the many settings in which such critical encounters with American culture have taken place. They are like moments of remembrance, for everyone who grew up in postwar Europe has them. They are the condensed memorable versions of the more continuing exposure to American culture that Europeans have all experienced. When taken together, they are like an album of vignettes vividly illustrating the ongoing process not only of the forms of reception of American culture but also of its selective appropriation—that is, of the ways in which American culture was redefined and made to serve the cultural needs of Europeans. Settings of reception, defined in such terms as class, age, gender, or ethnicity, then become the crucial focus for analysis.

Whatever the precise setting, such encounters always involve people who find themselves at the margin of established mainstream cultural modes and molds, not (or not yet) fully integrated into these dominant conventional forms. American culture, as they read it, provided them with alternatives of unconventionality, informality, and a sense of freedom of choice, all in marked contrast to cultural conventions they were expected to make their own.

In addition, there is a second reason to create this album of vignettes. The process of reception, or of cultural consumption, is a nut devilishly hard to crack. Whatever area of mass cultural production one investigates, whether world's fairs, film, television soap operas, or literary forms such as the romance, the mass consumption of these products remains an issue. It is one thing to explore the programmatic strategies of the organizers and producers of such forms of mass culture; it is a totally different thing to gauge what the audience chooses to get out of them. Work in these areas has produced interesting response studies, including investigations of housewives watching soaps and readers reading romances. As in the case of the European postwar reception of American mass culture, however, as the issue grows larger, it become more difficult to determine how to study the process of reception. A study of vignettes may be a promising approach.

After all, as narrative moments in stories told by Europeans, such vignettes are like second-order evidence of the reception of American culture. They tell stories of reception. They are recycled, or reconstructed, moments meant to convey remembrances of critical encounters with American culture. In that sense they are explicit indications of a process of reception. As such they are more open to research than are questions of first-order reception. It is difficult to see someone eating a hamburger in Paris as making a cultural statement, expressing an identity that challenges established conventions; it is much less difficult to interpret a narrative passage, whether in a film or in a book, that presents hamburger consumption in the light of a cultural peripety, willfully subverting European conventions of eating out. For that matter, it would be harder to prove a direct, first-order American influence on Alan Parker's style of filmmaking than it would be to trace his awareness of such influences. After all, he himself turns them into the stuff of narration. This much may be clear, then: to the extent that moments of the reception of American culture, presented in the dramatic light of moments of epiphany, have become a recurrent feature of European storytelling, they testify to a degree of self-conscious awareness of the American cultural impact that it would be unwise to neglect.

* * *

Condensed into single moments, points in time serving as *lieux de mémoire*, to use Pierre Nora's felicitous phrase, all vignettes of American culture's reception in Europe highlight what has truly been an ongoing process. Whatever conversion moments Europeans may vividly remember, they have all been more continuously exposed to an environment of free-floating cultural signifiers made in America. Confronted with an ongoing stream of vistas of the good life, as carried by media such as film, advertisements, television, and music videos, they have walked through a duplicate world of images as a continuing accompaniment to their lives. They never walked alone. Highly private as the consumption of American culture may have been—eavesdropping on AFN broadcasts late at night and against parental wishes, watching a Hollywood movie, or shutting out one's environment through the use of a Walkman—the cultural products that made for such private moments were at the same time consumed by many others, constituting a mass audience. These private moments, then, may well be seen as forms of collective behavior typical of contemporary mass societies. The very fact that the private consumption of mass culture is necessarily shared with many others gives mass culture its paradoxical quality of setting the public stage, giving an era its particular cultural flavor. Reminiscing, individual people become aware that they share similar cultural memories with others. They are able to reconstruct the feel of years past, evoking moments of cultural consumption that, it turns out, they shared with others. Everyone knows the exhilarating moments of discovering that others enjoyed the same film or rock song one thought one had enjoyed privately. There is the sudden sense of a joint return to a past that briefly comes to life again. That is why we now find Archie Bunker's chair, the throne of a world that he masterfully commanded, exhibited in the Museum of American History. Taken from the fictional world of a television series, it has entered the real world of historical artifacts. It serves to awaken the historical experience of a generation that collectively enjoyed an entirely imaginary world, vicariously spending part of their lives there.

In that sense modern mass culture, much of it in an American mold, has given our sense of history a particular coating. Huizinga bemoaned the fact that history as he conceived of it was losing form, escaping his capacity to recognize patterns of coherence and meaning; he must have been unaware of the new coat that contemporary mass culture was giving to our sense of history. As a shared repertoire of recollections allowing people to call forth an image of their own collective past, the mass-cultural mold is certainly a new form that history has assumed. It serves people as a switch that allows them to connect private memories with public memories. More important, such recollections often connect to historical events of a more traditional nature. For instance, the marked reorganization of the domestic sphere that America's rapid suburbanization engendered in the postwar years, especially the 1950s, constituted large-scale and anonymous forces of social change that historians would be hard-pressed to render in vivid forms of historical narrative. Using only the traditional tools of the craft, any historian, Huizinga included, would be unable to come up with narrative forms tellingly catching these processes. As he himself surmised in some of his musings concerning mass culture, however, the story of America's return to domesticity found its narrative forms precisely at that level. As it is, the process of social change was accompanied, if not actively promoted, by a host of Hollywood movies and television productions centering on the family home presented as the "natural" setting for the way that Americans structured their private lives. Collectively they set the cultural tone and gave the cultural feel to an era. To the extent that Americans now remember the era, it is by means of these mass-cultural representations. To the extent that Europeans remember the era, it is doubly vicarious: not only did these films and television programs allow them to look in on American family life, but they also provided European audiences with views of the good life, of single-family homes, cars in the driveway, "American kitchens," and husbands happily returning to the family fold. "Honey, I'm home!"

We all remember such historical configurations through the images that the mass media brought to our homes and are now the stuff of our historical memory. But mass culture mediates and shapes contemporary history in other ways, too. It is not only a matter of fictional representations, as in film or television sitcoms, that imaginatively reflect and capture the social and cultural trends of an era. Much of what actually happens, the day-to-day events that make up the daily news and that are conventionally seen as the real stuff of history, now reaches us almost instantly through the modern mass media in the form of newspaper photographs or television news flashes. Some of these images gain an iconic status, recapitulating an event in ways that leave an indelible imprint on our minds, as if on an etcher's plate. Often such images start leading their own lives, serving as summary recapitulations of recent history. Moreover, its place in the postwar world and in the communication networks spanning the globe means that America has been both a key player in many events making up recent history and a central provider of images representing those events. The images that acquire iconic status pop up time and time again. There is, to give just one example, the case of Nick Ut's photograph of napalmed Vietnamese children running in terror toward the eye of his camera. Many in the United States and Europe vividly remember the photograph. Interestingly, not unlike Archie Bunker's chair come home to a museum of history, the photograph was able to spawn its own afterlife as a factor of newsworthy history. Having become an emblem of the atrocities of the Vietnam War, it remained at the same time the picture of an individual girl in pain, creating an interest in her individual fate. In the fall of 1996 the public's reading of the photograph suddenly moved from the emblematic to the personal. The girl in the photograph reappeared on the stage of history as a woman of flesh and blood, individualized, no longer solely an icon. She came to a Veteran's Day ritual of remembrance at the Vietnam War monument in Washington, D.C., offering forgiveness.[25] A new meaning was added to an icon of mass culture that had long allowed us to give shape and form to our understanding of the Vietnam War. In a bitter irony, however, our empathy with this one victim of the war would never have been awakened had the mediation of an iconic photograph not first made her an emblem in our collective memories. Many others like her, similarly victims of the war, will forever remain faceless and nameless, never to draw our collective attention.

There are yet other ways in which the coat of mass-cultural memory is used to re-create the past. They resemble the ways in which the reception of American mass culture is recycled into individual vignettes, into those single moments of conversion that I talked about before. They are like a second-order, conscious use of the mass-cultural coat of history for the reconstruction of historical events. Again, the Vietnam War may offer apposite illustrations of what I have in mind. Surely Vietnam War movies in their own right are mass-cultural products adding to the sediment that mass culture leaves on our sense of history. Trying to evoke images of the Vietnam War, we often do so with the help of Hollywood's attempts to render that war. Nor does Hollywood shrink from adding iconic heroes to our store of recollections, for instance, in the form of Rambo as a latter-day raging Roland. Nonetheless, many of these films take us back to the historical event precisely by invoking collectively remembered mass-cultural products of the era. The music of the Rolling Stones and the Doors in Francis Ford Coppola's *Apocalypse Now* triggers historical connections in the minds of contemporary audiences. Similarly, the heart-rending finale of Michael Cimino's film *The Deerhunter* has the remaining protagonists, their voices wavering, sing Irving Berlin's "God Bless America." Grieving over those they have lost and attempting to reassert mutual bonds, they use a popular song richly evocative of their larger bonds with America. Tellingly, however, European audiences were strongly moved as well because they vicariously shared the musical repertoire and its associative force. Barry Levinson, in his *Good Morning, Vietnam,* made this connecting strategy the central ploy of his narrative. The high point of his film, a well-nigh transcendent moment, is his combined use of various tools from the realm of mass culture. In a sequence following Robin Williams's announcement of just another song in his radio program for the American forces in Vietnam, we hear the voice of Louis Armstrong singing "What a Wonderful World." A jumble of images from the Vietnam War accompany the lyrics, the sort of shots any prime-time television news program would show. Yet the structural logic of the sequence does not resemble only television news flashes. It is at the same time structurally similar to the standard music video, typically another jumble of images made coherent only by the accompanying soundtrack. Ironically, the clip from the film later became a hit as a music video disseminated worldwide through MTV, an American pop music channel. Merging the evocative force of Armstrong's voice with the logic of television footage to create something that clearly appeals to our familiarity with music videos, Levinson managed to use all these mass-cultural triggers to produce a moment of transcendence, a bitter comment on the horror of the war. It makes us sit back and reflect, despite what prewar critics of American mass culture had argued in their mood of cultural pessimism.

Were these critics alive today, what would they have to say to these new forms that now play a role in shaping our sense of the past? Many undoubtedly would characterize them as the ultimate victory of a cultural inversion they had been the first to see as typically American, an inversion that replaces reality with its fake representations. From Georges Duhamel and Simone de Beauvoir to more recent observers of American culture such as Jean Baudrillard and Umberto Eco, the language may have changed from the straightforward invective to more esoteric formulas such as *simulacrum* or *hyperreality*, but the diagnosis remains essentially the same. They all come up with their own variations on the old Marxian theme of false consciousness. Huizinga, too, would perhaps be reluctant to see present-day forms of historical awareness as worthy replacements for the historiographic forms whose decline and ultimate demise he observed or foresaw. Yet he may have come closest to a historiographic perspective that has been gaining adherents in recent decades. His almost sociological sense of the role and function of rituals, ceremonies, and public spectacles in late medieval Europe, as well as his keen sense of the role that modern mass media played in providing frameworks for identification and self-definition to mass audiences, took him to the threshold of an epistemological sea change in the historiography of collective consciousness. Huizinga would have had no quarrel with a current relativism that sees collective identities, whether of nations, ethnic groups, or regional cultures, as just so many constructions. He would have recognized the invented rituals celebrating and memorializing such identities as dramatic forms of history that he himself had studied. Nonetheless, he might have disagreed as to the implied voluntarism of this perspective and its attribution of historical agency. In Huizinga's case, in fact, the agency rested with historians. It was they who shaped history into larger narrative forms. Much current historiography, however, places the agency in history itself and explores it in terms of group strategies, struggles for cultural hegemony, and the invention of rituals meant to rally people around strategic readings of their collective identity.

This takes us back to a problem I raised earlier. Exploring the strategic agency behind the formation of group identities and frameworks for identification is only one issue. There is always the further question as to why, at the level of individual reception and appropriation of the rival constructions, people opt for particular readings of their collective identity. How do we explore the meanings and significance of such rival appeals at the point of reception? What messages and representations of reality do people store and digest to render meaningful life histories? As I argued before, the mass-cultural setting of our contemporary life is a powerful ingredient in these individual constructions. At the same time, however, as a setting that individuals have shared with countless others, it also provides them with a shared language of remembrance. If, to quote Carl Becker, everyone is his own historian, we have to go down to the level of individual historical awareness and try to fathom the sense of meaningful history at that level. It may be highly private, yet as a private construction it draws on repertoires widely shared with contemporaries.

If indeed mass-cultural products produced and disseminated under American auspices do function as the markers of time and the molders of the collective historical recollections not only of Americans but of Europeans as well, one further point is in order. The sense of history as I have explored it here is necessarily of a transient nature. It applies only to history as a shared experience, remembered collectively. As generations succeed one another on the stage of history, there is unavoidably a point in the past beyond which this repertoire of shared memories cannot stretch, a point following them like a ship's backwash. A century hence none of the markers of time and triggers of historical recollection, as I have explored them here, will still be operative. Does that mean that for future historians our history will be just like any other older stage of history? Undoubtedly, the feel that our recent history has to those of us who lived through it will be beyond retrieval. Yet the mass-cultural coating of our age will be there for later historians as a necessary resource. Much like cultural historians of our day and age, they will be able to return to films, recorded television programs, and music with a view to exploring their force in molding and reflecting collective identities.

Today, at any rate, contemporary historians are eagerly accepting the challenge to study the mass-cultural coat of our age. When they are involved in the production of television documentaries about recent historic episodes, they consciously draw on the repertoires of mass culture produced at the time. Thus, in the celebrated PBS/BBC series on the Great Depression, historical footage of farmers losing their farms is followed by a clip of Betty Boop, with the narrator reminding us: "Even Betty Boop lost her farm." The soundtrack sets the tone for recollection, playing the iconic musical reflection of the mood of the time: "Brother, can you spare a dime?" Other footage shows us Busby Berkeley choreographies, such as the celebrated "Remember my forgotten man." Not only do these ingredients take us back to mass culture popular at the time; more specifically, they make us aware that mass culture at its best is able to reflect the pressing concerns of a period. There are many more instances of this increased awareness among historians of the mass-cultural forms of history. In search of audiences that want to see their personal histories displayed, books, special exhibits, and, yes, entire museums are now devoted to the everyday lives of common people, showing the advent of mass-cultural products into their homes, work, leisure time pursuits, and so on. If mass culture has provided people with the rituals and ceremonies for the public display of their collective identities, the time has now come to display it in its own right.

11. Citizenship and Cyberspace

Citizenship, whatever else it may be, is also a state of mind. The communities with which people identify and through which they define themselves are always imagined communities. Whether it is the nation, the church, or a language community, in the last analysis they are always entities as people imagine them and represent them to themselves. People may put out flags on national holidays, engage in solitary prayer, or write a poem in a given language; these are all acts of communication taking place within a community of the mind. At times the symbols and rituals for the public display of people's affiliations with such larger imagined communities may have the quasi-official status of cultural ready-mades, repertoires for the cultural reproduction of communities. Every next generation is brought up acquiring these repertoires, singing national anthems, wearing green on St. Patrick's Day, or rallying at memorial places expressive of the mythical bonds of community. All such repertoires form the institutional setting for the collective celebration and reaffirmation of these communal bonds. As repertoires they are cultural constructs, if not inventions, that form part of larger collective strategies for tying people together within communities as conceived by organizing elites. These communities could be the populace of emerging nation-states, the working class, or youngsters affiliating with an emerging youth culture in the post–World War II era. They are all in a sense publics waiting to be mobilized by outside organizing efforts.

As the previous two chapters made clear, however, people's identities are always multiple and ultimately result from their individual explorations and affiliations. People are not unlike the shopping public in a mall, trying on different clothes of different styles, watching themselves change identity in the dressing-room mirror. Of the many identities lurking inside each of us, one or another may be triggered depending on the setting in which we find ourselves. Thus, a Frenchman visiting the United States may be surprised at finding himself affiliating with a larger Europe, seeing his identity as a European triggered rather than his narrower French national identity. The borderlines of the many imagined communities with which we are ready to identify ourselves cut across one another in a variety of intricate ways. At one point we may be ardently national—for example, when we root for our national teams in sports; at other points we may choose to emphasize regional affiliations, speaking the local patois with friends or family members and sliding back into an identity of primordial warmth. Or again we may find ourselves sporting affiliations that transcend the national, conceiving of ourselves in terms of race, or class, or sexual preference. What in the previous chapter I called the process of triangulation is always at work in each of us. We always measure our potential affiliation with larger cultural communities in terms of our other affiliations. As the two preceding chapters made clear, Europeans have increasingly woven an American cultural model into their explorations of meaningful affiliations and affinities. These chapters were case studies in the formation of transnational identities, taking America as the common point of orientation.

In the present chapter I focus on the emerging world communication structure of the Internet. From one perspective, the Internet can be seen as a new supermall catering to those shopping around for communities of like-minded spirits, allowing them to break out of the available frameworks for affiliation in their real-life settings, especially when these are felt as imposed from outside and stifling. In this view, the Internet is the new global site for the construction of imagined communities that are literally virtual, coming to life only on people's computer screens. From a different perspective, however, instead of being liberating in the sense of offering endless variety for creating new forms of cyberspace citizenship, the Internet may be only the latest medium for the global transmission of a culture crucially cast in an American mold. Rather than allow people's affiliations to multiply, it would narrow their options, subjecting them to an Americanization by stealth. My central question, then, concerns the extent to which the Internet is American in the way it may affect its users.

It is still too early to give a definitive answer. The Internet is too recent; the impact on its users keeps changing as its spreads around the world. My exploration therefore is of the Internet's potential, its promise and possible threats, as seen by the community of its users. I chose to look at the Internet's potential in terms of the dreams that it holds out for Americans and non-Americans alike. They are all dreams of perfect information as these have informed classic views of *Homo politicus* and *Homo economicus*, of the fully informed citizen and consumer. In the final section I focus on the dream of the Internet as potentially restoring the full body of human knowledge, the dream of perfect intertextuality, or in other words, "the dream of the lost library."

Dreams of Democracy

Given its auspices and early history, the Internet may appear as a paradox, if not an oxymoron. It originated as a cold war instrument, a military ploy to prevent the opponent from wiping out the U.S. government's command and communication structure in one devastating blow. It did this—and here is the paradox—through an act of preemption. Rather than allow the enemy to destroy the vital center, Pentagon planners chose to take away the center themselves, opting for a Hydra-like, many-centered web of communication. The evolving network technology of interlinked computers allowed them to do this. The Arpanet (Advanced Research Projects Agency Network), as the early secret military version was called, shared many of the same crucial features with the later public version that came to be known as the Internet. It was a decentered, if not entirely centerless, system—a web that would simply reroute communication flows if parts of it had been damaged. The paradox, as I pointed out, lies in the act of the government decentering itself, creating a structure that was in essence anarchic, doing away with structures of hierarchy, of super- and subordination, making for a potential equivalence of senders and receivers and an equality of flows of information. This potential of the system came fully into its own once the Net was opened up, first to universities and later to the general public.[1]

Once emancipated from its military-strategic rationale, the Internet became the chosen terrain for an academic community of mostly young intellectuals who infused the system with an ideology of late 1960s libertarianism. Despite the more recent growth of the Internet, driven by commercial motives, the early view of the Internet as a realm of liberty and equality, of antiauthoritarian if not antigovernment feelings, is still with us today. A blatant instance of this libertarianism turning to antigovernment subversion is the work of the so-called hackers; cracking the codes that protect secret government data banks, they turn the Net against government itself. It is an extreme case, yet illustrative of a more general underlying attitude shared by a population of Internet users. Jointly they have given a peculiarly American flavor to the Internet, a cultural imprint redolent with the long-standing rhetoric of American republicanism. As they conceive of the Internet—and later the World Wide Web—it constitutes not a virtual community but rather a virtuous community.

Admittedly, this idealist view of the Internet community represents a dream rather than a reality. For one thing, many users of Internet facilities participate for reasons totally unrelated to, if not actually at odds with, the republican impetus. More important, if the dream of republicanism assumes a community encompassing all humanity, as the concept of a World Wide Web seems to suggest, reality is a far cry away. In fact, on a worldwide scale, Internet users constitute a small and privileged group. As such, they are representative more generally of the way in which the fruits of Western civilization are shared out among the world population. Undeniably, however, as access to the Internet gradually extends across groups formerly excluded, it may well give them a taste of civic participation in a community that was previously always withheld from them. I myself, in a variety of settings that brought together young academicians from Second and Third World countries, have heard ample testimony to the liberating effect of Internet access on, for example, young women scholars in Islamic countries or young academicians working in the stifling bureaucratic and hierarchical university structures of countries that were until recently under the sway of the Soviet empire.

In extending its catchment area to become more representative of humanity across the world, the Web has become one of the central forces of a process commonly referred to as globalization. The following question thus arises here (as it does in other discussions of globalization): is the Internet also a force of the Americanization of the world? In other words, to what extent can we see the Web as a carrier of cultural values and a mental habitus that are recognizably American?

How American Is the Internet?

There are various ways of tackling this question. One pragmatic way is to look at the differential density in Internet use. A graphical representation of the traffic density along the channels of communication provided by the Internet would clearly show the United States to be the preeminent nodal point, with minor nodes showing up elsewhere in the network. The nodes are interconnected in the sense that traffic flows along the lines connecting them, but with nothing like the density that characterizes the nodal points. That is, the use of the Internet for interpersonal communication still tends to center on national societies as our present-day world knows them. Americans tend to communicate via the Internet among themselves more than with the outside world, and the same pattern holds for national societies elsewhere. Another possibly relevant measure might be called "wiredness," the percentage of a population with Internet access. Some of these other societies may be superior to the United States in this respect. Finland, for example, is more "wired" than the United States, yet in terms of the absolute density of traffic along the Internet, the former constitutes only a minor node compared to the latter. Thus, this imaginary exercise in graphical representation would highlight a position that America holds in many other ways as well and that we might appropriately call its imperial position. In this, as in many other respects, America constitutes a center in structures of communication that span the world, relegating other participants to a relatively peripheral place. It is a sender more than a receiver, in much the same way that Rome constituted the center of its imperial order.[2]

From this perspective, then, the Internet remains a communication tool used principally by Americans. They were the first to use it, and they still contribute the bulk of communication flowing along the Net. Given their originating role and the American auspices under which much current communication along the Net proceeds, does this mean that Americans have also been able to set a tone characteristic of conversations via the Net? In other words, have they been able to leave a cultural imprint on the use that others, outside America, make of the Net? This question suggests a second way of exploring the "Americanness" of the Internet.

As regards the tone and mode of messages spread via the Net, I suggest two aspects that might be seen as signs of an American imprint. One is the increased informalization of communication, and the other is what we may call the greater democratization or dehierarchization of communication that the Net appears to bring. A comparison with two older forms of communication will help to bring out more clearly what I have in mind: the art of letter writing and the telephone conversation. On the one hand, in terms of forms of address and linguistic mode, letter writing is clearly far more stylized and formal than average communication via the Net. The latter often reflects the informality of speech more than the formal code of written letters. It is in that sense closer to the directness of spoken telephone conversations. On the other hand, however, this very directness, verging on social intrusion, may keep people from using the telephone in situations of social inequality, such as structured hierarchical settings. As recent research has shown, in such situations people may be less hesitant to avail themselves of e-mail.[3] Recipients of their messages will read them and respond at a time of their own choosing. In that sense e-mail communication helps to lower social thresholds and ease exchange across hierarchical boundaries. Thus, e-mail messages constitute an intermediate form between the older modes of communication provided by the written letter and the telephone call. They resemble the latter in their greater informality of tone and style, but they are more like the former as a means of communication across hierarchical lines, only faster and therefore more efficient.

If informalization and democratization of communication do indeed characterize e-mail exchanges, can we then decide to see them as having arisen under American auspices? Could we not argue, in a McLuhanesque way, that the medium is the message, or in other words, that the nature of the medium determines its social and cultural impact, irrespective of who first set the tone? As in so many other instances of modernization, it is probably impossible to disentangle the two alternative explanations. We can only guess at what the typical mode of e-mail exchanges would have been had the idea and its implementation come from France or Japan rather than the United States. Nonetheless, as the history of many modern inventions illustrates, whether of the automobile, the camera, film, or other such technical contraptions, America has tended to diverge systematically from European countries by always aiming to make these novelties available and accessible to the many rather than the few. It went for user friendliness, mass marketing, and mass advertising, whereas in Europe these inventions were made to function in ways that would confirm rather than upset established social hierarchies. Many anguished European observers noticed the slackening of social restraints in the ways that Americans used their automobiles or flocked to watch the latest movies. More often than not they felt they were observing the ominous contours of Europe's future, and ironically, in many cases they were right. The joys of mass consumption would indeed come to Europe later, eroding the initial use of technical inventions for buttressing the symbolic capital of social elites. It was never solely a matter of Europe catching up with America in a parallel development toward becoming a consumption society; more often than not, before average European citizens could afford the luxuries of mass consumption, they had already acquired a taste for it and its democratic joys under the impact of views of the good life reaching them from America, through film, photographs, journalistic reports, and letters from friends and relatives who had migrated there. Since this was the case for inventions that were introduced more or less simultaneously on both sides of the Atlantic, the same trend should apply even more strongly to a novel means of communication such as the Internet, invented by Americans, imbued with their spirit of egalitarianism, and reaching others with its American imprint firmly established.

But surely the other reading—of the medium's being the message—cannot be entirely discarded. A mode of communication does in certain ways set the form and tone of its own use. A telephone conversation will never end using the words "Sincerely yours," nor will letters as a rule open with phrases like "Hello, this is so and so writing." It may well be, then, that a similar logic inherent to the medium has made for the greater informality and equality of exchange in e-mail communication. If this is true, then e-mail will in its own right serve as a force of informalization and democratization. As Sellar and Yeatman would have it, in their flippant *1066 and All That*, this is "A Good Thing."[4] Even so, given that e-mail can affect the quality of communication in positive ways, does it also have less positive consequences?

One worrisome consequence in this respect is the transient, ephemeral quality of e-mail communication. Unless properly stored, either saved electronically or printed out on old-fashioned paper, e-mail messages leave no trace. Here again, they are like telephone conversations. From a historian's perspective, this must affect our sense of history as well as our capacity to reconstruct the past. Of course, traditional archives can be shredded and recordings of Oval Office conversations can be erased as active manipulations by the parties involved, often in faint attempts to control the way they will go down in history. As active interventions, however, they do not logically follow from the inherent nature of the medium of communication. Matters are different in the case of e-mail or telephone exchanges. The medium in these cases does affect the historical status of the message.

There is another irony here. Much as the medium may inherently and independently determine the transience of the messages exchanged, the massive way in which American society has embraced this particular means of communication, with all its implied amnesia, may in the eyes of outsiders seem to confirm what older forms of a cultural critique of America have argued all along, that American culture is essentially ahistorical, lacking a sense of the present as adding to the store of history. Again this leads us to ask how American the Internet is. A recurrent theme in European critical observations of American culture is its lack of a sense of history and its blithe orientation toward the present and the future. The Internet, carrying everything before it in its advent as the preferred tool of communication among Americans, might well have struck such earlier observers as "typically American."

There is one more logical consequence of the inherent nature of Internet exchanges that might seem to confirm negative views of American culture. It appears as the negative side of the democracy of exchanges that the Internet provides. From this perspective, all messages are equivalent, regardless of their truth content. There are no gatekeepers of the sort used by older, more responsible forms of news dissemination, such as the press. Anything goes; anyone can join in. Truth now seems to find its confirmation more in the repetition of messages than in the traditional tests of checking sources, comparing views and versions, and the like. Thus, communities of like-minded Internet users often share a consensus view of reality that borders on a conspiracy view. For instance, surprisingly many black Americans have come to believe that the AIDS epidemic is the result of a white racist conspiracy. Similarly, well-known individuals can lend their alleged authority to the wildest rumors, seemingly confirming as truth their quasi-authoritative reading of certain events. Thus, the journalist Pierre Salinger made the news when he used the Internet to publicize his wild assertions concerning a missile that he said shot down the TWA passenger aircraft off the coast of Long Island in July 1996. Another infamous example is the *Drudge Report,* an electronic newspaper disseminating a wild hodgepodge of selections from established newspapers mixed in with rumor and gossip. Its editor, Matt Drudge, defends his editorial policy by characterizing gossip and rumor as information that has not yet been substantiated.

These are only a few examples of a certain view of the Internet that sees every user as his or her own journalist, all of them equally entitled to the free dissemination of their views. It seems to be a view of democracy gone haywire, only the latest confirmation of Tocqueville's more somber views of the evil potential of a society geared along egalitarian principles. As more optimist observers hold, however, such societies have within themselves sufficient vitality and means of redress to stand up to such excesses. Older and more respectable voices of public opinion, such as the press, analyze and warn against such trends.[5] Similarly, established legal institutions offer a recourse to offended parties. Thus, in the fall of 1997 Drudge was taken to court for slandering the former journalist and Clinton adviser Sidney Blumenthal, whom he had accused of marital violence.

In all these ways a balance may be found between the freedom of the Internet and a set of rules for morality and responsible behavior as these have applied to the older media of public opinion. In fact, various attempts at regulating the Internet have been undertaken in the United States under government auspices. Early enthusiasts may have seen the Net as a tool of antigovernment libertarianism, but government now appears to be striking back. Its first such attempt was centered on a concern shared by many Americans: the dissemination of sex-related material via the Net. It tried to restrict such material through the Communications Decency Act but failed. In June 1997 the Supreme Court declared the act to be unconstitutional. Nevertheless, the very attempt at legislative intervention raised the hackles of those who had cast themselves in the role of guardians of the early libertarian Internet culture.

A Libertarian Strikes Back

One voice raised on behalf of the republican vision of the Internet is John Perry Barlow's. Barlow is clearly among the early generation of Net enthusiasts who deserve the epithet "cyberguru." He represents the early frontier exhilaration of the "cybercowboys," also known as "cybernauts," the digital pioneers. He is a cofounder of a computer civil rights organization that intends to act on behalf of the interests of the citizens of cyberspace: the Electronic Frontier Foundation. From his self-chosen exile in Zurich he stood up in protest against the U.S. government's attempts to regulate the freedoms of cyberspace. He chose to do so by issuing, via the Internet, a Declaration of the Independence of Cyberspace.[6] It is a remarkable mélange of classic American political discourse, in the hallowed tradition of the American Declaration of Independence, and anti-Americanism. It shows an antigovernment cast of mind well-entrenched in America but now turned against the American government. A few quotations will serve to give the reader a taste:

> Governments of the Industrial World, you weary giants of flesh and steel, I come from Cyberspace, the new home of Mind. On behalf of the future, I ask you of the past to leave us alone. You are not welcome among us. You have no sovereignty where we gather.

> We have no elected government, nor are we likely to have one, so I address you with no greater authority than that with which liberty itself always speaks. I declare the global social space we are building to be naturally independent of the tyrannies you seek to impose on us. You have no moral right to rule us nor do you possess any methods of enforcement we have true reason to fear.

> Governments derive their just powers from the consent of the governed. You have neither solicited nor received ours. We did not invite you. You do not know us, nor do you know our world. Cyberspace does not lie within your borders. . . .

> We are forming our own Social Contract. This governance will arise according to the conditions of our world, not yours. Our world is different.

> Cyberspace consists of transactions, relationships, and thought itself, arrayed like a standing wave in the web of our communications. Ours is a world that is both everywhere and nowhere, but it is not where bodies live.

> We are creating a world that all may enter without privilege or prejudice accorded by race, economic power, military force, or station of birth.

> We are creating a world where anyone, anywhere may express his or her beliefs, no matter how singular, without fear of being coerced into silence or conformity.

> We believe that from ethics, enlightened self-interest, and the commonweal, our governance will emerge.

> In the United States, you have today created a law, the Telecommunications Reform Act, which repudiates your own Constitution and insults the dreams of Jefferson, Washington, Mill, Madison, DeTocqueville, and Brandeis. These dreams must be borne anew in us.

> Your increasingly obsolete information industries would perpetuate themselves by proposing laws, in America and elsewhere, that claim to own speech itself throughout the world. These laws would declare ideas to be another industrial product, no more noble than pig iron. In our world, whatever the human mind may create can be reproduced and distributed infinitely at no cost.

> These increasingly hostile and colonial measures place us in the same position as those previous lovers of freedom and self-determination who had to reject the authorities of distant, uninformed powers. We must declare our virtual selves immune to your sovereignty, even as we continue to consent to your rule over our bodies. We will spread ourselves across the Planet so that no one can arrest our thoughts.

We will create a civilization of the Mind in Cyberspace. May it be more humane and fair than the world your governments have made before.

Barlow's declaration can be seen as recent, if paradoxical, testimony to the continuing imprint of American political dreams. It is paradoxical because of its anti-American thrust, yet its view of cyberspace as a realm of republican virtue populated by "netizens" who constitute a community far transcending national borders, invokes a language of unmistakably American coinage.

As I argued before, however, the Internet is American on entirely different grounds as well. Anyone who surfs the Web is drawn into a world of information, blending commercial and other messages, that in most cases is clearly of American origin or at least cast in an American mold. For all its potential egalitarianism, the Internet in its present use clearly represents the structure of a web with a center dominating a number of peripheries. This view takes us back to the question of whether the process of globalization as facilitated by the Internet does not at the same time serve as an instrument for the center's Americanization of the peripheries. Given the Internet's openness of access, are there no ways in which the peripheries can strike back, penetrating right into the center for the dissemination of American mass culture?

Amstel Light: The Periphery Strikes Back

In the spring of 1997 an American friend sent me a clipping from, as he called it, an "alternative weekly" published in Washington, D.C.: the *Washington City Paper*.[7] His description suggested a smallish readership sharing tastes and views at variance with mainstream opinions, a public, in other words, that one could address in ways inconceivable for the larger population. The clipping contained an alarmist message from a group calling itself "Garrison Boyd and Americans for Disciplined Behavior." It sounded like some offshoot of the Christian Coalition. In bold print the message shouted "IMPENDING DOOM." It went on, surprisingly, to attack the city of Amsterdam for its "loathsome attitude of openness" and its "spontaneous social intercourse." To hammer the message home, it continued indignantly: "Ask yourself: do you want Amsterdam's reckless 'Open for Anything' culture here? No!" Yet the threat was imminent, doom was impending, for it turned out that the message was meant to warn Americans against Amstel beers as "the true embodiment of Amsterdam's recklessly open-minded behavior": "You must resist their seduction. You must say no to the Amstels from Amsterdam." The message finally referred to a Website—www.g-boyd.com—which, once opened, gave further stern warning against the evils of the various Amstel beers.

As I learned soon afterward, this was not a small advertising ploy aimed tongue in cheek at a limited in-crowd of cultural sophisticates. In fact, it was a $20 million campaign addressing Americans of every walk of life. As a piece in the media section of the *Village Voice* made clear, the campaign had penetrated as far as Times Square in New York, the iconic heartland of American billboard-size advertising.[8] In addition to huge billboards, the marquees of movie theaters on Forty-second Street that until recently had shown X-rated movies were now marshaled for a campaign against moral corruption coming from Amsterdam. "Do not look. Shield your eyes." "Openness is dangerousness."

Casting its product in the light of evil seduction, admonishing the public to avoid its beer at all cost, a Dutch brewing corporation, in collaboration with an American advertising agency, had opted for the ironic inversion of usual advertising strategies while parodying the tone of a moral crusade that had come to characterize much of American public discourse over the last two decades. The case is interesting for several reasons. First there is the multimedia aspect of the advertising campaign: from classic newspaper ads, to billboards, to movie theater marquees, to the Worldwide Web, Amstel's advertising ploy had become well-nigh inescapable. In addition to this high-saturation approach, however, there are other aspects of more direct relevance to my argument.

In recent years many students of the reception of forms of American mass culture abroad have emphasized what we may call the freedom of reception. They have pointed to the many inventive and imaginative ways in which people at the receiving end have given twists to the meaning of American mass culture, redefining it to make it function within the larger cultural context of their own daily lives. All such reception studies focus on the appropriation of American mass culture by publics exposed to it outside America's national borders. Thus, the study of problems of an alleged Americanization of national cultures outside America has served to redefine the problem in terms of the creative act of cultural translation. In terms of the many national contexts of reception, the research focus has thus become one of understanding the processes of what we might call the nationalization of American culture. Thus, for a country such as the Netherlands, the problem is not so much the Americanization of Dutch culture but rather the Dutchification of American mass culture.

Interestingly, the Amstel advertising campaign takes us one step further. Here the commodity to be sold is not American but Dutch, as are the auspices of the advertising campaign. Instead of exposing foreign publics to the seductive potential of American imagery, the Amstel campaign was aimed at Americans and based itself on images, prevalent among Americans, of Dutch culture as excessively open and permissive. The campaign then chose to recycle these images ironically, parodying the apocalyptic language of America's "moral majority" constituency. It testifies to a fairly uncanny reading of American culture by outsiders, who rather than passively receive American cultural values use them creatively in a parody of American cultural concerns beamed back at the American public. It was a case, one might say, of the periphery striking back at the empire.

Dreams of the Lost Labyrinth

As the example of Amstel beers may remind us, the Internet is being increasingly used for commercial purposes, for advertising, selling and buying, and the organization of business. The trend is very recent; its outcome, hard to predict. Clearly the Internet inspires dreams not only of democracy but also of a totally revamped and perfectly transparent market. The Internet may hold a promise of greater democratic participation, but it also promises greater access to and openness of the economic market. Again, in the eyes of non-, Americans, this may illustrate a peculiarly American tendency to conflate the spheres of politics and economics, conceiving of the public sphere of democratic politics as a market, not unlike the one where citizens meet as consumers.[9] In what follows, however, I intend to focus on a different dream, one as lofty as the dream of democracy and of a res publica in cyberspace.

The Internet has inspired dreams of the return to a world of total intertextuality, the reconstitution of the full body of human thinking and writing. It would be the return to the "City of Words," the labyrinthine library that, like a nostalgic recollection, has haunted the human imagination since the age of the mythical library of Babylon. Tony Tanner used the metaphor of the city of words to describe the central quest inspiring the literary imagination of the twentieth century.[10] One author whom Tanner sees as epitomizing this quest is Jorge Luis Borges. It is the constructive power of the human mind that moves and amazes Borges. His stories are full of the strangest architecture, including the endless variety of lexical architecture to which humanity throughout history has devoted its time—philosophical theories, theological disputes, encyclopedias, religious beliefs, critical interpretations, novels, and books of all kinds. While having a deep feeling for the shaping and abstracting powers of the human mind, Borges at the same time profoundly recognizes how nightmarish the resultant structures can become. In one of his stories, the narrator refers to the library of Babel as the "universe," and one can take it as a metaphysical parable of all the difficulties of deciphering humanity's encounters. At the same time, Babel remains the most famous example of the madness in humanity's rage for architecture, and books are only another form of building. In this library every possible combination of letters and words is to be found, with the result that there are fragments of sense separated by "leagues of insensate cacophony, of verbal farragos and incoherencies." Most books are "mere labyrinths of letters."

Since everything that language can do and express is somewhere in the library, "the clarification of the basic mysteries of humanity . . . was also expected." The "necessary vocabularies and grammars" must be discoverable in the lexical totality. Yet the attempt at discovery and detection is maddening; the story is full of the sadness, sickness, and madness of the pathetic figures who roam around the library as around a vast prison.[11]

What do Borges's fantasies tell us about the Promethean potential of a restored city of words in cyberspace? During an international colloquium in Paris at the Bibliothèque Nationale de France, held on June 3 and 4, 1998, scholars and library presidents discussed the implications of a virtual database on the Internet connecting the holdings of all the world's great libraries. Some saw it as a dream come true. In his opening remarks Jean-Pierre Angremy referred to the library of Babel as imagined by Borges while ignoring its nightmarish side: "When it was proclaimed that the library would hold all books, the first reaction was one of extravagant mirth. Everyone felt like mastering an intact and secret treasure." The perspective, as Angremy saw it, was extravagant indeed. All the world's knowledge at your command, like an endless scroll across your computer screen. Others, such as Jacques Attali, spiritual father of the idea of digitalizing the holdings of the new Bibliothèque Nationale, took a similar positive view. Whatever the form of the library, real or virtual, it would always be "a reservoir of books." Others were not so sure. They foresaw a mutation of our traditional relationship toward the written text, where new manipulations and competences would make our reading habits as antiquated as the reading of papyrus scrolls is to us.

Ironically, as others pointed out, texts as they now appear on our screen are like a throwback to scrolls and may well affect our sense of the single page. In the printed book every page comes in its own context of pages preceding and following it, suggesting a discursive continuity. On the screen, however, the same page would be the interchangeable element of a virtual database that one penetrates by using a keyword that opens many books at the same time. All information is thus put at the same plan, without the logical hierarchy of an unfolding argument. As Michel Melot, longtime member of the Conseil Supérieur des Bibliothèques, pointed out, randomness becomes the rule. The coherence of traditional discursive presentation will tend to give way to what is fragmented, incomplete, and disparate, if not incoherent. In his view, the patchwork or cut-and-paste approach will become the dominant mode of composition.[12]

* * *

These darker views take us back to my earlier discussion of America's imprint on the Internet. They are strangely reminiscent of an earlier European cultural critique of the ways in which American culture would affect European civilization. In particular, the contrast between reading traditional books and reading texts downloaded from the Net recalls a contrast between Europe and America that constitutes a staple in the work of many European critics of American culture. Europe, in this view, stands for organic cohesion, for logical and stylistic closure, whereas America tends toward fragmentation and recombination in a mode of blithe cultural bricolage, exploding every prevailing cultural canon in Europe. Furthermore, we can recognize the traditional European fear of American culture as a leveling force, bringing everything down to the surface level of the total interchangeability of cultural items, oblivious of their intrinsic value and of cultural hierarchies of high versus low.[13]

Nonetheless, the views summarized previously include no reference to America. Is this because America is a subtext, a code instantly recognized by French intellectuals? Or is it because the logic of the Internet and digital intertextuality have a cultural impact in their own right, similar to the impact of American culture, but this time unrelated to any American agency? At this point I will merely suggest a Weberian answer. There clearly seems to be a *Wahlverwandtschaft*—an elective affinity—between the logic of the Internet and the American cast of mind that allows an easier, less anguished acceptance and use of the new medium among Americans than among a certain breed of Europeans.

There is, it seems to me, a further way to explore this elective affinity. Most of the discussion at the Paris colloquium focused on the *use* of texts available via the Internet rather than on the *production* of texts—in other words, on the act of reading rather than writing. At one point, however, someone asked whether the logic of the Internet might not also lead to novel forms of literature. According to the report in *Le Monde,* no one could yet foresee its possible impact on creative writing, yet one could venture a little further than this. From a librarian's point of view, the Internet can be seen as having generated a virtual library in cyberspace, linking all available texts ever produced by writers. Through the use of keywords and related search techniques, visitors to this library can determine their own particular trajectories through the lexical labyrinth, producing textual collages to fit the particular needs of individual readers. In this case, it is individual readers who, on the basis of available texts, generate their own individual recombination and rearrangement of textual fragments. The logical next step, then, would be the production of precisely such a body of textual fragments as an act of creative writing, where the author would provide the keywords, known as hyperlinks, that would allow the reader to cruise through the textual fragments and to arrange them in any number of combinations. The result would be what we might call a hypertext novel.

As it happens, the challenge has been taken up. Hypertext novels do exist, not on the shelves of any physical libraries, but, as their logic dictates, in the virtual library of cyberspace. They can be downloaded as so many fragments and then, by clicking on any of the hyperlinks provided by the author, arranged by the individual reader sitting at his or her own computer.[14] This creative leap into cyberspace has something Promethean about it. It invites the reader to become his or her own individual author and to act out the dream central to an age that has proclaimed the death of the author. No longer must the reader be tied down to forms of narrative flow and structure set entirely by the author. The very logic of the hypertext novel demands that readers actively construct their own texts.

Again, this daring step was typically one for American writers to make first. Again, it seems to fit in with a more general American modularizing cast of mind, a greater willingness to break up coherent wholes and to let individual consumers recombine the fragments as they please. Nonetheless, the idea of the hypertext novel seems more daring than any actual examples I have seen. The idea ties in with the dream of the lost library, where an author would do no more than set the reader off on a journey through the labyrinth of the human imagination, out into uncharted territory. The idea is one of a text that is structurally open, fraying at the edges, providing hyperlinks into the unknown. The hypertext in its present form is a far cry from this, however. It is entirely self-enclosed, referring back only to its own constituent elements, allowing of no escape beyond the structural closure set by the author. It is reminiscent of the attempts to build a robot that does not simply reproduce humankind but improves on it. The result has always been of a Prometheus bound and shackled in retribution for his acts of hubris.

Like the robot, the hypertext novel is no more than a clumsy replica of books as we have always known and read them. The act of reading texts in their traditional form has always involved the active construction of hyperlinks. One book always reminds us of other books. Our mind produces its own links and associations. Reading one book, we get up and open other books to verify our associative hunches. We hear voices of other authors reverberating in unison with the voice of any particular author we happen to be reading. Sometimes the reverberation is a matter of authorial intent, and sometimes it is a case of the reader's mind wandering, but all reading is intertextual, all fiction a hypertext. Europeans have always produced fiction in a self-conscious awareness of its intertextuality, from Shakespeare and Cervantes to Julian Barnes and Julián Ríos. So have Americans. In their cultural games Americans may experiment in ways that strike Europeans as typically American, yet the dream of life in cyberspace is the contemporary version of dreams that we all share.

Perhaps I am being too postmodern here, reducing citizenship to the mental state of the individual, self-sufficient, and erudite mind, to an intertextuality in our mind that connects us to other minds, past and present, no matter where we are or under what conditions. Perhaps, but I cannot help being reminded here of some of the great prison writings, by the likes of Arthur Koestler, Antonio Gramsci, or George Orwell. As they make clear, whatever the duress of isolation and torture, the mind may find resources for survival in its interconnectedness with the minds of fellow human beings remembered through their words and works. Citizenship, in this final analysis, is a state of mind, a fragile and precious work of culture, sustaining us—at least the best of us—in the face of a breakdown of civil society, when we are confronted with whatever hardships those who see salvation in totalitarian projects impose on us, trying to tear apart our bonds with the past and with a community of kindred spirits. Killing fields appear all over this world, from Nazi gas chambers to the Soviet Gulag, Cambodian genocide, and the lethal pursuit of ethnic purity in the former Yugoslavia. Yet there have always been those whose minds never broke and who remained citizens of the world when all that remained was their inner city of words.

Notes

Chapter 1: Supranationalism and Its Discontents

1. See, e.g., E. J. Hobsbawm and T. Ranger, eds., *The Invention of Tradition* (Cambridge, 1983); E. J. Hobsbawm, *Nations and Nationalism since 1780: Programme, Myth, Reality* (Cambridge, 1990). The first book in particular has had a wide influence across such academic disciplines as history, anthropology, and cultural studies.

2. See J. Huizinga, *Verzamelde werken* (Collected works), 9 vols. (Haarlem, 1948–53), 4:497–554, 7:161, 266–78.

3. P. Berger, B. Berger, and H. Kellner, *The Homeless Mind: Modernization and Consciousness* (New York, 1973).

4. C. Baudelaire, *Selected Writings on Art and Artists*, trans. P. E. Charvet (Cambridge, 1972), 400, 401.

5. See R. Solá, "La France, le sol et le sang" (France, soil and blood), *Le Monde*, September 22–23, 1991, pp. 1, 8.

Chapter 2: Trespassing in America

1. On the history of such ideas, particularly of the melting pot, see W. Sollors, "A Defence of the Melting Pot," in *The American Identity: Fusion and Fragmentation*, ed. R. Kroes, 181–215 (Amsterdam, 1980).

2. J. Huizinga, *Verzamelde werken* (Collected works), 9 vols. (Haarlem, 1948–53), 5:333. The translation is my own, as are all subsequent translations not otherwise attributed.

3. J. Baudrillard, *Amérique* (Paris, 1986); U. Eco, *Travels in Hyperreality* (London, 1987).

4. As cited in G. Lenz, "The Politics of Traveling Theory: Revisions of Deconstruction, Postmodernism, and Neo-Marxism in Recent American Literary Criticism," in *Perceptions and Misperceptions: The United States and Germany: Studies in Intercultural Understanding*, ed. L. Bredella and D. Haack, 209–41 (Tübingen, 1988), 229.

5. The seminal book on the subject is J. Blair's *Modular America: Cross-Cultural Perspectives on the Emergence of an American Way* (New York, 1988).

6. Huizinga, *Verzamelde werken*, 4:497–554, 7:161, 420, 437–41; E. J. Hobsbawm and T. Ranger, eds., *The Invention of Tradition* (Cambridge, 1983).

7. G. Sorel, *Réflexions sur la violence* (Reflections on violence) (Paris, 1950).

8. See the interesting article by David Morley and Kevin Robins, "No Place Like *Heimat:* Images of Home(Land) in European Culture," *New Formations* 12 (Winter 1990): 1–24.

9. I. Howe, "In Defense of 'the Canon,'" *The New Republic,* February 18, 1991, pp. 40–49; A. Schlesinger Jr., *The Disuniting of America* (New York, 1991).

Chapter 3: Between Globalism and Regionalism

1. See E. Weber, *Peasants into Frenchmen: The Modernization of Rural France, 1870–1914* (Stanford, Calif., 1976).

2. D. Boorstin, *The Genius of American Politics* (Chicago, 1953), 103.

3. D. W. Brogan, *The American Political System* (London, 1943 [1933]), 94.

4. M. J. C. Vile, *The Structure of American Federalism* (London: 1961), 32.

5. M. Lerner, *America as a Civilizaton: Life and Thought in the United States Today* (New York, 1957), 182.

6. Ibid., 183.

7. F. J. Turner, *The Significance of the Frontier in American History* [1894], repr. in Turner, *Frontier and Section: Selected Essays of Frederick Jackson Turner,* intro. R. A. Billington (Englewood Cliffs, N.J., 1961), 37–63; see also Turner's "Sections and Nation," *Yale Review* 12 (Oct. 1922): 1–21, and his essay collection entitled *The Significance of Sections in American History* (New York, 1932).

8. A. von Steinwehr and D. G. Brinton, *An Intermediate Geography, with Lessons in Map-Drawing* (New York, 1870).

9. J. W. Redway and R. Hinman, *Natural Advanced Geography* (New York, 1898).

10. See National Geographic Society, *The Physiography of the United States* (New York, 1896).

11. G. Tucker, *Progress of the United States in Population and Wealth in Fifty Years, as Exhibited by the Decennial Census* (New York, 1843).

12. Those interested in the inner working of the U.S. Census Bureau should refer to W. F. Willcox, *Studies in American Demography* (Ithaca, N.Y., 1940), ch. 4, "Development of the American Census and Its Methods."

13. O. B. Baker, *Atlas of American Agriculture* (Washington, D.C., 1936).

14. O. B. Baker, *A Graphic Summary of American Agriculture Based Largely on the Census,* U.S. Department of Agriculture, Miscellaneous Publications, no. 105 (Washington, D.C. 1931); see also O. B. Baker, "Agricultural Regions of North America," *Economic Geography* 2–8 (Oct. 1926–Oct. 1932).

15. See, e.g., H. H. McCarty, *The Geographic Basis of American Economic Life* (New York, 1940). Interesting demographic work has been done by D. J. Bogue and W. H. Grabill in *The Population of the United States* (Glencoe, Ill., 1959). Arguably the most ambitious work in this vein is D. J. Bogue and C. L. Beale, *Economic Areas of the United States* (Glencoe, Ill., 1961).

16. H. J. Desmond, "The Sectional Feature in American Politics," *Transactions of the Wisconsin Academy of Sciences, Arts, and Letters* 8, no. 7 (1888–91); qtd. in F. Mood, "Origin, Evolution, and Application of the Sectional Concept, in *Regionalism in America,* ed. M. Jensen, 5–118 (Madison, 1951), 87.

17. Qtd. in F. Mood, "Origin," 89–90; emphasis added. For his delineation of the "underlying sectional areas," Libby looked at the way in which congressional district spokespeople cast their votes.

18. Turner, *Significance of Sections,* 23, 37.

19. Ibid., 50–51.

20. H. W. Odum and H. W. Moore, *American Regionalism: A Cultural Historical Approach to National Integration* (New York, 1938), 435.

21. N. M. Fenneman, *Annals of the Association of American Geographers* 4 (1914): 55–83.

22. John Leighly, *Annals of the Association of American Geographers* 27 (1937): 125–41.

23. C. L. White, E. J. Foscue, and T. L. McKnight, *Regional Geography of Anglo-America,* 3d ed. (Englewood Cliffs, N.J., 1964 [1943]), 5, 35.

24. See, e.g., A. S. Link and R. W. Patrick, eds., *Writing Southern History* (Baton Rouge, La., 1965); J. A. Hawgood, *The American West* (London, 1967).

25. W. P. Webb, *The Great Plains* (New York, 1931). For an early critique of this approach, see F. A. Shannon, *An Appraisal of Walter Prescott Webb's "The Great Plains": A Study in Institutions and Environment,* Social Sciences Research Council, Critiques of Research in the Social Sciences, Bulletin 46 (New York, 1940).

26. H. Kurath, "Linguistic Regionalism," in *Regionalism in America,* ed. M. Jensen, 297–310 (Madison, Wisc., 1951), 298.

27. G. Pickford, "American Linguistic Geography: A Sociological Appraisal," *Word* 12 (1956): 211–33.

28. H. Galinsky, *Regionalismus und Einheitsstreben in den Vereinigten Staaten: Ein sprachwissenschaftlicher Forschungsbericht* (Regionalism and the quest for unity in the United States: a linguistic research report) (Heidelberg, 1972), 22: "Are these sociolects nationally dispersed, and are they, therefore, variations on the national language, or are they, given their relative geographic concentration, to be seen as sociolinguistic variations of regional dialects?"

29. A. R. Maynes, *Rural Regions of the United States* (Washington, D.C., 1937), 19.

30. See Committee on Administrative Management, *Report of the President's Committee on Administrative Management* (Washington, D.C., 1937); J. W. Fesler, *Area and Administration* (Tuscaloosa, Ala., 1949). A good survey of this approach is given in H. Emmerich, *Federal Organization and Administrative Management* (Tuscaloosa, Ala., 1971).

31. A fascinating though highly partisan history of the early years of the Tennessee Valley Authority is D. E. Lilienthal's *TVA: Democracy on the March* (London, 1944).

32. L. Wirth, "The Limitations of Regionalism," in *Regionalism in America,* ed. M. Jensen, 381–93 (Madison, Wisc., 1951), 385.

33. P. H. Odegard and H. H. Baerwald, *The American Republic: Its Government and Politics* (New York, 1964), 40.

34. See, e.g., J. Gottmann, *Megalopolis* (New York, 1962).

35. V. O. Key, *Politics, Parties, and Pressure Groups,* 4th ed. (New York, 1958 [1942]), 268.

36. In M. Farrand, ed., *The Records of the Federal Convention of 1787,* 4 vols. (New Haven, Conn., 1911), 1:476.

37. A. O. Spain, *The Political Theory of John C. Calhoun* (New York, 1951), 133, 204.

38. Desmond, "Sectional Feature," 1.

39. Turner, *Significance of the Frontier,* 46, 54. On occasion Turner used different metaphors to convey this idea. In a later piece published in the *Atlantic Monthly* of January 1903, he referred to the early frontier, extending from the back country of New England down through western New York, Pennsylvania, and the South, as a "distinct belt of democratic territory" (repr. in Turner, *Frontier and Section,* 77–98; quotation on 81).

40. E. A. Shils, "Centre and Periphery," in *The Logic of Personal Knowledge,* ed. M. Polanyi, 117–31 (London, 1961); A. W. Gouldner, "Reciprocity and Autonomy in Functional Theory," in *Symposium on Sociological Theory,* ed. L. Gross, 241–71 (New York, 1959).

41. J. S. Mill, *"Utilitarianism," "On Liberty," and "Considerations of Representative Government"* (London, 1972), 395.

42. A. H. Heineken, *The United States of Europe (a Eurotopia?)* (Amsterdam, 1992).

Chapter 4: Immigrants and Transnational Localism

1. Stieglitz's photograph *The Steerage* has acquired its iconic status as a picture of immigrants even though the steerage passengers whom he photographed were most likely return migrants. Stieglitz was on his way to Europe when he took the photograph.

2. M. W. Sandler, *The Story of American Photography* (Boston, 1976), 106.

3. L. Adamic, *Laughing in the Jungle* (New York, 1932); repr. in part in *A Nation of Nations: Ethnic Literature in America*, ed. T. L. Gross, 69–83 (New York, 1971), 81.

4. P. Cresci, *Il pane dalle sette croste* (The bread of seven crusts) (Lucca, 1986), 239.

5. J. C. Schaap, "The Heritage of These Many Years," *Sign of Promise and Other Stories* (Sioux Center, Iowa, 1979), 244–55.

6. W. Wilterdink, *Winterswijkse pioniers in Amerika* (Winterswijk, 1990), 32–44.

7. The largest collection of letters to be published recently is W. Helbich, W. D. Kamphoefner, and U. Sommer, eds., *Briefe aus Amerika: Deutsche Auswanderer schreiben aus der neuen Welt, 1830–1930* (Letters from America: German immigrant writings from the New World, 1830–1930) (Munich, 1988).

8. See, e.g., R. Kroes, *The Persistence of Ethnicity: Dutch Calvinist Pioneers in Amsterdam, Montana* (Urbana, Ill., 1992).

9. H. J. Brinks, *Schrijf spoedig terug: Brieven van immigranten in Amerika, 1847–1920* (The Hague, 1978), 138; English-language translation, *Write Back Soon: Letters from Immigrants in America* (Grand Rapids, Mich., 1986).

10. The writer uses the Dutch word *lijkenis*, which is an unusual synonym for portrait and may well have been influenced by the English word *likeness*.

11. I have used quotation marks for those passages that were in English, but even the Dutch shows the impact of English, the writer having spent many years as an immigrant in the United States. The letter was written by one of two sisters from Friesland surnamed Tacoma.

12. M. Boekelman, "The Letters of Jane Aberson," in *Dutch Immigration to North America*, ed. H. Ganzevoort and M. Boekelman, 111–13 (Toronto, 1983), 113.

13. Schaap, *Sign of Promise*, 61–81.

14. Ibid., 64, 65.

Chapter 5: The Human Rights Tradition in the United States

1. J. P. Diggins, *The Lost Soul of American Politics: Virtue, Self-Interest, and the Foundation of Lieberalism* (New York, 1984); J. R. Pole, "The Individualist Foundations of American Constitutionalism," unpublished paper, 1987.

2. The term *propertarianism* was coined by Marcus Cunliffe for a course he taught at George Washington University, Washington, D.C., in 1984–85. The gradual erosion of this initially corporate view of property, assuming more radically individualist contours over the years, is well documented by Jeffrey Lustig in his *Corporate Liberalism: The Origins of Modern American Political Theory, 1890–1920* (Berkeley, Calif., 1982).

3. *Reynolds v. Simms*, 377 U.S. 533 (1964) 562.

4. See, e.g., G. F. Kennan, *The Cloud of Danger: Current Realities of American Foreign*

Policy (Boston, 1977), 43: "Those Americans who profess to know with such certainty what other people want and what is good for them in the way of political institutions would do well to ask themselves whether they are not actually attempting to impose their own values, traditions, and habits of thought on peoples for whom these things have no validity and no usefulness" (qtd. in A. M. Schlesinger, *The Cycles of American History* [Boston, 1986], 101).

5. H. J. Abraham, *Freedom and the Court: Civil Rights and Liberties in the United States* (New York, 1982 [1967]), ch. 4.

6. *Heart of Atlanta Motel, Inc., v. U.S.,* 379 U.S. 241 (1964).

7. *Public Papers of the Presidents of the United States, Jimmy Carter, 1978,* 2 vols. (Washington, D.C., 1979), 1:396.

8. The most vocal early opponents are to be found in Jewish intellectual circles associated with *Commentary.* A characteristic early blast is Nathan Glazer's *Affirmative Discrimination* (New York, 1976).

9. For these figures, see A. Hacker, ed., *A Statistical Portrait of the American People* (New York, 1983).

10. J. S. Quadango, "Welfare Capitalism and the Social Security Act of 1935," *American Sociological Review* 49 (1984): 632–47.

11. Cf. J. Rivière, *Les Etats-Unis à l'horizon de la troisième révolution industrielle* (The United States at the horizon of the third industrial revolution) (Nancy, 1986).

12. N. Glazer, "Individualism and Equality in the United States," in *On the Making of Americans: Essays in Honor of David Riesman,* ed. H. J. Gans, N. Glazer, J. R. Gusfield, and C. Jenks, 127–43 (Philadelphia, 1979), 139.

13. The initiative was sponsored by S. I. Hayakawa, sociolinguist and former U.S. senator from California. Its adoption meant the elimination of bilingual voting forms and bilingual education, among other things.

Chapter 6: Ideology

1. See P. G. Kielmansegg, "Der Gesellschaftsvertrag soll ohne Unterschrift gelten" (The social contract is to apply unsigned) *Frankfurter Algemeine Zeitung,* April 24, 1999, p. 44. My discussion draws on his arguments.

2. See ibid.

3. J. Higham, *Strangers in the Land: Patterns of American Nativism, 1860–1925* (New Brunswick, N.J., 1955).

4. See, for instance, J. O'Sullivan, "America's Identity Crisis," *National Review,* November 21, 1994. In discussing the views of multiculturalists, he argues: "'Traditional values' are certainly a component of 'Americanism.' But there are also history, language, customs, agreed methods of settling disputes, songs, tales, poems, collective memory, loyalties, and allegiances. In this respect, the immigrant is not an American, and if he arrives in a context of multiculturalism, he may never become one. Nor may his children" (45).

5. For a cogent analysis of Bacon's views, see H. Barth, *Wahrheit und Ideologie* (Truth and ideology) (Erlenbach/Zurich, 1961).

6. C.-A. Helvétius, *De l'esprit* (on the soul) (Paris, 1758), 551.

7. F. Bacon, *The Works of Francis Bacon,* ed. J. Spedding, R. L. Ellis, and D. D. Heath, 14 vols. (London, 1879), 1:129.

8. K. Marx, in *Karl Marx/Friedrich Engels: Historisch-kritische Gesamtausgabe. Werke, Schriften, Briefe* (Karl Marx/Frederick Engels: historical-critical edition: works, writings, correspondence), ed. D. Rjazanow, 11 vols. (Frankfurt am Main/Moscow, 1927–35), 5:21.

9. Qtd. in Barth, *Wahrheit,* 220.

10. G. F. W. Hegel, *Hegels Werke,* 20 vols. (Berlin, 1840–52), 9:535–36.

11. C. Geertz, "Ideology as a Cultural System," in *Ideology and Discontent,* ed. D. E. Apter, 47–77 (New York, 1964).

12. C. van Heek, *Verzorgingsstaat en sociologie* (The welfare state and sociology) (Meppel, the Netherlands, 1972), 18.

13. D. Apter, "Introduction: Ideology and Discontent," in *Ideology and Discontent,* ed. D. Apter, 15–46 (New York, 1964).

14. D. P. Moynihan, *Counting Our Blessings: Reflections on the Future of America* (Boston, 1980), 88.

15. M. Janowitz, *The Social Control of the Welfare State* (Chicago, 1976), xvi.

16. T. Skocpol, *Protecting Mothers and Soldiers: The Political Origins of Social Policy in the United States* (Cambridge, Mass., 1992).

17. E. D. Berkowitz, "Current Developments in the Welfare State: An International and Historical Perspective," in *Social and Secure? Politics and Culture of the Welfare State: A Comparative Inquiry,* ed. H. Bak, F. van Holthoon, and M. Krabbendam, 160–75 (Amsterdam, 1996), 161.

18. E. D. Berkowitz, *America's Welfare State: From Roosevelt to Reagan* (Baltimore, 1991); L. R. Jacobs, "The Cultural Crisis of the American Welfare State: Barriers to National Health Care Reform," in *Social and Secure? Politics and Culture of the Welfare State: A Comparative Inquiry,* ed. H. Bak, F. van Holthoon, and M. Krabbendam, 357–82 (Amsterdam, 1996).

Chapter 7: Neopopulism and Neoconservatism in the United States

1. M. B. Katz, *The Undeserving Poor: From the War on Poverty to the War on Welfare* (New York, 1989).

2. D. P. Moynihan, *Family and Nation* (New York, 1986); T. Sowell, ed., *American Ethnic Groups* (Washington, D.C., 1978); I. Katznelson, *Schooling for All: Class, Race, and the Decline of the Democratic Ideal* (New York, 1985); S. M. Butler and A. Kondratas, *Out of the Poverty Trap: A Conservative Strategy for Welfare Reform* (New York, 1987).

3. W. J. Wilson, *The Declining Significance of Race: Blacks and Changing American Institutions* (Chicago, 1978); W. J. Wilson, *The Truly Disadvantaged: The Inner City, the Underclass, and Public Policy* (Chicago, 1987).

4. S. Steele, *The Content of Our Character: A New Vision of Race in America* (New York, 1990).

5. J. Sleeper, *The Closest of Strangers: Liberalism and the Politics of Race in New York* (New York, 1990), 315, 314.

6. A welcome initiative to reintroduce these older perspectives is W. Sollors, ed., *Theories of Ethnicity: A Classical Reader* (New York, 1996).

Chapter 8: National American Studies in Europe, Transnational American Studies in America?

1. H. Melville, *Clarel: A Poem and Pilgrimage in the Holy Land,* part 4, canto 21, in *The Writings of Herman Melville,* ed. H. Hayford, A. A. MacDougal, H. Parker, and G. T. Tanselle, 25 vols. (Evanston, Ill., 1991), vol. 12, 2:158–59.

2. T. Dreiser, "Life, Art and America," *The Seven Arts* 1 (Feb. 1917): 363.

3. G. Steiner, "The Archives of Eden," *Salmagundi* 50–51 (Fall 1980/Winter 1981): 57–89.

4. Qtd. in D. Echeverria, *Mirage in the West: A History of the French Image of American Society to 1815* (Princeton, N.J., 1957), 32–33.

5. D. J. Boorstin, *The Image: Or What Happened to the American Dream* (Harmondsworth, U.K., 1963 [1962]), 183.

6. The quotations are from André Siegfried's preface to A. Philip, *Le problème ouvrier aux Etats-Unis* (The labor problem in the United States) (Paris, 1927) xi, xv.

Chapter 9: Traveling Theories, Traveling Theorists

1. J. Verne, *Paris au XXe siècle* (Paris in the twentieth century) (Paris, 1994).

2. A good illustration of this angle of perception is Serge Guilbaut's *How New York Stole the Idea of Modern Art: Abstract Expressionism, Freedom, and the Cold War* (Chicago, 1983).

3. M.-G. J. de Crèvecoeur, *Letters from an American Farmer* (London, 1912) 39, 42; emphasis added.

4. Ibid., 40.

5. Ibid., 39.

6. A. de Tocqueville, *De la démocratie en Amérique* (On Democracy in America), 4 vols. (Paris, 1839–40), vols. 1, 5.

7. Le docteur René Lefèbvre [E. Laboulaye], *Paris en Amérique* (Paris in America) (Paris, 1879), 389.

8. J.-J. Ampère, *Promenade en Amérique* (Travels in America), 2 vols. (Paris, 1855); A. de Chambrun, *Impressions of Lincoln and the Civil War: A Foreigner's Account* (New York, 1952); O. Comettant, *Voyage pittoresque et anecdotique dans le Nord et le Sud des Etats-Unis d'Amérique* (A picturesque and anecdotal voyage in the American North and South) (Paris, 1866); E. Duverger de Hauranne, *Les Etats-Unis pendant la Guerre de Sécession* (The United States during the War of Succession) (Paris, 1990 [1866]); X. Eyma, *Les deux Amériques, histoire, moeurs et voyages* (The two Americas: history, morals, and voyages) (Paris, 1853).

9. Qtd. in D. Lacorne, J. Rupnik, and M. F. Toinet, eds., *L'Amérique dans les têtes* (The imagined America) (Paris, 1986), 61.

10. Qtd. in ibid., 62.

11. I fast-forward to the post–World War II area for no reason other than that I explored French views of America during the interbellum in a previous publication (*If You've Seen One, You've Seen the Mall: Europeans and American Mass Culture* [Urbana, Ill., 1996]). Here I refer to some of the leading French voices from the interwar years in different contexts. (See the previous and following chapters.) In this chapter my interest lies in pursuing the ways in which French repertoires in the perception of American modernity, established in the nineteenth century, can still be recognized in the decades following World War II.

12. A. M. Schlesinger Jr., *The Disuniting of America* (New York, 1991).

13. Ibid., 15.

14. S. de Beauvoir, *La force de l'âge* (Prime of life) (Paris, 1960), 160.

15. J.-P. Sartre, *Situations III* (Paris, 1949), 82.

16. Ibid., 84.

17. Ibid., 96.

18. Ibid., 91.

19. Qtd. in M. Contat and M. Rybalka, *Les écrits de Sartre* (Sartre's writings) (Paris, 1974), 122.

20. S. de Beauvoir, *L'Amérique au jour le jour* (America day to day) (Paris, 1954 [1948]), 27.

21. S. de Beauvoir, *La force des choses* (Force of circumstance) (Paris, 1963), 130–33.

22. M. Crozier, *Le mal américain* (The Trouble with America) (Paris, 1980).

23. M. Crozier, *The Trouble with America,* trans. Peter Heinegg (Berkeley, Calif., 1984), 85.

24. T. Morgan (*né* Sanche de Gramont), *On Becoming American* (New York, 1988 [1978]).

25. Ibid., 4, 72, 310.

26. E. Morin, *Journal de Californie* (California journal) (Paris, 1970), 250.

27. J. Baudrillard, *Amérique* (Paris, 1986), 156, 167.

28. U. Eco, *Travels in Hyperreality* (London, 1987), 37, 43.

29. Qtd. in ibid.

30. P. Bourdieu, "Questions aux vrais maîtres du monde" (Questions to the true masters of the world), *Le Monde, sélection hebdomadaire,* October 23, 1999, pp. 1, 7.

31. Ibid., 7.

Chapter 10: America and the European Sense of History

1. R. Kroes, *If You've Seen One, You've Seen the Mall: Europeans and American Mass Culture* (Urbana, Ill., 1996).

2. Ibid., 22.

3. Ibid., 82–84.

4. J. H. Huizinga, *Amerika levend en denkend: Losse opmerkingen* (Haarlem, 1927), 126; English-language translation, *America: A Dutch Historian's Vision, from Afar and Near,* trans. Herbert H. Rowen (New York, 1972), 312.

5. J. H. Huizinga, *In de schaduwen van morgen* (In the shadows of tomorrow) (1935), *Verzamelde werken* (Collected works), 9 vols. (Haarlem, 1948–53), 7:313–424.

6. J. H. Huizinga, *Over vormverandering der geschiedenis* (On the changing form of history) (1941), *Verzamelde werken,* 7:192–207.

7. J. H. Huizinga, *Nederland's geestesmerk* (The Dutch cast of mind) (1935), *Verzamelde werken,* 7:279–313.

8. Ibid., 312.

9. Huizinga, *Amerika levend en denkend,* 165–66.

10. Albert Camus, *American Journals* (London, 1990), 42.

11. Ibid., 32.

12. Qtd. in A. Visson, *As Others See Us* (Garden City, N.Y., 1948), 149.

13. A. de Tocqueville, *De la démocratie en Amérique* (On democracy in America), 4 vols. (Paris, 1930–40), 3:272–76.

14. J. Huizinga, *Amerika dagboek, 14 april–19 juni 1926* (American journal, April 14 to June 19, 1926), ed. A. van der Lem (Amsterdam, 1993), 44; emphasis added.

15. Huizinga, *Amerika levend en denkend,* 175, 176.

16. J. Huizinga, *Mensch en menigte in Amerika* (Man and the masses in America), *Verzamelde werken,* 5:395.

17. Interestingly, this observation is from Huizinga's first book on America, *Mensch en menigte in Amerika, Verzamelde werken,* 5:332–33.

18. Ibid., 5:290.

19. Ibid., 5:335.

20. Huizinga, *Amerika levend en denkend,* 15.

21. Ibid., 21.

22. Huizinga, *Amerika levend en denkend,* 28.

23. Ibid.

24. J. Huizinga, *Amerika dagboek,* 93.

25. See Jan Scruggs, "A Child of War Forgives . . . ," *USA Today,* November 11, 1996.

Chapter 11: Citizenship and Cyberspace

1. I am aware that I emphasize one particular reading of the origins of the Internet. There are rival views. For a good discussion of these alternative readings, see Roy Rosenzweig, "Wizards, Bureaucrats, Warriors and Hackers: Writing the History of the Internet," *American Historical Review* 103 (December 1998): 1530–52.

2. A recent book-length study of telecommunications and the Internet confirms the picture as briefly sketched here. The study, *TeleGeography 1999,* was written by the Washington-based research firm TeleGeography, Inc., and was produced as an analysis of today's communication landscape for companies in the industry. For a summary of its main findings, see Victoria Shannon, "What's Lurking behind Those Slow Downloads," *International Herald Tribune,* May 27, 1999, p. 7. As John Carr points out in an interesting article on these issues: "In the Internet's own organisation, and in the values and assumptions which underpin it, one thing stands out: the net is American. . . . more than half of internet users today are in the US" (John Carr, "Age of Uncertainty: Anarchy.com," *Prospect,* June 1999, p. 2).

3. B. J. van den Hooff, *Incorporating Electronic Mail: Adoption, Use, and Effects of Electronic Mail in Organizations* (Amsterdam, 1997).

4. W. C. Sellar and R. J. Yeatman, *1066 and All That: A Memorable History of England* (London, 1930).

5. The *New York Times,* for example, denounced Drudge's journalistic style in an editorial piece entitled "WWW.Internet.anarchy" (qtd. in *Le Monde, sélection hebdomadaire,* August 30, 1997).

6. <http://numedia.tddc.net/scott/declaration.html>.

7. *Washington City Paper,* June 27, 1997.

8. Leslie Savan, "Morality Plays on 42nd Street," *Village Voice,* June 16, 1997.

9. I have argued this point more at length in my *If You've Seen One, You've Seen the Mall: Europeans and American Mass Culture* (Urbana, Ill., 1996), chapter 5: "The Fifth Freedom and the Commodification of Civic Virtue." For an excellent survey of the way business is increasingly availing itself of the Internet, see "Business and the Internet: The Net Imperative," a special survey published in *The Economist,* June 26, 1999, pp. 72–116.

10. Tony Tanner, *City of Words: American Fiction 1950–1970* (New York, 1971).

11. For the Borges quotations, see ibid., 41.

12. For my summary of the proceedings at the Paris colloquium, I have used a report published in *Le Monde, sélection hebdomadaire,* June 20, 1998, p. 13.

13. For a fuller analysis of the metaphorical deep structure underlying the European critique of American culture, I refer the reader to my book *If You've Seen One.*

14. A site specializing in hypertext novels is <http://www.eastgate.com>.

Index

ROB KROES is the chair of American studies at the University of Amsterdam. He is a past president of the European Association for American Studies (1992–96) and the author, coauthor, or editor of thirty-one books, including *The Persistence of Ethnicity: Dutch Calvinist Pioneers in Amsterdam, Montana* (1992), *If You've Seen One, You've Seen the Mall: Europeans and American Mass Culture* (1996), and *Predecessors: Intellectual Lineages in American Studies* (1999).

Typeset in 10.5/12.5 Adobe Minion
with Minion display
Composed by Jim Proefrock
at the University of Illinois Press
Manufactured by Thomson-Shore, Inc.

University of Illinois Press
1325 South Oak Street
Champaign, IL 61820-6903
www.press.uillinois.edu